IF WAR
SHOULD
COME

THE TIMES

If War Should Come

The Origins of the Second World War, from The Times Archive

Mark Barnes

The Author

Mark Barnes has spent 45 years in the newspaper industry, the vast majority of them working in picture libraries. He has contributed to print and digital editions of *The Times* and provided features, reviews and photography to a number of other publications and websites. His previous book *The Liberation of Europe* was published in 2016.

ACKNOWLEDGEMENTS

I am immensely grateful to my colleagues at News UK who have been such a valued source of assistance and encouragement with this book. Andrew Sims, Nick Mays, Chris Ball, Lily Carlton, Steve Baker, Richard Hodson, Michael-John Jennings, Sue DeFriend, Lee Chilvers, Anne Jensen, Liane MacIver, Joanne Lovey, Chris Whalley and Robin Ashton.

Thanks go to Charlotte Stear at Crécy and to Mark Nelson.

I'm grateful to Jack Beckett, Michael Bone, Jim Grundy, Phil Hodges, Christina Holstein, Innes McCartney, Frances and Roger Morris, Scott Smith, Matthew Swann, Paul Theobald and Simon Thomson for their help and encouragement.

Beers are owed to Lance Flower, who knows his GDP from his IPA, while continued allegiance is due to our fellow purveyors of Legra Random Waffle in Leigh-on-Sea: Geoff Baker, James Baker, John Baker, Phil Cunningham, Stephen Firminger, Mark Flower, Rob Lawrence, Chris Levell, Ted Meadows and Steve Robinson.

Love to my son and daughter and their partners; James Barnes and Sophie Lawson, Emily Barnes and Jack Hall, to my mother Joyce Barnes and to my dear Francheska Bedding.

For my grandson Leonard James Hall.
Always.

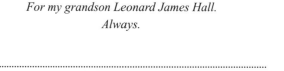

PHOTOGRAPHS

Half-title page: Bill Warhurst's picture of Vickers Medium tanks of the Royal Tank Corps passing St Nicholas' church at Elmdon in Essex was taken on 9 September 1937. *Bill Warhurst [TT]*

Main-title page: William Horton's stunning image of HMS Hood shining a light on the Silver Jubilee Review of 1935 also appears on page 109. *William Horton [TT]*

Contents page: Men of 1st Battalion South Staffordshire Regiment demonstrate the new Boys Anti-Tank Rifle for the media at Aldershot on 21 January 1938. The weapon was heavy and firing it produced a shoulder crunching recoil. *Cathal O'Gorman [TT]*

Rear cover: Renault R35 light tanks negotiate a mountain road during the French army's Alpine manoeuvres of August 1938. *Jack Barker [TT]*

Endpapers: Renault R35 tanks parade down the Champs-Élysées on Bastlle Day 1939. *M Fryszman [KN]*
German artillerymen enjoy a roadside meal watched by an audience of admiring children during the remilitarisation of the Rhineland on 7 March 1936. *Stanley Devon [KN}*

Contents

There was no mistaking who occupied Printing House Square in the spring of 1924. The signage was a leftover from the Northcliffe era and would soon be replaced by something much more discreet in the shape of a fine clock (below left) that became a notable casualty of the Luftwaffe in 1940. Some of the decorative metal work survives in the News UK Archives. [TT]

Edward Risley and Bill Warhurst were the first two photographers employed by *The Times*. Risley died young in 1926 but Warhurst went on to have a superb career. Both men had sons who became successful photographers with the paper. [TT]

Things look busy in this view of *The Times* picture library at Printing House Square in 1927. Head librarian Maud Davies has interrupted sorting negatives to take a phone call. *Cathal O'Gorman* [TT]

INTRODUCTION

IN the late summer of 1939 the GPO Film Unit set out to make a public information film to reassure the British public looking nervously at the prospect of conflict with Nazi Germany that their lives were in good hands. *If War Should Come* ran for ten minutes with a script read by the actor Jack Livesey dubbed over a medley of Elgar's finest. Spitfires and anti-aircraft guns give way to people building Anderson shelters and scenes of evacuee children enjoying their supper. The stentorian Livesey reverts to calmer tones at the end, reminding his audience 'No-one in this country of ours wants war. But if war should come, don't be alarmed. Keep a good heart. Whatever happens, Britain is a nation prepared.'

The film was backed up by a leafleting campaign run by the Lord Privy Seal's Office, but events overtook both the film and the leaflet and hasty revisions were applied to reflect the horrible reality that it was not so much a case of *if* but *when* war would begin.

This book examines the reality behind the claim that Britain was a nation prepared. An additional subtitle for this story might have been 'a study of obsolescence' because much of the weaponry and equipment on view proved inadequate for the trials to come. The government was supported by a large section of the press to present the image that Britain possessed the military might to defend both the country and the empire and it is fair to ask what else would they have done? But we have to balance this with what we know about the people who voiced their concerns at the time and the inconvenient truth that the state of military preparedness in the United Kingdom was far from ideal.

This is not a book about the Nazis or their creed, nor is it another run through events such as the Abdication Crisis. Instead it concentrates on how Britain and, to a lesser extent, France, were confronted with the next world war even as they struggled to recover from the first one. To understand why there was a Second World War we have to look back to the finale of the Great War, a terrible conflict still in our thoughts a century on. It was an industrial conflict gripped by rapid advances in modern weaponry – poison gas, machine guns, aeroplanes, flamethrowers, submarines and the tank. There was progress in medicine and other benign corners of science but the war is remembered principally in the most simplistic terms for its unprecedented level of death and destruction. In attempting to draw a line under it, the men who gathered to sign the Treaty of Versailles and others that followed created new frontiers that were to have tragic consequences for Europe just twenty years later.

There was much sadness when the very last old soldiers of the Great War faded away and this has brought the Second World War into focus, especially when we consider that the precipitous events featured in this book happened eighty years ago. My mother was a young girl throughout the war years, only starting working as a teenager in 1943. She is 90 years old at the time of writing. The remaining people who actually fought the war are even older and many have left us, including my father who died in 1992 aged 73. Our physical connections to those times are becoming ever more tenuous.

When I was growing up the war was a much more recent experience for the people around me and its legacy was

The Paris office of *The Times* was at 8, Rue Halévy. Operations were run from there by Victor Barker whose son, Jack, became a photographer for the paper. He would take many of the memorable images used in this book. *Jack Barker [TT]*

everywhere. Although new movies about it were less common, all the old gems were regularly shown on the telly. When the cricket was rained off the BBC could always show *Dunkirk* or *The Dam Busters* in its place. Films are entertainment but learning the history was another matter. My father insisted upon it and gave me Cornelius Ryan's *The Longest Day* to read when I was eleven. I loved it and still do, but there was much more to learn. When ITV produced the classic *The World at War* series it was a revelation to the younger me, and it has stood the test of time.

For my father, the war was the biggest event in his life, but like many who had lived through it, he preferred to brush off the worst of those six years as if they had not been such a trial. His father was killed at sea and his brother had fifteen minutes of fame as a war hero. My dad was a 20-year-old conscript in the late spring of 1939 but was no longer fit for any military service by VE Day. His army pay book reveals travels to far-flung corners of the British Empire and surviving photos and letters concentrate on the little things that keep us grounded in knowing who we are and where we are from.

He only ever told me humorous things about scorpions in his boots, frying eggs on vehicle bonnets and having to wear a London busman's uniform coat in lieu of army issue. The most useful souvenir he had of his service was a pair of wellington boots issued when he was guarding the Norfolk coast in 1940. I went with my dad to Anzio in 1975 but the trip did not go well because he didn't find the graves of the lads he kept in mind. I intend to go back for him one day.

The war was still a thing of the future when Neville Chamberlain attempted to avert it. Although he had been too old for

Left: The press pack at work during the General Strike in May 1926. Although there would be marked progress in the development of plastic-based films in the years up to 1939, the plate cameras used by these men would hardly change in real terms and press photographers would continue to favour glass plates over other formats well into the 1950s. *[TT]*.

Below: The physical demands of preparing images for publication meant that prints were often used and abused, but some proved useful for reference purposes. This one dating from June 1935 shows the line-up of ships during the Atlantic Fleet visit to Southend-on-Sea marking the Silver Jubilee of King George V. The unmarked aircraft carriers are *Furious* and *Courageous*. *William Horton [TT]*

military service, he well understood that the horrors of the Great War should never be repeated and the British public were firmly behind him. Anti-war sentiment was universal and many, including visionaries like H.G. Wells, cherished the hope that the conflict had been a war to end war. The policy of appeasement was not without its dissenters, of course, and Winston Churchill, the man we keep as their champion, continues to brood over those times from his place on the back of our £5 notes. But he was not alone and leading Labour figures led by the Gallipoli veteran Clement Attlee were equally as critical, albeit tinged with additional disdain for the manner of Chamberlain's approach to domestic politics.

Appeasement was strongly supported by much of the British press, led by *The Times* under the editorship of Geoffrey Dawson, a man with strong connections to the political establishment, basking in confidences as much as he enjoyed the rounds of country pursuits bagging pheasants and hooking trout. In earlier years Dawson had benefited from the patronage of the imperial heavyweight Lord Milner when he was busy stirring up Boer resentment in South Africa in an attempt to force-feed them a British imperial vision they could not stomach. As a champion of empire, Milner has roads named after him across Britain and there is one not far from the location of the News UK photo archive.

Lord Milner collected a 'kindergarten' of talented young men in tune with his ideals and it was via this route that Dawson became editor of *The Times*, not once but twice. His first tenure was during the proprietorship of Lord Northcliffe, where the two men gradually took divergent paths. After Northcliffe's death the paper passed to the altogether more accommodating John Jacob Astor V, a Great War veteran of considerable means who gave Dawson the platform he wanted while the descendant of the paper's founder, John Walter, managed the business.

The Times seemed in every sense to be an organ of the establishment and Dawson was more than happy to project it from within his position as a friend of people who really mattered. As the menace of Nazi Germany grew ever clearer, Dawson tempered the paper's coverage of Hitler's excesses so as not to undermine the appeasement policy of Neville Chamberlain and Dawson's close friend Edward Wood, the ennobled Lord Halifax, Britain's Foreign Secretary.

Although the press of that era has long enjoyed the collective 'Fleet Street', in actual fact *The Times* was based a short distance away on Queen Victoria Street in a warren named Printing House Square. My very first job was at *The Observer* in 1975, housed in the typically grim 1960s vintage offices that replaced it. *The Times* had, by then, decamped to Gray's Inn Road. This move had taken place primarily because, in 1966, the paper was sold to the Canadian press baron Roy Thomson. He had bought *The Sunday Times* from its long-standing owner, Lord Kemsley, in 1959 and now created Times Newspapers Ltd. It was the merger of these two papers under one roof that saw the coming together of the picture archives featured in this book.

Lord Kemsley, James Gomer Berry, worked with his brother William to build the Allied Newspapers empire. They acquired *The Sunday Times* in 1915 and steadily added to their collection of national and regional titles. By the start of the Second World War the company they built was the largest media group in the United Kingdom, but by then the brothers had caused great surprise when they split their business. William, Lord Camrose, took the *Daily Telegraph*,

while Lord Kemsley kept hold of the rest. He would eventually rename the group after himself and build new premises where he acted as editor in chief of *The Sunday Times* alongside the imposing figure of W.W. Hadley. Such was his confidence, the proud press baron would have 'A Kemsley Newspaper' emblazoned across the mastheads of his leading titles.

For a 'picture paper' he enjoyed the success of the *Daily Sketch*, a populist read founded in Manchester by Edward Hulton. The paper had changed hands before it came to the Berry brothers but under them it thrived, employing some of the best photographers of the period between the wars, including James Jarché, William Field, Stanley Devon and the young Geoffrey Keating. They were working for a title that had borrowed and adapted the famous slogan of the *New York Times*, trumpeting the *Sketch* as 'The Picture Newspaper with all the News and Pictures Fit to Print.' They even advertised it in *The Times*!

The busy pool of staff photographers was managed by Tom Noble providing images principally for the *Daily Sketch*, but also the *Sunday Graphic* and other titles in the group. Noble kept his men on the go at all times. There was always something to do. He would call on a number of regular freelancers when necessary and they could be sure of seeing their work used. In his entertaining autobiography, Stanley Devon tells us they were known as spacemen.

Across the city, *The Times* had made progress with photography since the end of the Great War when, under Lord Northcliffe, the paper ceased its reliance on using occasional photos from its sister paper, the *Daily Mail*, and employed its own team of photographers. The first had been the pioneering Edward Risley, but, soon, Bill Warhurst, Stanley Kessell and William Horton joined him. Cathal O'Gorman and Eric Greenwood came on board a short while afterwards. Another important name was Jack Barker. With his father, Victor, employed as manager of the paper's Paris office, he was ideally placed to cover many of the major events happening in Europe before the German invasion of France in 1940. Like many of his colleagues from that era he was still hard at work in the late 1960s. They were all gone by the time I started out on Fleet Street but my former colleague, Mick Bone, has memories of Stanley Devon coming into the TNL picture library to cadge a cup of tea while bemoaning the simplicity of modern 35mm cameras making the job so much easier for younger photographers.

In my previous book, *The Liberation of Europe 1944– 1945*, I looked at the great campaign to end the Second World War in Europe conducted from D-Day until the total collapse of the Nazi regime in the spring of 1945. Gathering the images for it was relatively straightforward because the collections for the campaign were almost entirely homogeneous within the wider News UK picture archive. For this book I have had to research through a great many prints and negatives that survived the effects of wartime bombing. Subsequent and unfortunate deletion programmes known as 'thinning out' occurred not long after the Second World War and were repeated during the early 1970s when the merged picture archives of *The Times* and *Sunday Times* were shoehorned into one space, the sacrifices allowing room for expansion.

Although progress in the application of plastics led to the introduction of 35mm and improved 120 roll film formats during the 1920s, press photography was still dominated by the glass plate; a thin pane of glass coated with light-sensitive emulsion placed into a 'slide' holder that fitted into the bulky

The networking skills of the future Lord Kemsley, Sir Gomer Berry, are apparent in this image from November 1932. Aside from a couple of earls, this gathering for a shooting party on the estate of Lord Burnham near Beaconsfield included Berry (fourth from right) with a future Prime Minister of France, Pierre-Étienne Flandin (fifth right) and the increasingly powerful Neville Chamberlain (second right). *Robert Chandler [KN]*

The new frontage of Kemsley House pictured on 28 April 1939. The building was badly damaged by bombing on 24 September 1940, killing the photographer Charles Maxwell, who was on Home Guard duty, and destroying an unknown number of glass plate negatives. *Alfred Harris [KN]*

Then, as now, selling newspapers was a highly competitive business that often called for a bit of initiative. This enterprising duo found a novel way to reach customers aboard the many ships lined up for the Coronation Review of 1937 at Spithead. The ship in the background is the unfortunate RMS *Lancastria* that would be sunk off St Nazaire with tremendous loss of life in June 1940. *News UK Archive*

The Times made regular use of join-ups, the merging of two images to make a wide shot. This image was used across the full width of the picture page and shows the scene on The Mall on 15 April 1936 where the cortege carrying the coffin of the late German ambassador, Leopold von Hoesch, began it's long journey home to Dresden. A critic of Nazi policy, von Hoesch died of a heart attack on 10 of April and his demise proved convenient for Hitler who quickly replaced him with the ardent Joachim von Ribbentrop who was, to say the least, far more on message with Nazi ambitions. *Stanley Kessell [TT]*

The Times was a leading exponent of technological progress in many areas of newspaper production. The paper even developed its own typeface, in 1931, and Times New Roman remains in use around the world, but no longer where it was launched. Infrared photographic processes and new printing methods were given much prominence but the company also had a firm eye on its long-term future with the construction of a new press hall that was officially opened by Neville Chamberlain on 1 December 1937, when he started the presses rolling after a celebratory dinner. To the left of Chamberlain is the proprietor, John Jacob Astor V, and next to him is the editor Geoffrey Dawson. The paper's manager, John Walter, whose ancestor founded the paper in 1785, stands at the top of the stairway. *William Horton [TT]*

cameras of the day. Press photographers would carry a number of prepared slides to quickly change over after each exposure. Plate cameras were robust but needed to be treated with respect. Professional newsmen quickly learned to judge distances and in this way they could pre-set their camera to be ready for action. Once processed, the plates were handled with differing degrees of care. They were routinely broken and often stored on open shelving with all the attendant perils this implies. A typical quarter plate negative is roughly the same size as a CD case. There are over four million of them in the News UK picture archive.

Photographic prints were generally seen as one-use-only assets and the production methods of the hot metal era often ensured this was so. Prints we now treasure were abused with abandon. They might be folded across blocks for cropping purposes and artists masked out bits they didn't want or painted on what editors preferred to see. Large prints were usually scored with a blade so they could be folded into standard files, although *The Times* librarians preferred to file theirs in a separate system to keep them whole. Printing standards were generally superb but things were sometimes rushed. The same applies to negative processing where the vagaries of 'dip and dunk' were the order of the day. Many plates betray thumbprints of the people handling them set permanently in the wet emulsion before drying.

Indexing glass plates was a challenge and it was found expedient to scratch a file number and sometimes a caption into the emulsion using the point of a compass or the nib of a fountain pen. Daybooks were kept to log the material coming in and most papers eventually resorted to a card index for their archives. Quite a lot of the early indexing was done retrospectively but the librarians soon caught up and found the most convenient solutions to caring for an ever-increasing amount of material.

The Great War occurred at a time when newspapers were in their pomp, without serious rivals from other forms of media. The conflict was recorded with a mixture of good, bad and terrible journalism, while still photography and flickering moving pictures truly found their feet as enduring mediums of

Mr Chamberlain was given a commemorative clock resembling the one installed outside Printing House Square as a memento of the occasion. *[TT]*

record. Newspapers were still at the top of the tree at the start of the Second World War, but cinema newsreel and the new realm of television were other outlets for imagery. Although television was suspended during hostilities, newsreel had a massive part to play, providing us with iconic moments from the war. Radio was a direct conduit to hearts and minds and would be used by politicians and propagandists to sell their version of events.

The importance of newspapers had hardly dimmed when I started work in 1975 but the climate has changed in this age of 24-hour news and social media. Demands on picture libraries and archives have altered beyond recognition in the period since digital cameras brought an end to reliance on wet process photography in the mid-1990s. The days of sending out dozens of print files for use by picture editors were ended by the introduction of seemingly unlimited digital archives and that process continues. What was once a labour-intensive trade has diminished in the digital age. At one point there were a good thirty or more picture and reference librarians working at the now demolished plant at Wapping in East London. There are eight of us left. This is a time when picture archives have to sing ever louder for their suppers and this book is as much a showcase as it is an exercise in recalling dramatic moments of our history.

Press photographers had much to keep them occupied during the uncertain summer of 1939. Leslie Hore-Belisha had moved from heading up the Ministry of Transport to the War Office and was persuaded to invoke memories of the militia to get a quarter of a million young unmarried men into uniform. One of them was my father, a trainee sports journalist just beginning to make his way on Fleet Street when other matters intervened. As war loomed, he remembered returning to his office to be met by the boss standing gravely in the newsroom. 'Barnes, you have to go!' My dad and his army mates smile out from a few surviving photos and I honour them all to this day. This book is dedicated to the militiamen of the 7th (Stoke Newington) Battalion of the Royal Berkshire Regiment. Above all it is in memory of my father, who made me a newspaperman and a lover of history. Although he wasn't perfect, he was my dad and the love never fades. This one is for you, Barney.

Mark Barnes
March 2021

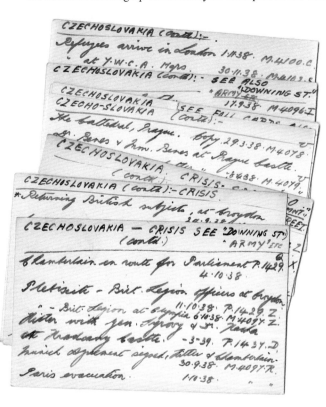

Typical Kemsley index cards like these from the period of the Munich Crisis can present challenges for modern-day librarians attempting to de-cypher some of the entries. Many of the Kemsley cards from the period were written retrospectively. *Mark Barnes*

The French photographer and inventor Édouard Belin is credited with inventing wirephoto technology with the advent of his Bélinographe as early as 1907. The system went through a succession of improvements over the decades before the Second World War, with companies such as AT&T leading the way. The British withdrawal from the Rhineland in December 1929 provided the perfect opportunity to show off the wonders of this modern technology. A breathless caption tells us: 'These pictures were taken by plane to Strasbourg and transmitted by wire via Berlin, a distance of about 1,000 miles – a new triumph for the *Daily Sketch* system.' Charles Maxwell's original image does not survive in print or negative form and this blurry-looking version lacks a lot of detail, but this print showing how the wirephoto was received in London is historic in its own right. An artist has amended parts to hide wonky elements. *Charles Maxwell [KN]*

Right: Allied Newspapers made extensive use of aeroplanes to beat deadlines, although sometimes with tragic consequences. The nuptials of the Kaiser's grandson Prince Wilhelm of Prussia and Dorothea von Salviati on Saturday, 3 June 1933 were a case in point. Bertram Wilson covered the civil and religious ceremonies in Bonn for the next day's edition of the *Sunday Graphic*. The published caption celebrated how the exposed plates were 'Flown by Captain AJ Styran to Heston (337 miles) in 135 minutes – a remarkable average of 2½ miles per minute.' The 38-year-old Wilson and the popular air racer 'Bill' Styran were killed on a similar mission when their plane crashed returning from covering the unveiling of the R101 memorial in France the following October. *Bertram Wilson [KN]*

A NOTE ON LAYOUT AND SOURCES

I have elected to place certain events happening concurrently into overlapping chapters in the hope of simplifying a narrative that would otherwise become fragmented. This means events such as those in Abyssinia and Spain can be kept in an easy to follow order rather than have them spread across several chapters. As ever, any errors are strictly my own.

The images in this book are from the News UK photographic archive. *The Times* images are shown as [TT]. Kemsley Newspapers material appears as [KN]. All such images are copyright of Times Newspapers Ltd. Photographers are identified when known. Additional images are credited to their provider.

Cutting-edge wirephoto technology at Kemsley House in July 1938. The Berry brothers' Allied Newspapers set great store in wiring images across their empire, predominantly from Glasgow and Manchester to London, but the vast majority of copy negatives made of wired photos were not retained during revisions of the photo archive made after the Second World War.
Charles Maxwell [KN]

The sinking of the liner *Athenia* on the first day of the war served to underscore the value of wirephotos, when this image of survivors arriving in Greenock was transmitted to London. *[KN]*

Photographers at the *Daily Sketch* often carried Leica cameras for assignments where bulky equipment was likely to be a hindrance, but even top-notch pros like Stanley Devon never really got to grips with them, preferring the larger formats they had grown up with. This sequence was taken in a No 37 Squadron Handley Page Harrow bomber at RAF Feltwell in January 1939. Working with an unfamiliar camera in a notoriously chilly Harrow must have been a challenge but he had a plate camera, as well, to do the kind of shots he preferred. Stan's ability to take consistently good pictures of RAF subjects led to him being snapped up by the Air Ministry to become an official photographer at the start of the war. *Stanley Devon [KN]*

This book was made possible thanks to the technology for making digital scans of prints and negatives. This image of the Processing Department of Allied Newspapers dating from 1927 had lengths of gummed paper attached to the glass side to mask out areas the end user did not want. The author washed this off carefully using boiled water. The plate had also suffered damage to the emulsion during processing and ironically the worst of it is on the right, where the chap is retouching another plate. Thanks to imaging software it was possible to overlay a picture of the author's hand (inset) to replace the ruined original. The finished work allows to us to enjoy this wonderful photo in full. *William Field [KN] / Andrew Sims*

The strength of the alliance between Britain and France was underlined on Bastille Day, 14 July 1939, when a detachment of the Irish Guards were given the honour of marching at the head of the *Défilé*. The temptation to invoke the spirit of Napoleon Bonaparte led to quite an operation to get this montage into the *Daily Sketch* the next day. Glass plate negatives of the parade were flown to London where they were processed and printed, allowing an artist very little time to execute the image painted directly onto this photograph before the presses rolled that evening. *M Fryszman [KN]*

1

MAKING GERMANY PAY

························

O N 11 November 1918, the much-travelled Canadian 116th Infantry Battalion arrived at the outskirts of Mons in Belgium. The men had come far in the time the battalion had been engaged on the Western Front and are representative of the millions who descended on that corner of Europe from across the world to endure 'the war to end all wars'. The battalion's dead can be found in cemeteries large and small from Vimy Ridge to Cambrai and the Hindenburg Line. A memorial tablet to the 116th is affixed to a hotel standing close to the sprawling Supreme Headquarters of the Allied Powers in Europe, an organisation borne out of an even more terrible war to come.

Hardy souls can brave the traffic to visit another memorial just opposite, marking where British cavalry had their first brush with the enemy on 22 August 1914. It is a convenient spot to take a somewhat simplistic glance at a war that more or less ended where it began after four years of unparalleled death and destruction. But the real history of the Great War is a much more complicated story than battlefield coincidences suggest. Mapping the peace was just as great a challenge to the politicians and soldiers attempting to pick up the pieces.

Germany was in chaos during the final weeks of the war and faced years of internal conflict as the power of Paul von Hindenburg and Erich Ludendorff fell away in their attempts to keep control. They had, through the Supreme Army Command, the *Oberste Heeresleitung* (OHL), long held sway over the Kaiser and politicians, but people were starving and anger at Prussian militarism became increasingly open. With Hindenburg largely operating as a figurehead, his deputy, Ludendorff, dominated a succession of politicians, but at the end of September 1918 he suddenly declared the military situation hopeless and called for a truce. The American president, Woodrow Wilson, demanded immediate constitutional changes in Germany based on his well-publicised Fourteen Points. The country would have to become

Below: U-Boats were required to surrender at British ports following the Armistice. Over a hundred and fifty of them were gathered at Harwich. Nearest the camera is the U-117, a Type UB III coastal torpedo attack boat built by Blohm und Voss at Hamburg. She was under the command of the highly decorated *Kapitänleutnant* Erwin Waßner, a veteran submariner who became the first post-war German Naval Attaché to London. U-117 was scrapped at Felixtowe in 1920. *[KN]*

a genuine parliamentary democracy before there could be any serious discussions about peace.

Ludendorff and the Kaiser cajoled Prince Maximilian von Baden to take the reins as chancellor. He represented a kind of halfway house between the de facto dictatorship of the OHL and the parliamentary system Wilson demanded, and Ludendorff hoped this would be enough to get talks started. For Ludendorff, creating a facade of what he called 'parliamentarisation' would keep him firmly in charge and having civilians nominally in control offered the excuse he was taking his orders from an elected government. On this basis he was able to propagate the 'stabbed in the back myth' central to far right propaganda in the years that followed.

But in a sequence of three notes, Wilson ended by demanding the abdication of the Kaiser and the imposition of a truly democratic republic before there could be peace. This was too much for Ludendorff, who ordered the army to fight on. The new chancellor was appalled and called on a wavering Kaiser to dismiss Ludendorff. On 26 October the Supreme War Lord informed the First Quartermaster General that he had lost his trust. Lieutenant General Wilhelm Groener replaced him.

There were problems elsewhere as mutiny fomented within the High Seas Fleet. Facing imminent defeat, naval commanders had ordered their ships to sail for a final clash with the Royal Navy. But the sailors at Wilhelmshaven and Kiel balked at such a proposition and mutinied at the end of October. Disaffection spread. The mutiny had a domino effect on German politics, bringing socialist agitation out into the open. The danger of a total breakdown was on the cards. With revolution in the air, Baden met with the leading social democrat Friedrich Ebert to discuss how to take things further. Baden planned to persuade Wilhem II to abdicate in favour of a regency under his second son, Prince Eitel Friedrich, but Ebert was convinced that only the complete removal of the monarchy would forestall socialist revolution similar to Russia.

Resistance to the Allied powers had broken down elsewhere. Bulgaria and Turkey were already out of the war and the Austro-Hungarian Empire collapsed on 31 October when Hungary split from the union. This, in conjunction with defeat at Vittorio Veneto, sealed an armistice with Italy.

The utterly dismayed Kaiser had been encouraged to stand and die with his armies, but instead he abdicated on 9 November as Baden gave way to allow Ebert to become chancellor. That same day a republic was proclaimed in Berlin by Philipp Scheidemann speaking for the various social democrats who dominated the Reichstag in an attempt to counteract the activities of communist leader Karl Liebknecht, who had recently been released from prison and who declared a socialist republic of his own from the former Kaiser's palace on the same day. Wilhelm left for exile in the Netherlands on the 10th. The transfer of power to Ebert had seen the constitutional change demanded by Woodrow Wilson as the basis of any truce arrangements.

Matthias Erzberger of the Catholic Centre Party led the small group who negotiated the Armistice for Germany. He found little room for manoeuvre with an obdurate Ferdinand Foch leading the Allied delegation. The Germans had made the tortuous journey to the railway siding at Compiègne on 8 November, where the two parties rendezvoused. Foch presented his list of demands and the Germans were given seventy-two hours to accept. They had little choice under the circumstances and messages from both Ebert and Hindenburg instructed Erzberger to sign. The Armistice came into effect at the eleventh hour of the eleventh day of the eleventh month of 1918. Some Germans never forgave Matthias Erzberger for his apparent treachery. Followers of the far-right Organisation Consul murdered him in 1921. Philipp Scheidemann, the man who had proclaimed the German republic, only just escaped a similar fate in June 1922 when he was attacked with prussic acid.

Peace with the Allies came as Germany hovered on the brink of all-out civil war. Fighting spread across the country as Freikorps units swelled by disaffected war veterans took on the communists. Street fighting and brutal murders followed, exemplified by the deaths of Karl Liebknecht and Rosa Luxemburg during the Spartacist Uprising in January 1919. Battles at Munich and elsewhere saw cities changing hands as left and right fought for supremacy. Against the background of all this the victorious Allies set out to exact punishment on Germany for the Great War just ended. They would come to the table with differing ambitions and the result would see a peace imposed on Germany fostering a new ultra-nationalism that proved disastrous for Europe and the world within twenty years.

An uncertain world staggered on. Long-cherished hopes of true nation status for the Poles and Czechs needed to be addressed. A myriad number of other ethnic and territorial issues were yet to be resolved. But with Russia mired in civil war and the dread fear of revolution fluttering hearts in every European capital, the gathering of the victors to agree what became known as the Treaty of Versailles was looked on as the chance for a genuine and lasting peace supported by the creation of an international body that could arbitrate disputes and administer solutions. But the talks took place without Russia and came to be dominated by the degree of punishment France in particular wished to mete out on Germany for costing her so much in blood and treasure.

The French hoped to push their frontier with Germany as far as the Rhine, giving them increased security alongside control of strategic coalfields and industries. But this was dependent on pledges of mutual support from Britain and especially the United States. For France the support of the Americans was crucial. But although Woodrow Wilson had espoused the creation of the League of Nations, he faced opposition from American legislators who wanted to keep the United States away from the mess of further European entanglement.

The Americans were even more strident in their opposition to the League possessing the right to direct member states to take military action. To do so would override the primacy of the Constitution and the authority of Congress. This and other aspects of Versailles led the United States to seek a separate peace with Germany that wasn't ratified until 1921. The Americans never joined the League of Nations, dealing it a mortal blow, but it was to be a slow death.

The evaporation of American support was devastating to French aspirations. The alternative of a buffer state dominated by Paris proved impossible, so the French settled for the demilitarization of the Rhineland backed up by promises of support from London in the event of renewed aggression by Germany. The Saarland was placed under a French mandate and the territories lost in the war of 1870 regained.

The months it took to secure agreement in Paris saw bitter arguments over the level of punishment Germany would receive. Millions of gold marks in hard cash were only part of the equation. Aside from consignments of coal, raw materials, industrial chemicals and machinery, the Germans were to be stripped of their offensive military power. They would have no air force, no modern capital ships or submarines. Their army would be limited to the size of a defence force of 100,000 men, leaving her neighbours secure. She could have no general staff or armoured vehicles. Germany would lose her colonies and surrender her lead in many fields of science and industry. Adding insult to injury, a great many patents were confiscated, including the wonder drug aspirin.

The British delegation was based at the Hotel Astoria in Paris, where a team of lawyers, linguists, diplomats and economists pored over the fine print assembled in the halls of the Quai d'Orsay, where the principal negotiations took place. A party of Girl Guides travelled out from London to act as messengers. Between them they generated a mountain of paperwork but there were anxious moments when agreement seemed improbable and yet it all came together, somehow.

The leading British economist John Maynard Keynes described Versailles as a 'Carthaginian peace' and German reluctance to agree to the full terms led to the Allies threatening to resume hostilities. This was enough to persuade Admiral von Reuter to order the scuttling of the interned High Seas Fleet at Scapa Flow. But the Germans were in a hopeless position and having spoken impassionedly about the injustice of it, Friedrich Ebert reluctantly agreed to send a delegation to sign the treaty. Ferdinand Foch had led the Allied armies to victory in 1918 and was instrumental in settling the Armistice. He was unconvinced by the terms of the treaty, saying 'this is not peace. It is an armistice for twenty years.' Foch was to die ten years before his prophecy became fact.

Symbolism was everything and the chance to reverse the humiliation of 1870–71 was not lost on the French. Abject defeat on the battlefield in the Franco-Prussian War was made worse by the peace imposed on France by Otto von Bismarck. A payment of 5 billion francs and the loss of Alsace-Lorraine was a bitter pill to swallow, while the sight of the King of Prussia crowned Kaiser of a united German Empire in the Hall of Mirrors at Versailles was too much to bear. Redress was finally at hand. The great occasion took place in the very same room on 28 June 1919. It was precisely five years to the day since the assassination of Archduke Franz Ferdinand of Austria had precipitated the war.

There was jubilation in Paris and London at the signing of the treaty. National celebrations were to follow. In Paris, the first peacetime *Quatorze Juillet* for five years saw a massive outpouring of pride in France's military triumph. Britain enjoyed its own Peace Day; a public holiday with parades and celebrations on 19 July. The military parade in London saw contingents from the victorious Allied forces marching through the capital to the delight of vast crowds. But things were not always so cheery. A searchlight station on Parliament Hill was set alight during late night festivities and attending firemen were impeded by revellers. Rioting veterans disrupted festivities in Luton and burned down the town hall. Peace Day offered brief respite from the pain of recession, the spectre of mass unemployment, and longer working hours for those lucky enough to have a job to go to. Britain approached the next decade amid a strong feeling of disillusionment.

The events of 1919 dragged on as Germany struggled to reboot itself in the reality of post-war Europe. An abortive attempt at a union with Austria was snuffed out when Allied fears of Pan-Germanism led to the enforced creation of an Austrian republic. This was ratified with the signing of the Treaty of Saint-Germain-en-Laye on 10 September 1919. The republics of Czechoslovakia and Poland had come into being with sizeable German minorities within their newly defined borders. The end of 700 years of Habsburg rule and the imposition of a weak Austrian state shorn of its former institutions and much of its traditional economy fired the indignation of its ethnic German populace, many of whom found common cause with the extremism espoused by nascent National Socialism.

In Germany, amid all the political violence of competing ideologies, grievances over the crippling terms of Versailles united opinion. On 21 September 1919 Philipp Scheidemann summed up the deep sense of injustice felt across the political spectrum on the day he became head of the National Assembly, saying 'Which hand, trying to put us in chains like these, would not wither? The treaty is unacceptable.' Injured pride helped fuel resentment that grew in intensity as time wore on. But misgivings over the perceived iniquities of Versailles would not be exclusive to disgruntled Germans alone.

Germany's unwillingness to pay reparations would lead to disputes between the Allies. Britain saw a reinvigorated German economy as good for business, a position that was bound to meet with disapproval across the Channel. With their finances in a total mess at the end of the war, the British needed all the opportunities for trade they could muster. Cuts in wages and rising unemployment caused hardship and intense bitterness in a land Lloyd George had hoped would be 'a fit country for heroes to live in.' Crippling reparations could only hinder the chances of a rejuvenated Germany being open to imports of goods the British desperately needed to sell.

Business was business but, for France, with swathes of the country ravaged by war, reparations meant much more than mere compensation. Britain may have suffered air raids with loss of life and property but it was a drop in the ocean compared to the scale of destruction of critical industrial and agricultural lands of her ally across the English Channel. The French saw Germany's failure to pay as something much more significant. Germany's reluctance to accept any guilt for its war of conquest implied a willingness to try again some day. The scars of 1870 and now the Great War left France determined to insure no more German armies would sweep across her borders. Breaking German industrial and military power was central to this. Moneys drained from her neighbour could not be spent on armaments and the means to deploy them.

The Spa Conference of 1920 and the London Conference in 1921 sought to implement a workable payments schedule. Germany had to come up with 132 billion gold marks, the equivalent of 33 billion US dollars, to pay for the civilian damage her war of aggression had caused. But the waters were already muddied. The figure was divided into three bonds in a bid to mask the unpalatable truth from the public in Britain and France that as things stood, Germany could never pay such an enormous sum. The London schedule required the Germans to come up with 50 billion gold marks.

Regardless of the cut in reparations, the Germans still struggled to pay their dues. By the end of 1922 the French had reached the limit of their patience. The Allies met in London where the new Italian Prime Minister, Benito Mussolini, caught the eye of the British press. No agreement was reached, so they decided to try again early in 1923. Failure to enforce a payment plan at the next summit in Paris saw reluctant but drastic action by President Poincaré to send an army into the Ruhr to take control of the coal and raw materials owed to France for her own reconstruction. The Germans argued that the French action, supported by a Belgian contingent, diverted the very resources the country needed to expand industrial growth in order to stimulate trade. There was sympathy for this viewpoint in London and Rome, but this was mitigated by long-standing suspicion the Germans were hiding assets abroad.

A photographer working for *The Times* recorded the scene as French tanks rolled into Essen. Details on Monsieur Gouville are sketchy in the extreme and he only seems to have supplied images from the initial invasion and from two months later when clashes between workers at Krupp and French troops led to a number of deaths. Pictures from other agencies highlight the atmosphere of mutual loathing between the local populace and the French, but our man Gouville did not capture anything as candid or as emotive. Passive resistance was encouraged and there were protests elsewhere in Germany. With the Weimar economy in tatters, the seizure of raw materials was just about the only way the French could ensure the Germans met their obligations. Hundreds of miles to the south, an aspiring politician wallowed in indignation at the shame heaped on Germany. France had secured the lasting enmity of Adolf Hitler.

With an economy already teetering on the abyss, the French invasion precipitated disastrous hyperinflation in the Weimar Republic. By November of that year a single US dollar was worth 4.2 billion paper marks. Workers paid by the hour saw their wages vanish before their eyes while the story goes that restaurant customers were wise to pay for their meals in advance. German banks printed worthless notes with eyewatering denominations running into tens and hundreds of millions of marks. In the absence of precious coal claimed by France, a lot of it found use on the nation's fires.

The Dawes Plan of 1924 went some way to improve matters. A committee led by US Brigadier-General Charles G. Dawes called for the withdrawal of foreign forces from the Ruhr and changes to how reparations were paid. But for all the good it did the Dawes Plan could only be seen as temporary. The plan hinged on the Germans taking on huge loans from American banks to pay their reparations and this in itself would be undone by the Wall Street Crash five years hence. Dawes shared the 1925 Nobel Peace Prize for his efforts and rose to be Vice President of the United States alongside Calvin Coolidge.

Reparations were important but so, too, were borders. Settling frontiers once and for all was seen as a way to improve understanding between former enemies, removing the scope for future conflict. The British, French, Belgians and Italians met with the Germans at Locarno in Switzerland in October 1925. The Locarno Treaties arising from the summit saw Germany guarantee her post-Versailles borders in the West in addition to a further treaty guaranteeing peace between France, Belgium and Germany. There was to be no such security for Germany's eastern neighbours at Locarno. Lacking crucial support from the British, who doubted the value of any agreement while so many Germans lived within their borders, the Czechs and Poles had to settle for arbitration conventions backed up by the Permanent Court of International Justice. The French reaffirmed mutual assistance pacts with Czechoslovakia and Poland but how effective these would be was put to the test in 1938. The seeds of appeasement had been planted. The Locarno Treaties were signed in London on 1 December 1925.

In 1929, Dawes' colleague Owen D. Young, the founder of the Radio Corporation of America, led efforts to settle the issue of reparations once and for all. The plan required Germany to pay 112 billion gold marks at a rate of two billion per annum from 1930 onwards. Once again, the plan relied heavily on loans made by American banks and would see final payment due in 1988. But the Wall Street Crash and subsequent Great Depression would interfere with the schedule, compelling the American banks to withdraw millions of dollars from abroad to shore up the US economy, effectively curtailing German ability to pay. By this time the Germans were agitating to suspend payments altogether. President Herbert Hoover had already called for a moratorium of one year.

Allied occupation forces were withdrawn from the Rhineland. British units centred on Cologne and then Wiesbaden had been progressively run down from corps, to divisional, to brigade strength by the end of 1929. Nevertheless, the British had become quite comfortable in their home from home and even had their own newspaper. Relations with the locals were good but the departure of occupying forces was as welcome in Germany as it was in London, where the expense could be cut from the defence budget. A second British Army of the Rhine would enjoy a much longer stay after 1945.

There had been little progress two years on from the Young Plan. A seven-power conference held in London in the summer of 1931 expressed good intentions but with Britain and France struggling to repay their own war debts to the Americans, the summit at Lausanne in the summer of 1932 represented a line in the sand. The conference between Britain, France and Germany led to an understanding that a suspension of German reparations could be set in place if the Americans restructured the outstanding loans of her one-time allies. But Congress wasn't having any of it and notions of bad faith on the part of Britain, in particular, gave ammunition for the isolationists. Britain still owed the United States over £800 million in 1934 at a time when a pound sterling exchanged for 5 US dollars. The impact of the Great Depression followed by the Second World War would see that money absorbed into the even greater sums owed at the end of 1945. It would take another sixty years to repay.

With Hitler in power a year after Lausanne the Nazis refused to pay another pfennig and they tore up the Locarno Treaties. By that time Germany had paid less than a quarter of the reparations set out in 1919. The post-Second World War Federal Republic was required to continue interest repayments on loans taken out for reparations once reunification had taken place in 1990. The final instalment was made on 3 October 2010.

The notion that the terms of Versailles were harsh in the extreme was not just felt by the Germans. Many leading figures in Britain believed it to be the case. Four years after Lausanne, Ramsay MacDonald, who had been at the conference, expressed pleasure at seeing the treaty 'vanishing'. It is difficult to argue with the suggestion that the implementation of Versailles was a root cause of the very circumstances the treaty was designed to prevent.

The last year of the Great War had seen the sequence of massive offensives launched by the Germans from 21 March 1918 lead to a break in the 'stalemate' of trench warfare. Allied retreat turned into the glory of the Hundred Days, when, from 4 August 1918, the Germans were thrown back way beyond the start lines of the so-called *Kaiserschlacht* – the Kaiser's Battle. By the end of September Ludendorff knew his plans had failed while Germany itself was on the brink of chaos. Defeat was now inevitable. The Armistice that began at 11am on 11 November 1918 was met with joyful scenes in London. *[KN]*

News of the Armistice caused thousands of people to pour onto the streets of the capital. Crowds rushed to Whitehall where *The Times* takes up the story: 'For a time, Downing Street was kept clear; then the human torrent could be held in check no longer, and a cheering, triumphant crowd assailed the approach to No 10.' Important personages were greeted with enthusiasm. 'But it was for Mr Lloyd George that the crowd was waiting. A few minutes before 11 o'clock he appeared at the door – and the storm broke.' David Lloyd George appeared to be overwhelmed by the reception he received. '…Then he spoke to probably the most enthusiastic audience he has ever addressed - ' At 11 o'clock this morning the war will be over. We have won a great victory and we are entitled to a bit of shouting.' *[KN]*

Flag-waving nurses celebrate the happy news at the London Hospital in Whitechapel. *[KN]*

It appears the glorious news has yet to sink in for these sailors and soldiers photographed at a London railway terminus. *[KN]*

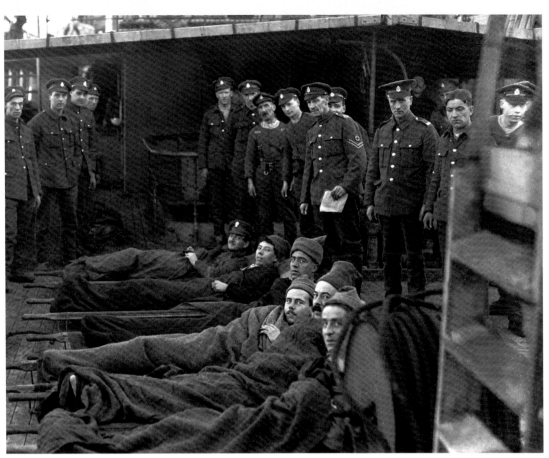

Some of the last men to be wounded before the Armistice returned home on 24 November 1918. *[KN]*

The defeat of Germany at sea was encapsulated in the surrender of U-Boats at Harwich which began arriving on the days following 21 November. The submarines were met by launches ready to put armed men aboard. These German sailors gathered on an unidentified U-Boat appear to be relaxed about their situation. *[KN]*

The virtually new U-141 glides into Portsmouth past Nelson's flagship HMS *Victory* to the satisfaction of a group of Boy Scouts and other onlookers. One of three Type 139 long-range cruiser submarines built at Kiel, this vessel only entered service in 1918 and did not achieve any successes against Allied shipping before the cessation of hostilities. Her commanding officer was *Kapitänleutnant* Constantin Kolbe. U-141 was scrapped at Upnor in 1923. *[KN]*

The war's end saw an immediate cutback in the production of war matériel. These newly unemployed munitionettes are queuing for assistance at King's Cross Labour Exchange. *[KN]*

A dismal scene in Whitehall on 7 February 1919 where a large party of soldiers waited to be demobilised in front of the old Admiralty and opposite the War Office. *[KN]*

While some counted themselves lucky to escape military life, there was intense frustration for reluctant warriors eager to get home. Police broke up groups of Canadian and American servicemen gambling near the YMCA Eagle Hut at the Aldwych on 9th March 1919. Two men were arrested, but a large group of others were unimpressed and a brisk fight known as the Battle of Bow Street took place (above). A riot by Canadian troops at Epsom, in June, left a policeman dead and others injured. *[KN]*

But there was other fighting to do. On 9 April elements of the North Russia Relief Force sailed from Tilbury to assist covering the withdrawal of British and Allied forces supporting faltering White Russian efforts to halt the advance of Lenin's Bolsheviks. These veteran officers appear to be in good spirits despite the uncertainty of their mission. A good number of men of all ranks who enjoyed life on campaign were happy to go to Russia, but the *Daily Express* was less certain, recalling Bismarck in exclaiming: 'The frozen plains of eastern Europe are not worth the bones of a single British grenadier.' The final withdrawal from Murmansk was completed on 12 October 1919. The Termination of the Present War (Definition) Act 1918 would keep some men in uniform for a considerable time to come. Britain's war with Germany would not legally end until 10 January 1920 under the terms of the Act and the conflict with Turkey had another four years to run before it, too, had concluded. The Act also declared 31 August 1921 as the date the Great War itself was officially ended. *[KN]*

Conflict had broken out in Ireland after the government formed by Sinn Féin called for independence on 21 January 1919. This image shows the Mark IV Male tank HMT *Scotch & Soda* positioned on the Sarsfield Bridge in Limerick during the general strike that took place in April 1919. Local trades unions formed a self-proclaimed soviet on 15 April in protest against the imposition of martial law. The tank shown was one of a small number deployed by the British in Ireland. It was operated by the 17th Battalion of the Tank Corps, a unit also equipped with armoured cars that were found to be much more useful given the fluid nature of the conflict. *[KN]*

A ration party from the Buffs betray a sense of cheerful wariness while going about their business in the city. The Limerick Soviet ran until 27 April 1919. *[KN]*

Back in London there were plenty of comings and goings to keep press photographers busy. It was a case of happy returns for these veteran soldiers of the London Scottish when they arrived at Charing Cross on 16 May 1919. The Cockney Jocks marched out into a sea of people amid a tumultuous welcome from Londoners. *[KN]*

Although it took months to negotiate the Treaty of Versailles, the impact of German bombing in 1940 has reduced the number of images available to us showing the great effort that went into achieving a settlement. Happily, a sequence of images showing aspects of the backstory of the negotiations survives. The *Daily Sketch* photographer sought out people performing vital tasks at the Hotel Astoria, where the British delegation had taken up residence.

Right: The head of British archives at the Astoria was Miss Bigby. She is pictured with some of the team of clerks and Girl Guides working at the hotel. *[KN]*

Linguist and librarian Irene Boyle is pictured at her desk. Bound volumes of *The Times* can be seen to her right. The practice of keeping editions of the paper in this form continues at News UK to this day. *[KN]*

William Malkin was a legal advisor at the Foreign Office who would travel to Munich with Neville Chamberlain in 1938 and prepare British officials for the Nuremberg Trials after the Second World War. *[KN]*

A smiling Marshal Ferdinand Foch is pictured followed by his chief of staff, General Maxime Weygand. Foch was unhappy with the results of the Versailles Treaty and said famously, 'This is not peace. It is an armistice for twenty years.' He died in 1929, missing his prophecy becoming fact. *[KN]*

This otherwise uncaptioned image shows members of the reparations committee enjoying a lighter moment during proceedings in Paris. *[KN]*

Come the great day when the treaty was signed, other photographers recorded the dramatic scene in the Hall of Mirrors while the *Daily Sketch* snapper was left kicking his heels. He photographed comings and goings of the great and the good and found people of interest to record. Just some of many interested onlookers attending the treaty negotiations included this group of French soldiers taking five to chat and enjoy a smoke. Several of these men have suffered severe facial injuries. 28 June 1919. *[KN]*

With the job done the three most powerful men in the world could step out into the sun to bask in the glory of their achievement. David Lloyd George, Georges Clemenceau and Woodrow Wilson go for a stroll in the warmth of the Paris afternoon accompanied by a posse of minders. *[KN]*

Celebrations soon broke out in London as news spread across the Channel. The war really was over, but for thousands of men like these amputee veterans there were other battles to come amid the uncertainty of Lloyd George's much paraphrased 'land fit for heroes'. *[KN]*

Members of the Women's Royal Air Force enjoy the day. Their service was disbanded in 1920 as defence cuts bit hard, but the name was revived in 1949 and remained in use until 1994, when the separate women's service was merged with the RAF. *[KN]*

The fun went on into the night as a huge crowd stayed on in Trafalgar Square as Nelson looked down on the festivities. *Robert Field. [KN]*

Below: A tumultuous victory celebration was held in Paris on Bastille Day. Thousands of Allied troops and leading military figures marched through the Arc de Triomphe and down the Champs-Élysées led by a group of wounded veterans, the *mutiles*. German guns and kit were heaped around the arch to display the depth of the great victory France had secured over her enemy. The stain of the Franco-Prussian War of 1870 had been removed at last, but the cost was immense in blood and treasure and there was much to be done to rejuvenate a nation exhausted by war. *[KN]*

The situation was no better in Britain but the government hoped a grand day of celebration would lift spirits, as long as it was just the one; the struggling economy came first. 19 July 1919 was eventually chosen as Peace Day, with events held across the country. Contingents from the victorious allies were invited to take part in a massive victory parade through London. The vast crowd reserved an ecstatic greeting for Britain's war-winning military commanders, Field Marshal Sir Douglas Haig (above left) and Admiral of the Fleet Sir David Beatty (left). *[KN]*

Below: Fifteen thousand military personnel took part in the parade. Naturally pride of place was given over to the British who put on a fine show for their sovereign. King George V takes the salute while Queen Mary looks on. *[KN]*

Allied forces taking part in the parade were led by other giants of the Great War era. General John J. 'Black Jack' Pershing led the American Expeditionary Force and had been against agreeing to an armistice until the Kaiser's armies were pushed back on to German soil. Although his insistence on outmoded frontal assaults were criticised then and since, Pershing's popularity was such that he became the only living US general to achieve the six-star rank of General of the Armies. The other holder is George Washington, who was promoted posthumously in 1976 during bicentennial commemorations of the Declaration of Independence. *[KN]*

French cavalrymen pass down Whitehall. *[KN]*

A musician from the US 3rd Division – the *Rock of the Marne* – takes a break. The caption writer for this image was impressed with the soldier's Boston haircut. *[KN]*

Men of the US 4th and 6th Divisions take a break during a halt at the new Cenotaph on Whitehall. The first incarnation of Sir Edwin Lutyens' masterpiece was purely temporary. A permanent stone monument was unveiled on Armistice Day in 1920. *[KN]*

A good many nations were represented in an event that would not be repeated until the parade held in a much-changed world of 1946. A Belgian colour party (top left) proved popular while a group of Italians were noted for coming through the war without injury. The small Japanese contingent was led by Colonel Nobuyuki Abe, seen following the standard bearer, a future prime minister of his country who was fortunate to avoid a war crimes conviction at the end of the Second World War. *Thomas Houlding, [KN]*

Peace Day celebrations were not just confined to the land. The Atlantic Fleet dropped anchor in the Thames and such was the level of interest in seeing the great capital ships that a special train service was instituted between London and Southend-on-Sea, where the battleships and battle cruisers could be viewed from the town's famous pier, or, better still, from a pleasure boat. This image shows HMS *Royal Oak* dropping anchor as she lines up ahead of *Revenge* and *Resolution*. *Thomas Houlding, [KN]*

The Courageous-class aircraft carrier HMS *Furious* was launched as a battlecruiser in 1916 but was converted to her new configuration along with two sister ships in her class. She holds the distinction of being the vessel on which Squadron Commander Edwin Dunning made the world's first deck landing on a moving ship in 1917. Sadly, he was killed making a repeat attempt, adding an unwanted first to the ship's fine record. This image shows her at a halfway house stage of having separate decks for landing and take-off. This arrangement was clearly unsatisfactory so she was refitted with a through deck between 1921 and 1925. *Furious* was used to experiment with a range of aspects of carrier operations before the Second World War and took part in several actions against German targets, including attacks on the *Tirpitz*. She was sold for scrapping in 1948. *Thomas Houlding, [KN]*

The arrival of the fleet was a huge event in Southend, where a souvenir brochure was produced to help visitors identify the ships anchored in the Thames Estuary. More humble vessels occasionally upstaged the mighty capital ships, including this fast coastal craft, one of the 'submarine chasers' used to depth charge enemy U-Boats. In the background are the dreadnought battleship HMS *Orion* flying the flag of Rear Admiral Sir Douglas Nicholson and one of her sister ships that had recently been consigned to the Reserve Fleet. *Thomas Houlding, [KN]*

The Peace Day parade had been marred by the non-appearance of Canadian units because they had already returned home. Indian troops were missing as well because the date for the event had been brought forward and their ship did not arrive in time. It was decided to hold a separate parade for the Indian Army on 4 August and *The Times* was confident the men taking part would be keen to display their loyalty to their king-emperor. We've seen enough of parades, so this shot of Indian troops camping in Hyde Park offers a welcome change of scene. *[KN]*

There were other troops enjoying the sights and sounds of the capital that summer. These German prisoners of war are pictured passing through Trafalgar Square at the start of their return home to an uncertain future. *[KN]*

Other Germans continued to be of interest. A provision of the Treaty of Versailles had ordered for alleged German war criminals to be put on trial, but there was little enthusiasm for the process amongst the Allies or in Germany, where the authorities refused to extradite their citizens to face trial in foreign countries. Attempts to extradite the former Kaiser from the Netherlands failed and he would remain in exile for the rest of his life. A long list of suspects was submitted to the government in Berlin early in 1920 and a small number of cases were heard at Leipzig in May 1921. Men accused of mistreating prisoners of war or, more seriously, submariners charged with sinking hospital ships faced a panel of judges where most were found innocent, while some received relatively light sentences. Britain's chief observer at Leipzig was the Solicitor General Sir Ernest Pollock (pictured in 1923) who was 'much impressed' by the proceedings, although he was aware that the British public 'may have desired and expected more startling sentences.' He recognised the German sense of injustice, predicting 'a wide-reaching and permanent effect' in the country. That the process was unsatisfactory was obvious to all and sundry and any further attempts to bring Germans to trial were abandoned in 1922. The lessons learned would help shape the Nuremberg Trials that followed the Second World War. [TT]

Members of the London branch of the Italian Fascist Party raise a salute as they pass the Cenotaph en route to Westminster Abbey, where they laid a wreath at the Tomb of the Unknown Warrior. Afterwards the *fascisti* knelt in salute within the abbey grounds. *The Times* described the group of around fifty Blackshirts singing their 'wonderful marching song' and the scene at Noel Street, Soho, where they gathered afterwards for speeches and singing accompanied by an orchestra. 5 November 1922. [TT]

By December 1922, Germany's failure to fulfil her obligation to pay reparations led to a conference of four Allied leaders in London to address the situation. While there was a general agreement that the Germans needed to pay up, there were differences over the best way to proceed. In addition to defaulting payments of hard cash, the Germans had failed consistently to supply the coal and timber due to France. The belief that the Germans were playing games and attempting to divide Allied opinion was strong but while the British favoured giving them a break, the French were in no mood for such ideas, certain of the conviction that German refusal to accept defeat and the need to pay for the consequences of their war of aggression was at the centre of all the issues. The London conference held on 11 December was adjourned without agreement but the leaders agreed to present a united front and come up with proposals at a second summit held in Paris in January 1923. The conference gave London a brief look at the new Italian leader, Benito Mussolini, pictured laying a wreath at the Cenotaph. *[TT]*

Mussolini's fascists had come to power amid violence but there were other places on the map where incidences of extreme intolerance gave songwriters of the day plenty of inspiration. It might seem bizarre to a modern audience to see Gertrude Lawrence, a first-rank entertainer of the day, dressing up in Ku Klux Klan robes emblazoned with a swastika to poke fun at far-right extremism, but this happened on the London stage in 1923. She appeared in the music and comedy review *Rats* at the Vaudeville Theatre alongside Herbert Mundin. The show took an irreverent look at current events and mixed digs at the state of the railways with a whimsical piece of satire called *The Ku Klux Klan Foxtrot*, with lyrics and music by Ronald Jeans and Philip Braham. It is convenient to suggest the appearance of the swastika shows awareness of something ominous on the horizon, but just how bad things would get was anyone's guess. *[TT]*

Allied leaders reconvened in early January 1923 to deal with the Germans but failure to agree sanctions angered the French, leading Prime Minister Raymond Poincaré to order the invasion of the Ruhr to extract the reparations owed to his country in the form of coal stocks and hard cash. The prize: king coal. *M. Gouville [TT]*

Germany had to be taught a lesson. The photographer Monsieur Gouville covered the invasion for *The Times* when troops from the 32nd Infantry Corps supported by Renault FT tanks rolled into Essen. *M. Gouville. [TT]*

Right and below: French troops of the 32nd Infantry Corps in Essen. *M. Gouville. [TT]*

The humiliation felt by Germans over the invasion helped propel impressionable youngsters like these into the arms of the National Socialists. *M. Gouville [TT]*

Feelings boiled over during a protest on Altendorferstrasse by workers at Krupp. French troops and engineers had arrived to confiscate vehicles and machinery at the works when sirens turned on at the orders of the management sent thousands of men on to the street. Reports of the incident varied, but Monsieur Gouville captured the scene just moments before the French opened fire, killing thirteen and wounding many more. *M. Gouville [TT]*

The unintended result of the occupation was to accelerate the effects of hyperinflation. Although the French succeeded in getting some of the coal and moneys owed, their actions precipitated a collapse in manufacturing just when profits from it might have contributed towards reparations. German banks began printing currency in huge denominations, but the money was increasingly worthless as price rises outstripped the value of new notes before the ink had dried. *Mark Barnes*

The French commander took the wise decision not to interfere with the funeral arrangements for the victims. A large crowd turned out to pay their respects to the dead. Although passive resistance against the French was encouraged, there were well over a hundred deaths in incidents where troops opened fire. *M. Gouville [TT]*

There was trouble elsewhere. The murder of an Italian general attempting to arbitrate a border dispute between Albania and Greece caused uproar in Italy, where condemnation of the Greeks led to angry demonstrations. Amid demands for an official Greek apology, together with a huge payout in compensation, Mussolini saw an opportunity to inflate his reputation by ordering Italian forces to launch a punitive occupation of Corfu. The Italians invaded on 31 August 1923 in an operation that killed a number of civilians. It was now the turn of Mussolini to face condemnation from the League of Nations, but the failure of Britain and France to put any pressure on Rome ended any significant response from a League already proving weak in the face of the sort of aggression favoured by Mussolini. His profile was enhanced at the expense of Italy's erstwhile friends in London and Paris who urged Athens to submit to most of his original demands. The Italians withdrew at the end of September, giving Mussolini the appetite for more adventures. Italian troops are seen coming ashore on 31 August. [TT]

British business was perfectly capable of getting things done while the politicians continued to do a lot of talking. Direct communications between Britain and Germany offered hope of greater political understanding while offering potential for improved trading links at a time when the economies of both London and Berlin could do with all the help they could get. Sir John Denison-Pender, chairman of the Eastern Telegraph Company, is seen handing over the first message sent via the new Dumpton Gap-Emden cable from the company's headquarters at Electra House in Moorgate on 12 February 1924. Sir John carried the wishes of the City of London, telling his opposite number in Germany that the reopening of direct telegraphic communication would 'Materially assist towards that re-establishment of complete trade relations with the countries of Europe which is so much to be desired.' [TT]

Despite continued differences over how to deal with Germany's ability to pay reparations, it was recognised that the parlous state of the Weimar economy was a major factor in delays of payments from Berlin. Hyperinflation reached a peak by the end of 1923 and recovery was essential to any hope of reparations being met. Something had to give, so a committee of financial experts convened to suggest ways Germany could make realistic payments. The committee, headed by US Brigadier-General Charles G. Dawes, recommended complete withdrawal of foreign troops from the Ruhr, Allied supervision of the Reichsbank, and hefty loans to Germany by Britain and the United States to make things happen. The Germans had to pay a billion marks in the first year. Dawes was awarded the 1925 Nobel Peace Prize for his efforts. He is pictured at the Vintners Hall in London in 1929 when serving as US Ambassador to the United Kingdom, following his term as Vice President of the United States alongside Calvin Coolidge. [KN]

Dawes shared the Nobel Peace Prize with Sir Austen Chamberlain, who did much of the serious talking at Locarno where Germany's western borders were settled, but territorial issues with her eastern neighbours were fudged, leaving scope for future trouble. He is pictured with a group of contented signatories in the garden of No 10 Downing Street on 1 December 1925. The front row includes the Belgian Foreign Minister Emile Vandervelde, French Prime Minister Aristide Briand, German Chancellor Dr Hans Luther and British Prime Minister Stanley Baldwin. Behind them the group includes Edvard Beneš of Czechoslovakia on the left, German Foreign Minister Gustav Stresemann and the Polish Prime Minister, Count Skrzynski. Behind them are Sir Austen, on the left, and Winston Churchill.

Below: Enterprising people possessing a degree of confidence found ways to profit from Germany's defeat, although the wait for a windfall could be lengthy. The raising of the scuttled German fleet at Scapa Flow was of frequent interest to *The Times* and 1926 proved to be a busy year with ongoing efforts to salvage the 26,000-ton battlecruiser SMS *Hindenburg*. The ship would not budge despite a Herculean effort that cost the entrepreneur Ernest Cox tens of thousands of pounds. Although other ships of varying sizes had been raised, the *Hindenburg* refused to unstick until 1930. It took a further two years to break her up. *William Horton [TT]*

The General Treaty for Renunciation of War as an Instrument of National Policy, better known as the Kellogg-Briand Pact, was signed in Paris by France, Germany and the USA on 28 August 1928. It was co-authored by the American Secretary of State Frank B. Kellogg and the French Foreign Minister Aristide Briand. The pact was met with great enthusiasm and is seen as a precursor of the United Nations Charter. Over sixty countries would eventually sign up but the strength of it would be put to the test on numerous occasions during the decade to follow. Kellogg and Briand were awarded the Nobel Peace Prize in 1929. *F.R. Donovan [KN]*

A significant result to arise from Locarno was the agreement for the withdrawal of occupation forces from the Rhineland. The British had, in any case, steadily reduced the number of troops stationed in Germany and the garrison had withdrawn from Cologne to Wiesbaden in December 1925. Life in the Rhineland seems almost idyllic for these young soldiers of the Prince of Wales's Volunteers (South Lancashire Regiment). Perhaps they were reading they would soon be going home.
Patrick Brown [KN]

Afternoon tea is served in the NAAFI to men of the 2nd Battalion Royal Welch Fusiliers based at Gheluvelt Barracks at Biebrich. *Patrick Brown [KN]*

Things were even more civilised in the Sergeants' Mess of the Corps of Military Police. *Patrick Brown [KN]*

Below: The British began packing up to return home in September 1929 but routine work continued until the end. The 8th King's Royal Irish Hussars last field exercise was held on the Exerzierplatz near Wiesbaden at the beginning of September in the presence of Lieutenant-General Sir William Thwaites, General Officer Commanding-in-Chief of the British Army of the Rhine. The regiment would return to fight their way into Germany with their Cromwell and Challenger tanks in 1945. *Stanley Kessell [TT]*

The British hadn't just brought horses with them. This Rolls-Royce armoured car of the Royal Tank Regiment is the subject of scrutiny. *Stanley Kessell [TT]*

Getting everything ready to depart created the need for help from local labour because there were not enough British personnel to do the work. Soldiers and German civilians are seen hard at it in the Royal Army Ordnance Corps packing case factory at Dotzheim. *Stanley Kessell [TT]*

Service life in Germany clearly had its merits. *Patrick Brown [KN]*

A soldier sees his wife and child to the railway station at the start of their journey home to Britain. *Charles Maxwell [KN]*

The British in Cologne had produced their own newspaper that morphed eventually into *The Cologne Post and Wiesbaden Times*. The last edition was published on 3 November 1929. It would be five years before more British troops would serve on German soil during the period of the Saarland plebiscite, an event we will see in the next chapter. *[KN]*

The city of Aix-la-Chapelle had been a favoured home of Charlemagne and under its German name of Aachen had been at the centre of the short-lived Rheinische Republik instigated by Konrad Adenauer in 1923. He would go on to be the first chancellor of West Germany in 1949. Belgian troops had occupied Aachen and they are seen saying farewell to the city in December 1929. The demilitarization of the Rhineland was not destined to be permanent. *Bill Warhurst [TT]*

Although political violence continued to bedevil Germany a decade on from the end of the Great War, there was time for former enemies to enjoy fraternal associations. One old soldier who found a warm welcome in Britain was General Paul von Lettow-Vorbeck, who had led the undefeated Schutztruppe fighting against the British, Belgians and Portuguese across the length and breadth of East Africa between 1914 and 1918. Lettow-Vorbeck enjoyed intense and mutual loyalty from the African askari troops in his modest force and earned the lasting admiration and friendship of his greatest foe, Jan Christian Smuts. It was Smuts who invited Lettow-Vorbeck to attend a dinner for 800 Africa campaign veterans in London in December 1929. The event was crowned when Smuts returned his old enemy's medals that he had lost during the war. Lettow-Vorbeck was a convinced monarchist who loathed the Nazis. Adolf Hitler's effort to woo him with the offer of the ambassador's post in London was allegedly met with a forthright 'Go and fuck yourself!' The top-hatted general is pictured after laying a wreath at the Cenotaph. *Stanley Kessell [TT]*

Adolf Hitler was in power and already creating ripples of fear at home and abroad in the early spring of 1933. The benefits of trading with a resurgent Germany were attractive to big business but there were other considerations. Incidences of repression of Jews in the wake of the Enabling Act becoming law in Germany brought an immediate response from Jewish communities around the world. In Britain traders organised a boycott of German goods, but general disbelief that a state apparatus could become so evil extended to a sceptical press; indeed, the *Daily Express* headline of 24 March exclaimed 'Judea Declares War on Germany', reflecting the divisions in forming a response to Nazi excesses. This image was taken in Whitechapel in April where there appears to have been much less doubt about Hitler's intentions, but his long-term aims would prove to be far worse than even his more astute critics expected. *Edward Taylor [KN]*

Trade was one thing but cultural links with Nazi Germany could be just as problematic. The distinguished actor Werner Krauss came to Britain to star in *Before Sunset* at the end of September 1933, where he received a respectful reception for his theatrical achievements. But Krauss was a vocal supporter of the Nazis and a staunch anti-Semite, and his presence on the London stage met with opposition. Protesters disrupted his performance at the Shaftesbury Theatre on 28 September when they heckled and scattered anti-Nazi leaflets ('We want British actors for British plays. Not Nazi actors.') The press placed much emphasis on the professionalism of the cast, who carried on regardless amid stink bombs and frequent disturbances in the gallery, where what *The Times* drama critic described as 'fanatical youths' were given short shrift by equally determined theatregoers. Krauss is pictured in a defiant mood the next day accompanied by his wife Maria (left) and fellow cast member Peggy Ashcroft, who had appealed to the protesters for fairness. The next performance passed off peacefully thanks to the presence of thirty policemen in the theatre. *Reginald Coote [KN]*

Sporting links presented other imagery that continues to raise eyebrows over eighty years later. Here we see the German visitors before their rugby match against France at Parc des Princes on 24 March 1935. *Les Bleus* ran out 18-3 winners with tries from Maurice Celhay and Armand Vigneau. *F.R. Donovan [KN]*

A leading British witness to the fading charm of Weimar Germany as it succumbed to Nazi supremacy was the writer Christopher Isherwood whose accounts of life in Berlin introduced a range of characters, to love or loathe in equal measure. The alluring Sally Bowles remains the best known, while the sinister Mr Norris was based on the colourful rogue Gerald Hamilton, who had worked in Germany as *The Times* sales representative. Isherwood (left) is pictured with his close friend W.H. Auden. *Robert Field [KN]*

In time the façade of normality would be in evidence across the spheres of trade and communications. This *Lufthansa* Junkers Ju 52 was preparing to leave Croydon with the night mail to Berlin at 2200hrs on 7 May 1934. *William Horton [TT]*

But the ascendency of the Nazis would have other consequences. A fading example of Anglo-German reconciliation was an annual memorial service held at the graveside of two Zeppelin crews at Potters Bar that had regularly been attended by British and German dignitaries. By 1936 the event was a much more politicised German affair. *The Times* report of the commemoration held on 8 March recorded the attendance of a party from Arnold Leese's Imperial Fascist League in support of their Nazi benefactors, but surviving images only show the principal German attendees. Military Attaché Major-General Leo Geyr von Schweppenburg is on the left. To the right of him is the diplomat Prince Otto Christian Archibald von Bismarck. In the centre is the ill-fated German Ambassador Leopold von Hoesch, whose death we saw in the introduction. Schweppenburg is pictured with Naval Attaché Captain Erwin Waßner, a recipient of the *Pour le Mérite*, who was the commander of the submarine U-117 we saw surrendering at Harwich in 1918. Schweppenburg will be seen again later. *Geoffrey Keating [KN]*

2

THANK GOD FOR THE FRENCH ARMY

....

WHILE defeat may have presented Germany with an extremely harsh future, there was not much to smile about for the victors as the bill for post-war recovery hit home. One way to save money was through drastic cuts in military expenditure. With the war over, hundreds of contracts for hardware and other essentials were cancelled as Britain's armed forces steadily reduced back to peacetime levels.

The army returned to its traditional role of garrisoning the homeland and policing the empire. It had to find men to carry out occupation duties in Germany while the worsening situation in Ireland demanded boots on the ground. It was Winston Churchill, no less, who suggested basing the defence budget on the principle there would be no major war for ten years. This was accepted despite intense objections and the precipitous decline in Britain's military power was set in train. The cost saving was immediate. Defence spending plummeted from over £750 million in 1919–20 to less than £200 million by 1922. (In percentage terms, defence spending had always been the subject of fluctuation. Just 3.69 per cent of Britain's GDP was allotted to defence in 1900 but the Second Anglo-Boer War saw that figure rise to 6.4 per cent in two years. This had shrunk to a modest 3.15 per cent by 1914 and reached a whopping 47 per cent by 1919.)

Fortunately for the Exchequer, there was to be no repeat of the arms race of the kind fought by Britain and Germany before the Great War. Although there were other powers in attendance, the Washington Naval Conference of 1921–22 is remembered for removing the prospect of similar rivalries exploding between Britain, the United States and Japan. The three countries may have emerged victorious from the Great War but there were growing tensions between them as the Americans sought to match the ambitions of an expansionist Japan looking on jealously at US and European possessions in Asia.

The terms agreed at the conference limited the number, tonnage and armament of battleships that were still the primary capital ship dominating the seas – although aircraft carriers were beginning to make an appearance and they, too, were included in the agreement. By limiting the size and power of the battle fleets of her potential enemies, Washington kept the numbers game in favour of Britain for a little longer, with the Royal Navy retaining twenty-two battleships and battlecruisers totalling 558,950 gross tonnage. Four of them were to be

Below: King George V balked at the deafening engine noise, the fumes and much more besides when he had his first tank ride in 1916. The king is seen here with Queen Mary watching from a discrete distance as a Medium Mark C put on a show for the royal party on 21 May 1922. The type first appeared in 1918 but the Armistice saw an end to a contract to build 600 that year and the volume the Tank Corps hoped to receive was whittled down to a meagre fifty. The Mark C has the distinction of being the only type to appear in London's Peace Day celebrations of July 1919 and that same year a number were stored in central Glasgow during violent disturbances dubbed the Battle of George Square, but they were never deployed. The last surviving Mark C was scrapped in 1940. *[TT]*

replaced by two new battleships entering service in 1927 and more would appear after the naval treaties of 1930 and 1935, but the Royal Navy's ageing fleet of Great War era capital ships would find themselves exposed from 1939 onwards.

The agreements made in Washington could be considered a harbinger of the end of Britain's naval pre-eminence, but there were other ramifications that would impact on world events. Running in tandem with the treaty was Britain's decision not to renew her alliance with Japan, choosing instead to develop relations with the Americans, in part to placate Commonwealth leaders anxious over Japan's military ambitions triggering a war with the United States. Britain's subsequent cancellation of the alliance added fuel to the fire of distrust burning in Tokyo and fed the rise in the ultra-nationalist militarism that led to Japan waging war against the British Empire in 1941.

Defence costs were also a target of the Committee on National Expenditure chaired by Sir Eric Geddes, the man whose organisational genius had been central to the success of the British railway network on the Western Front. Geddes had the army in his sights and *The Times* of 16 March 1923 highlighted how the millions of pounds saved led to an alarming drop in manpower to a point where the 'limit of safety' had been reached. There was growing anxiety within the army that further cuts would prove precipitous with a reduction of 55,000 men in the Estimates for that year. 'No fewer than 1,500 officers had fallen before the Geddes Axe.' Sir Eric's no-nonsense approach gave the nation a name for stringent cost-cutting that would stay in use for decades to come.

Churchill's Ten Year Rule was only abandoned in 1932, but the impact of the Great Depression put the brakes on any improvement to the UK's defence capability. A deep opposition to war was entrenched across the country and rearmament was a dirty word. In that year defence spending had shrunk to a little over £100 million. The year 1936 would see defence expenditure shrivel to just 2.9 per cent of GDP. The rise of Adolf Hitler had seen Winston Churchill revise his views on military expenditure, but he was powerless to influence decisions from his position on the political margins. His time as a prophet of doom was about to begin.

While the 1920s had seen a rapid decline in strength, towards the end of the decade the British Army began experimenting with mechanised warfare. A brigade-size formation was set aside to develop tactics and operational procedures for armour accompanied by infantry riding in specialised vehicles creating a mutually supporting structure backed up by artillery and other essentials. Unfortunately, there were dissenting voices within a conservative British Army that favoured something much less radical and despite the clear success of the experiments the Mechanised Force was disbanded in 1929. Even had the army intended to press on with expanding mechanisation there simply wasn't the money to build the necessary hardware. Although Vickers built a number of fully tracked artillery tractors known as Dragons, it was smaller vehicles, the tankettes, that found favour and were ordered in quantity. This sort of armour proved popular in other countries but the fad had run its course by the beginning of the Second World War. The bottom line is tankettes were a cheap option and the tracked vehicles Britain should have developed would have to be bought from the United States as the Second World War progressed.

Others looked on at what the British were doing with interest, but to suggest a blueprint for the *Blitzkrieg* was sketched out on Salisbury Plain is wide of the mark. Both the French and Germans had developed mechanised formations of differing capabilities by 1939. But Britain did not go anything like as far and the lessons of the late 1920s had to be relearned the hard way once hostilities commenced.

It was just a little ironic that Douglas Haig should die just as the mechanised warfare experiments were bearing fruit. He had commanded the largest British army to ever take the field and saw it through to a great victory despite the best efforts of the Germans and the politicians looking anxiously over his shoulder. By accepting attrition, Haig succeeded in damning himself in the memoirs of the political enemies who outlived him. He was no military genius but Haig was attracted by the potential of war-winning weapons and it was the 'all arms' tactics using armour, aviation, artillery, infantry and cavalry that won the war for the British Empire in 1918 and the essence of it would be readily adapted by the Germans in 1939.

Haig was firmly in the sights of the two most prominent military theorists of the era, Major-General J.F.C. Fuller and Basil Liddell Hart. The former was a tireless evangelist for mechanised warfare but his reputation was blighted by his unrepentant support for fascism. Fuller's vision for armoured formations was beyond the means of the defence budget just as much as it was a leap into the dark for many of his erstwhile colleagues in the upper echelons of the army. 'Boney' Fuller was fortunate not to find himself in detention along with Oswald Mosley and other fascists when they were rounded up in 1940. An ardent anti-communist, he went so far as to claim the wrong side won the war in 1945 and was a severe critic of Churchill and Roosevelt, quite apart from his feelings towards Stalin.

The prolific Basil Liddell Hart had been an infantry officer during the Great War and had seen enough of it to become involved in developing new instructions for infantry training afterwards. He, too, espoused an all-arms method of warfare centred on mechanisation that struck many a chord at the time and since. He was attracted to the unconventional warfare of T.E. Lawrence and became his biographer, but had also written a much-admired life of William Tecumseh Sherman, a man poles apart from Lawrence of Arabia.

Liddell Hart moved from the *Daily Telegraph* to become Military Correspondent of *The Times* in March 1937, using his authority to gain access to movers and shakers in the period of rearmament and reorganisation. Another *Times* writer enthused that the publication of a Liddell Hart book was 'an event' and there is no disputing he had cemented his position as the go-to commentator on military matters at such a critical time in history. He must have been a busy man because he was never free long enough to sit for a *Times* staff photographer. But Liddell Hart's place is contentious. His post-Second World War reputation was built on the myth he manipulated that his theories had a direct influence on German thinking, especially on tacticians like Heinz Guderian and Erwin Rommel, when in fact the Germans had arrived at the *Blitzkrieg* via a range of influences and their own experiments.

A greater amount of mechanisation might have been the ideal solution for the British Army had the money and vision been there. It is fair to point out that for all its qualitative superiority in armoured fighting vehicles, the German army remained reliant on the horse at every stage of the war to come and would eagerly make use of the large number of motor vehicles captured from the enemy. The Germans simply never had enough trucks. Versions of tankettes would stay in British service until well after the Second World War, the best known being the Bren or Universal Carrier. Motorisation, the replacement of horse transport with wheeled motor vehicles, did go ahead, but it, too, would take time and money. Mechanisation and motorisation may sound similar but, in military terms, they are not the same thing and the distinction would confuse press photo caption writers for years to come.

The following decade would see an emotional defence of the horse in the order of battle as wheels and tracks replaced hooves, but the poor state of the British defence industry and the lack of cash to splash on it would hobble efforts for rapid improvement. It was not the will of the public for Britain to rearm and this state of affairs would continue almost to the point of no return. With faith in British sea power as strong as ever, it fell to the likes of Winston Churchill to point to who would guarantee the defence of the democratic West; the mighty army across the English Channel. He spoke of the threat the Nazis posed to peace on 23 March 1933 when he said: 'There are a good many people who have said to themselves, as I have been saying for several years – thank God for the French Army.' He expanded on his views later that year, describing France as the 'sole great surviving democracy' and the 'strongest military power' in Europe. While these assessments would come back to haunt him in 1940, Churchill's admiration for the French Army was both genuine and enduring. But the reality behind the mistaken optimism he held in 1933 invites closer examination.

Just as the British had their own difficulties, French generals were mired in a struggle over money and doctrine between the wars. But the greatest impediment to rearmament in France was the state of domestic politics where divisions were stark. Governments came and went through a revolving door as the Third Republic staggered from one crisis to the next. There was violent opposition to rearmament amongst factions who either saw the military as a threat to their powerbase or in the other extreme as a possible weapon of repression. A stagnant birth rate hindered both industrial expansion and military development in France. There were not enough people to fill the ranks of workers and soldiers needed to rejuvenate the country's fortunes. The Germans had no such difficulties.

France's generals were steeped in their own brand of conservatism that was rooted in positional warfare. The political champion of their vision was André Maginot, a charismatic veteran of Verdun who managed to retain a little more respect than many of his political colleagues. France would sit safely behind her eastern frontier protected by a network of impregnable fortifications. The Maginot Line cost a whopping three billion francs to construct but, fatally, it was never extended to run along the Belgian border to the sea. This was due as much to a strong belief in the Franco-Belgian alliance as it was faith in natural barriers barring any German incursion. French strategy hinged on being able to advance a large army into Belgium should the old enemy come again. But in October 1936 King Leopold III declared his country neutral, withdrew from the alliance with France, and repudiated Locarno. It was a gift for Hitler. Maginot died in 1932 and did not see the subterranean world named in his memory. It was an outstanding feat of construction, but with Belgium neutral, the very foundation of French defensive strategy was in tatters. Leopold had spoken for a people who were sick of their country being a convenient battlefield for its neighbours but the ramifications would prove to be immense.

Developments in armoured warfare and combat aviation, meanwhile, were virtually ignored in France. The Armée de l'Air withered as vested interests within the aircraft industry, political interference and the myopia of the generals created an unpalatable cocktail set to leave a horrible taste. The multitude of factors that led France to be so woefully unprepared for war in 1938, let alone a year later, do not appear evident at first glance in the photographs taken by the Paris-based Jack Barker of *The Times* during his regular attendance of army exercises. Closer inspection shows ageing weapons and obsolete kit amid the smattering of new light tank designs that were doomed to fail in 1940.

The story of the rise of Adolf Hitler and his henchmen has filled the shelves of libraries and will not be repeated in fine detail here. The Nazis rode on the back of a mixture of political violence and populism seemingly unstoppable by 1931. The democratic parties of Weimar were simply no match for the tactics of Hitler and his supporters, who played on grievances over Versailles and fear of communism while preaching anti-Semitism. Armed groups were involved in conflict across the country and as fears of all-out civil war grew Hitler felt emboldened to go for the presidency, but he lost the election in March and April to Field Marshal Paul on Hindenburg.

The Reichstag elections that followed in July 1932 took place against a background of worsening violence as storm troopers fought regular gun battles with their communist opponents. The Nazis continued to increase their share of the vote and secured their position as the largest party in the Reichstag at the next round of elections in November of that year. An alliance between the communists and social democrats might have been effective against the Nazis but Moscow had demanded the destruction of political moderates, leaving the left little option but to resort to worsening violence against their rivals to achieve their aims. This played into the hands of the Nazis, who secured changes in the law to see special courts in session to try offenders for political violence. While the courts sentenced both Nazis and communists, matters were resolved in January 1933 when Hitler became chancellor and quickly ordered an amnesty for his supporters. Repression of the communists was intense but the violent situation blinded moderate parties to the danger and when the opportunity presented itself, Hitler was able to make an audacious grab for absolute power.

Whoever it was who started the Reichstag fire on 27 February 1933, the result was perfect for Hitler. Within a month he instituted the Enabling Act, giving him full power to carry through his schemes and the rest, as they say, is history. With Hitler's installation as dictator of Germany the scene was set for the slide to world war, but there were plenty of opportunities for him to expand his realm before the first German troops crossed into Poland on 1 September 1939.

Bill Warhurst of *The Times* had his first encounter with Nazi theatre when he covered the death of Paul von Hindenburg in August 1934. He attended the lavish funeral of the late president at Tannenberg, the scene of his great victory over the Russians in 1914. Adolf Hitler wasted no time in combining the offices of president and chancellor, becoming *Führer und Reichskanzler*. Hindenburg's death had come just a month after Hitler had purged rivals from the Nazi apparatus with the infamous Night of the Long Knives. He had the support of the army and held a plebiscite giving him near unanimous approval for his assumption of sole power. By the end of the year he would begin flexing his muscles on the international stage.

The Treaty of Versailles gave the League of Nations the mandate to govern the Saar territory of Germany for the fifteen-year period the region's coal output was given over to the French in war reparations. At the end of this period a ballot had to be held offering people the choice of retaining the mandate, returning to German control, or unifying with France. There had been broad-based political support for reunification with Germany before the Nazis came to power, but with Hitler as Führer, his regime's repression of opponents quickly impacted on events in the Saar where democrats and anti-Nazis faced intimidation. The Nazis quickly gained control of the political agenda as the sole champions of German unity.

At the end of 1934 the League voted to send in troops to monitor the Saar, but they were never intended to act as a police force. Britain and Italy provided the largest contingents under the overall command of a British general. Although the result was a foregone conclusion, the Nazis' belligerent behaviour had caused anger and alarm in Paris, raising concern France would send in troops. The Nazis could not afford any French military intervention so they played a typical game of brinkmanship, upping and lowering the crescendo of their activities while keeping a cautious eye on French intentions. The local Nazi leadership softened its tone and banned the wearing of political uniforms for the period of the plebiscite. Voting took place on 13 January 1935, resulting in near universal support for a return to Germany.

There was extensive press coverage of the ballot. It gave the British media the chance to get a closer look at the Nazis just as Hitler's fear and suspicion of a free press morphed into open hostility. Both *The Times* and the *Daily Sketch* sent photographers to record the activities of the peacekeepers and the referendum campaign in detail. Jack Barker travelled from Paris where he crossed paths with his opposite number, Geoffrey Keating. Happily, a large amount of their work survives. Images of British troops marching through streets bedecked in swastikas make for interesting viewing. Neither *The Times* nor the *Daily Sketch* sent photographers to cover the Berlin Olympics held the following year. Nor did they attend the huge Nazi rallies at Nuremberg. But we are getting ahead of ourselves, because, as we shall soon see, the year 1935 had more up its sleeve.

Italy's place as one of the victors of 1918 and the country's position as a friendly power made the imposition of right-wing dictatorship awkward but far from impossible for London and Paris to treat with while Italy remained watchful of German expansion. Their occupation of Corfu in 1928 coupled with virtual control of Albania had shown the Italians were keen to dominate their neighbours, but given Rome's concerns over Austria they were seen as a counterbalance to Nazi ambition. Mussolini himself wasn't above explaining his policies in *The Times* and was more than happy his 'political and polemical manifestations' were followed so attentively at Printing House Square. He reminded the paper in June 1925 that:

> Even the Italian opposition now recognise the great historical importance of the Fascist experiment which has to be firmly continued in order not to fail in its task of morally and materially elevating the Italian people, and also in the interest of European civilisation.

But as much as Mussolini's brand of fascism attracted approval from all manner of onlookers, amid humorous quips about the trains running on time there was a dark side to contend with. Mussolini looked on jealously at the established European colonial powers and wanted to recreate a glorious Roman empire of his own.

The Italians had long bridled at a devastating defeat at the hands of the Ethiopians in 1896 and although Rome enjoyed an African foothold in Somaliland it was to neighbouring Abyssinia, modern-day Ethiopia, that Mussolini looked upon to expand his empire. In what became a typical manoeuvre for fascist dictators, border incidents were set off to ratchet up tensions and a full-on battle had taken place at Wal Wal in 1934.

The Italian invasion of Abyssinia in October 1935 is characterised by the use of poison gas, which, along with a campaign of indiscriminate bombing of civilian targets, sent alarm bells ringing way beyond the Horn of Africa. In London the war was debated in both Houses of Parliament, where there was a tangible air of disbelief that such a civilised nation as Italy could be so brutal. The Italians deliberately bombed the few hospitals in the country to scare away Western witnesses. Journalists from the democratic West were feared and top of the list was George Lowther Steer, a young South African adventurer working for *The Times*.

The paper's coverage of the war is mapped for us by news photography. Steer was based with the Ethiopians and either took his own or supplied images he acquired. He was joined for a while by a stringer, Walter Holmes, and, a little confusingly, he shared facilities with the Reuters correspondent Christopher Holme. Steer enjoyed the confidence of Emperor Haile Selassie and took considerable risks to report on the hopeless struggle faced by the hotchpotch Abyssinian army fighting a superior Italian force deploying chemical weapons. Steer held a deep respect for many of the fighters he encountered and retained warm affection for Ethiopians in general. He saw something noble in the futility of defending a progressive and yet somewhat antediluvian kingdom against the cruelty of an unashamedly racist European invader. Frederic Roper of the *Daily Sketch* may well have gained a similar impression as he recorded military parades and other ceremonials in Addis Ababa as war loomed. He took several rolls of film with a Leica that gave him problems, but he overcame them to produce some fascinating work.

Meanwhile, *The Times* sent out Bill Warhurst to cover things from the Italian side. He sailed from Naples with part of the invading army down the Suez Canal and out to the war zone. J.W. Eggitt of the *Daily Sketch* photographed a number of Italian troopships at Port Said while the British did nothing to stop them passing through. The League of Nations voted for an arms embargo against both sides, but it was bound to hurt Abyssinia the most. The League also imposed economic sanctions against Italy but they were never carried out with much conviction, although Britain supported them.

The major consequence was open hostility towards Britain on the part of the Italians. And yet some in London and Paris sought to end the war as neatly as possible; the proposed Hoare-Laval Pact of December 1935 would have seen the partition of Abyssinia in favour of the Italians, but the plan was leaked in the French press. Outrage at the sell-out of the Ethiopians led to the resignation of both Samuel Hoare and Pierre Laval, but their careers were far from over.

Bill Warhurst spent time in the van of the Italian army and snapped many of the principal characters prosecuting the war, including Marshal de Bono, Count Ciano, and Mussolini's sons Bruno and Vittorio. The Duce's boys had a high old time of it enjoying their part in the bombing campaign. While Bruno was a serious pilot who was killed on active service in 1941, Vittorio thought it was all a bit of a hoot, describing his war as 'exceptionally good fun.' Sadly, a number of Bill's images are uncaptioned but one showing him with a group of Italian officers enjoying a hearty lunch sets the tone. Others picture Warhurst and his companions following the war by donkey, while still more featuring Italian armoured vehicles and other hardware betray a good deal of the inadequacies that would dog the Italians in Greece and the Western Desert a few years hence.

From this distance the mismatch between the conquering Italians and the Ethiopians is stark and the result was a foregone conclusion. It was a confusing struggle that saw Nazi Germany arming Abyssinia in response to Italian attitudes over their designs on Austria. Imperial Japan, once the model for progress in Abyssinia, had also supplied arms even though Tokyo had given the Italians a free hand. The war gave vent to the prejudice of Evelyn Waugh, who considered George Steer to be an inferior little colonial. The man himself stayed on until the very end, marrying his bride at the British embassy amid the chaos and violence of Addis Ababa as the city fell to Mussolini's invaders. Haile Selassie went into exile, arriving in London in June 1936 to a warm welcome from ordinary Londoners but something of a cold shoulder from the British establishment. He sent out the prescient warning that after Abyssinia there would soon be new targets for fascist aggression. He was not wrong for within a few weeks civil war had broken out in Spain, sparking intervention by the competing ideologies of Rome, Moscow and Berlin.

A glance through the daybooks of *The Times* and Kemsley Newspapers shows how the beginning of the Spanish Civil War saw a rush of interest to get in on the action. They reflect a common approach to long-running stories where the opening shots are covered with gusto before a gradual dip takes hold unless something truly newsworthy happens within the context of events. While correspondents from British newspapers covered the war in earnest, news photography was often bought in from a number of agents, for sending out photographers to cover things was an expensive business. Irun was conveniently close to the French border and Jack Barker recorded events there before the city fell to the Nationalists in September 1936. Gerald Cook of the *Daily Sketch* was there, too. Sadly, all the negatives he brought back were destroyed in 1940.

Jack Barker described his experiences with Franco's forces in an account entitled 'the fight for Irun, with the Nationals on the Northern front', received at Printing House Square on 27 August 1936. He talks of following ammunition convoys carried by mules along a track bombed regularly by government aircraft:

> I counted five air raids on my way back. The Spanish Foreign Legion had been spotted by the reds and was the subject of concentrated bombing. They were fortunately under cover and there were no casualties as far as I know.

But it was tough going:

> I walked over 50 miles over 12 hours to get to Oyarzun and back. The climb over four passes was very hard… This has been the hardest trip I have experienced… How I got back on the Pamplona road seems extraordinary to me as I was suffering terribly from heat, especially thirst.

In time a French blockade made access more difficult, but the stream of refugees crossing into France were good subject matter and would remain so for the duration of the conflict. In addition to his own images, Barker was able to tap into official sources and buy pictures from adventurous Brits following events from Gibraltar and the Spanish ports. He acted as liaison for a number of men working on opposite sides of the political and military divide in Spain, including the veteran correspondent E.G. de Caux who was based in Barcelona, where he endured continuous battles to get his work past the rigorous censorship demanded by the local authorities. He was relieved to get out of Spain in August 1938 and looked forward to a rest at the French spa town of Bagnoles de l'Orne. Another *Times* man covering events was David Scott from the Paris office, who Barker would have known well. Scott had made a name for himself covering the epic salvage of bullion from the SS *Egypt* at the beginning of the decade. He produced some important reports from the Basque Country, including encounters with the legendary blockade-runner 'Potato' Jones.

Jack Barker received regular packages of images showing events in Republican areas. He was frustrated at first by the quality of the material, at one time describing a large pack of images as 'old and useless'. He also had to instruct his supplier, M. Casses, to employ better captions to explain the context of what people hundreds of miles away in Paris and London were looking at.

Censorship was intense as the main protagonists sought to manipulate coverage. News had become a weapon and perhaps the best-known example of this occurred at Guernica. German and Italian bombers pounded Durango on 31 March 1937 but substantive news of the attack barely filtered out. The attack on Guernica by the Germans on 26 April 1937 might have gone the same way, but The Times correspondent George Steer was there to cut through pro-Nationalist spin to get the real story out to the world. Spain was at the centre of an ideological struggle where both the Germans and Italians sent substantial forces to support Franco's armies. The Soviet Union supplied a significant amount of arms and knowhow to the Republican government including a number of aircraft with their crews. But it was the fascists who benefited the most as both Mussolini and Hitler flouted the non-intervention pact sponsored by the League of Nations in both deeds and spirit.

The major European powers, including the Nazis, sent warships to enforce a blockade to stop arms and supplies reaching the protagonists. German sailors would die as a result, but the cynicism of the fascist dictatorships knew no bounds as tons of war matériel reached Franco's armies. Fifty thousand Italian troops fought in Spain as 'volunteers' and while their presence drove in the wedge in relations between London and Rome, the democratic governments pursued friendship with Italy as a counterbalance to the growing menace of Germany. Although the Italians and Germans had their differences, especially over Austria, there was concord over support for Franco. In their minds Bolshevism or communism simply had to be defeated and the Spanish battleground was the place to do it.

Although the Republican government had a mandate, divisions within Spain were strong and this was also the case within the rainbow of parties fighting the Nationalists. Like the

Catalans, the Basques were a sizeable minority within the country and the war offered the opportunity to proclaim their own republic. This would soon draw the attention of the Nationalists as General Mola sought to crush the young state using the full might of the thousands of 'volunteers' in his army, supported by yet more flying in support. The Condor Legion included a thinly disguised air group of the German *Luftwaffe* using the conflict in Spain to experiment with tactics and weaponry for future employment in the *Blitzkrieg*. Many of the best-known aircraft of the assault on Poland and in the West were trialled in Spain. Some would be found wanting and need further development or re-tasking altogether, but the Nazis' principles of air warfare were set in place by the end of the conflict.

The Germans used a mixture of high explosive and incendiaries to destroy Guernica. Without any notable anti-aircraft defence to thwart them, the bombers were able to attack the town in relays. News of the bombing reached George Steer and other correspondents who headed to the scene, where they found much death and destruction. But the wheels of propaganda and disinformation were already in place. While Steer pursued the truth, another correspondent, Henri de Vilmorin, was claiming the destruction was caused when Republican forces had continued a scorched earth policy seen elsewhere. For Steer the discovery of bomb parts stamped with German manufacturers marks was evidence enough and he was able to get his story out. Vilmorin continued to send reports and photographs in to *The Times* via Barker in Paris. The pictures all came from official Nationalist sources.

A direct consequence of *The Times'* publication of Steer's reports from Guernica occurred on 4 May 1937 when a furious Adolf Hitler abruptly cancelled a proposed interview with the paper's Geneva correspondent, Harold Daniels, which had been due to go ahead after lengthy negotiations. Relations between the paper and Berlin deteriorated further on 15 May 1937 when George Steer's account of witnessing the interrogation of a German fighter pilot was published. Joachim Wandel had been shot down near Larrabezua and admitted escorting Condor Legion bombers on the Guernica raid when mention of it was discovered in his diary. Wandel used the rehearsed deception of claiming to be a paid volunteer recruited in Berlin rather than a serving member of the *Luftwaffe*, explaining how he had come to Spain via Rome. Although he was subsequently sentenced to death by the Basque authorities, 'Gnom' Wandel would go on to be an ace with seventy-five victories and a recipient of the Knight's Cross at the time of his death in Russia in 1942.

Steer's report also told of a similar route to Spain taken by Hans Sobotka, a Heinkel He 111 crewman who had been shot down when bombing Bilbao on 12 April. The report went to on to detail how Germans and Italians were openly fighting in Spain, with Italian tanks carrying national markings at the battle for Truende while Italian infantry had flown the Italian flag. German fury at Steer's report would see the confiscation of copies of *The Times* of 15 May along with other British papers that had repeated the story.

The activities of the Condor Legion over Spain were a signpost to the immediate future of Europe and beyond. Strategic bombing theories of the Italian Giulio Douhet allied to the statements of men such as Stanley Baldwin set the tone for fear of aerial bombing of cities. The British Prime Minister offered a bleak future in 1932 when he said, 'I think it is well also for the man in the street to realise that there is no power on earth that can protect him from being bombed. Whatever people may tell him the bomber will always get through.' The movie version of H.G. Wells' *Things to Come* had done the rounds of the cinemas, presenting a nightmare vision of bombing and poison gas. Although the fear of gas was to prove unfounded, the *Luftwaffe* used Spain to finesse the methods to carry out the kind of bombing that would be seen at Warsaw and Rotterdam.

George Steer had come to Spain following the tragic deaths of his wife and child during childbirth but he threw himself into his work and developed a strong affinity for the Basques, barely disguising his support for their cause. He had a busy time on the front line witnessing the efforts of the blockade-runners bringing scant relief to Basque fortunes. While he was no longer an official correspondent of *The Times*, the paper's foreign editor Ralph Deakin approved of his work. But the nature of the war made it essential to tell the story from both sides. Both Steer and *The Times* were subject to intense suspicion from the Nationalists and it is likely that their Italian friends had influenced thinking, having been on the sharp end of Steer's reports from Abyssinia. James Holburn had begun to cover events from the Nationalist perspective and he tended to offer an uncritical window on Franco's activities. Other British papers favoured this perspective and were prepared to swallow Nationalist lies about Guernica and much else besides.

The Times management struggled increasingly with Steer's stance in the face of establishment fear of communism. The Nationalists and their supporters were standing up to Moscow and this reflected the attitudes of many of the paper's readers. Steer's coverage was frowned upon by the Chamberlain administration as the British policy of appeasement evolved. The paper's editor, Geoffrey Dawson, enjoyed close ties with the government and *The Times* would play a role in the Munich Crisis to come. The paper dropped George Steer because his anti-fascist stance angered Berlin and Rome at a time when British diplomats were doing their best to build workable relationships with dictators.

George Steer leaves our story, but his coverage had influence on one man in particular whose rendition of the horror of the bombing became perhaps the most iconic painting he produced. Pablo Picasso's mural *Guernica* was exhibited at the Paris International Exposition in July 1937, reflecting the short amount of time it took him to complete the work. The mural travelled to England in September 1938, where art critics gave it a mixed reception. Alfred Harris photographed it at the Whitechapel Gallery for the *Daily Sketch*. He appears to have taken only a single half-plate frame. After this the painting went on a tour of Liverpool, Leeds and Manchester, where it helped to raise funds for refugees and others affected by the conflict.

At this stage photographic coverage of the war by Jack Barker and others centred on humanitarian aspects. Refugee Basque children were camping in Hampshire and they made for good imagery. Out in Spain, James Holburn had given way to Kim Philby, who continued reporting from the Nationalist viewpoint despite his true beliefs. In January 1939 he sent an image from the fall of Barcelona showing the German panzers used by Franco's army, but to be fair the same picture shows Russian-built tanks the Nationalists had captured in numbers from the Republicans. Perhaps this otherwise bland image best illustrates the fate of Spain as a laboratory for the vested interests of foreign dictators. Philby himself escaped an ironic death when he survived shelling by Russian-made artillery that killed his companions.

Madrid surrendered to Franco on 28 March 1939 after his enemies had begun fighting amongst themselves. The war ended on April Fool's Day. There was residual coverage of former prisoners of war as fortunate survivors of the International Brigades returned to Britain keeping up their spirit of defiance to the end. Tragic as events in Spain were, eyes had already moved closer to Nazi Germany and it was there that the immediate future of Europe was decided.

The Washington Naval Conference had serious ramifications for the Royal Navy. The treaty agreed in the United States set limits on the number, size and armaments of battleships in addition to placing limitations on the newest form of capital ship; aircraft carriers. Opening in November 1921, Washington was the world's first arms limitation treaty and met with immense support from across the spectrum of British politics and a public determined to see no more wars. The British delegation was led by Arthur Balfour, who returned to London on 14 February 1922 to something of a hero's welcome. Andrew Bonar Law, US Ambassador George Harvey and David Lloyd George came to meet him at Waterloo. *[TT]*

Below: A large crowd turned out for the launch of the battleship HMS *Rodney* at Birkenhead on 17 December 1925. The design of both *Rodney* and her sister ship, *Nelson*, were subject to the Washington Naval Treaty limiting the weight and armament of capital ships to a maximum of 35,000 long tons and 16in guns. The Nelson class was something of a compromise; both ships were based on the projected N3 class that had been on the drawing board before Washington. There would have seen four massive ships armed with nine 18in guns and a displacement of 48,000 long tons. In the event, the Nelson class included the armament and features from the cancelled G3 class of battlecruisers that, like the N3, had also fallen victim to Washington. *Rodney* took five years to build at a cost of over £7.5 million. She was in use throughout the Second World War and was pretty worn out when decommissioned in 1946. *Stanley Kessell [TT]*

Fitting enormous 16in guns into *Rodney*'s turrets began a year after her launch. *William Horton [TT]*

The terms of the Washington Naval Treaty gave leeway for cuts, but it was the fall of the 'Geddes Axe' that caused the most alarm in military circles in the spring of 1923. Sir Eric, himself, had been charged with slashing public spending across the board and took no prisoners in his quest. *[KN]*

The rhomboid monsters of the Great War era had given way to the conventional look of tanks we can identify with today by the summer of 1925. This Vickers Medium is seen fording the River Wylye at Codford in Wiltshire. Continuous cuts in defence spending would see this design soldier on until the Second World War, when a number saw service in the home defence role. *Bill Warhurst [TT]*

The army's qualified interest in mechanisation saw the appearance of a number of vehicles that aroused a degree of publicity, but they did not all go into regular service. One that made it was the Vickers Medium Artillery Tractor, a type that would acquire the name dragon, literally a play on *drag gun*. Enthusiasm for such technically challenging equipment did not reach the Treasury and while the army's Manual of Military Vehicles of 1930 noted that the 'Necessity of mechanising the artillery had become apparent' it lamented that 'the dragon, however, is a highly specialised and costly vehicle.' A simpler and cheaper alternative was required and the manual's authors opined that the Citroën Kégresse half-track was seen as the way forward. But the army wouldn't get them, either. Field Marshal Lord Methuen and General Alexander Godley, the GOC of Southern Command, are seen admiring dragons at Burgeston Field in September 1924. *Bill Warhurst [TT]*

The Times military correspondent Lt-Col Frederic Walker's report of an exercise held around Andover on 21 September 1925 reflected on the Official History of the British campaigns of 1914 written by Brigadier General Sir James Edmonds. The exercise was based on maintaining manoeuvrability rather than descending into 'siege warfare in the field', the fate of Field Marshal Sir John French during that precipitous period of the Great War. 'The question arises whether the monotonous horror of that trench warfare is likely to be repeated in the future, or whether, by skilful use of new inventions which increase speed of movement and deadliness of weapons (combined with protective armour for those who handle them), the issue between great armies can be determined rapidly by other methods.' Someone who understood all this was French's successor, Field Marshal Earl Haig, who had led Britain's largest ever army to its great victory in 1918. *The Chief* had been invited to view the exercise at a time when he was deeply involved in veterans' affairs but like so much else, his views on what he witnessed were not made known. *Bill Warhurst [TT]*

Much effort was put into finding solutions to military mobility. The Tank and Tracked Transport Experimental Establishment at Farnborough gave a demonstration of new designs for delegates of the Imperial Conference amid clouds of dust in Long Valley at Aldershot on 21 May 1927. Stanley Kessell used considerable skill to get this superb panned image of the Vickers Reconnaissance Car, the prototype configuration of what became the D3E1 Wheel-cum-Track Machine. This was intended to resolve problems with track-wear affecting the endurance of armoured vehicles, an issue that is still with us ninety years later. *Stanley Kessell [TT]*

One design that didn't go the distance was a pioneer of the tankette concept, a small thinly armoured vehicle operated by one or two men that found favour in several countries, including France and Italy, during the 1930s. We shall see their versions later. The brains behind it was Major Giffard Le Quesne Martel, whose home-built prototype was in competition with a tracked vehicle produced by Sir John Carden and Vivian Loyd, who were destined to have great success with their designs after being bought out by Vickers. A one-man operated prototype of Martel's vehicle was followed by eight production versions that made room for two men (seen here) when it was accepted a single operator could not drive and use a weapon at the same time. *Stanley Kessell [TT]*

A recipient of the DSO, the MC and Mentioned in Dispatches five times during the Great War, Martel was a gifted engineer and tank pioneer who acquired the nickname 'Slosher' thanks to boxing skills he was not shy in using. He busied himself in tank development throughout the 1930s and held divisional command with the BEF in 1940, where he led an attack that gave Erwin Rommel a fright. He headed up the British Military Mission to Moscow for a year and had a bit part in the Battle of Kursk – the largest tank battle in history. He retired as a lieutenant general and died in 1958. He is pictured at a parade in London in 1941. *[TT]*

Below: This image shows the Morris-Martel Mk I attempting to keep up with a Vickers Medium Mk Ia tank. A Crossley-built version of Martel's machine was also on display. *Stanley Kessell [TT]*

A few months later the Experimental Mechanised Force were putting some of this shiny new kit through its paces. Stanley Kessell was on hand to record vehicles crossing the River Avon at Amesbury in July 1927, where the crew of a Carden Loyd Mk V tankette were having a miserable time. Despite the ducking one of their vehicles received at Amesbury, Carden and Loyd had hit on a winning formula. Their tankette designs were favoured over Martel's and work with Vickers would see a range of armoured vehicles that proved lucrative to the company, with sales and licencing agreements as far afield as Japan. Sir John Carden was killed in an air crash in 1935 but Vivian Loyd continued working after leaving Vickers and went on to produce the Loyd Carrier during the Second World War. In this image the soggy tankette has been pulled clear of the river by a Vickers Medium tank.
Stanley Kessell [TT]

Although it had shrunk immeasurably since 1918, the RAF battled to secure a role for itself in the face of near constant attacks from jealous admirals and generals keen to carve up the world's first independent air force. That they failed owed much to the tenacity of Marshal of the Royal Air Force Lord Trenchard; forever considered the father of his service. 'Boom' Trenchard sought to engender the 'air spirit' in the RAF by initiating centres for training aircrew and technical staff imbued with pride in their uniform and organisation. His success says as much about him as the people serving under him. He is seen when, as Air Chief Marshal Sir Hugh, he inspected apprentices at the No 1 School of Technical Training at RAF Halton, near Wendover in Buckinghamshire, in 1924. Trenchard's efforts to protect his service came at a cost and the RAF would struggle to progress through the difficult years when financial restrictions stifled expansion and modernisation, but young lads like these on parade would form the backbone of the service in the difficult years ahead. *[TT]*

Money was found to build facilities to defend the capital and one of these was at a former home defence fighter base at RAF Hornchurch in Essex. The station had only re-opened in the spring of 1928 and had recently dropped the wartime name Sutton's Farm. There were regular air manoeuvres designed to test defences for London and these usually proved attractive to press photographers. This image shows Armstrong Whitworth Siskin IIIA fighters of No 111 Squadron getting going aided by a Hucks Starter. *[KN]*

These pilots seem fairly pleased with how things had gone. *[KN]*

The decade following the Great War had seen many aviators and aircraft celebrated for daring exploits. Air races and record attempts were fertile ground for a publicity conscious RAF, but there was a serious side in respect of the many technological breakthroughs linked to the effort. The Schneider Trophy was, perhaps, the pinnacle of air racing and the competition is indelibly linked to the designer R.J. Mitchell, whose Supermarine floatplanes won the trophy outright after their third win in a row in 1931. He is seen here at Calshot during the 1929 competition when Flight Lieutenant Dick Waghorn won with an average speed of 328mph in N247. This, however, is the second aircraft, N248, receiving some TLC despite being disqualified, although it broke two world records on its runs. Today, this aircraft is on display at Solent Sky in Southampton. R.J. Mitchell's most iconic design will appear later on in our story. *James Jarché [KN]*

Naval matters had returned to the top of the international agenda by January 1930. The major maritime powers accepted that the agreements reached in Washington eight years earlier were in need of an upgrade to preclude any rekindling of an arms race. They had failed to reach a consensus in Geneva in 1927, but the conference that took place in London between 21 January and 22 April set limits on the number of heavy and light cruisers operated by the UK, Japan and the USA. The treaty also set a maximum limit on the tonnage of a submarine and the calibre of gun they could use. This effectively killed off the development of large, heavily armed long-range 'cruiser' submarines by Britain and France. Among other things, the treaty also limited the size and armament of destroyers. It was a busy four months for the delegates, seen listening to the opening address made by King George V in the Royal Gallery of the House of Lords. *Bill Warhurst [TT]*

Below: The Modified K-class submarine HMS *K26* was a victim of the agreement reached in London because she exceeded the maximum displacement set down by the delegates. *K26* was the last of a class beset by accidents leading to them being dubbed the 'Kalamity Klass' by unimpressed sailors. Admiral Jacky Fisher was most definitely not a fan, thinking the use of steam power to be nonsensical. *K26* had enjoyed success carrying out the longest voyage by a submarine to date when she made the return trip from Britain to Singapore via staging posts of the empire. Some 20,000 miles later her crew were no doubt very glad to see Portsmouth in this picture taken on 13 August 1924. *[TT]*

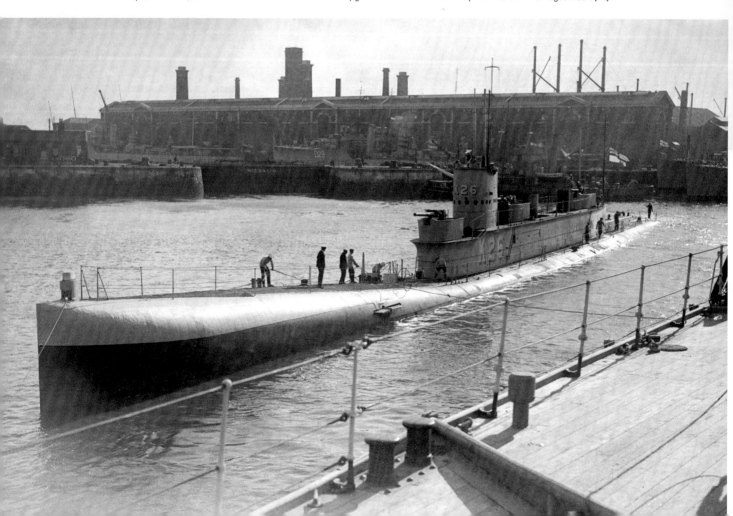

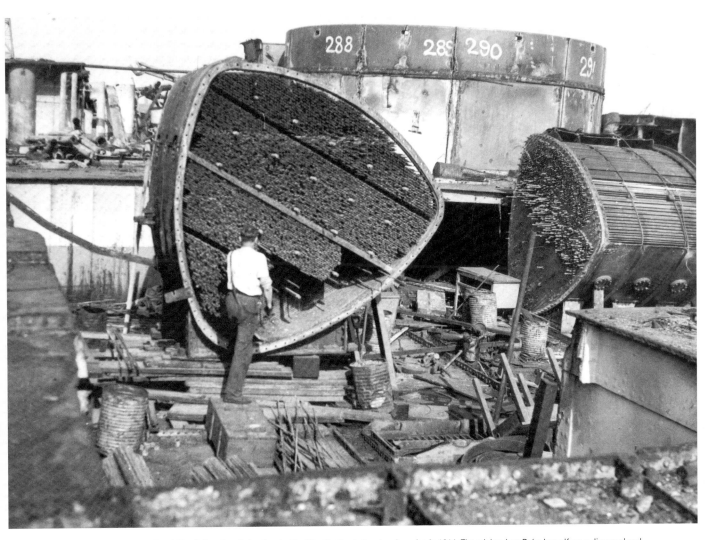

Other victims were the Royal Navy's four *Iron Duke*-class battleships that had all entered service in 1914. The mighty *Iron Duke*, herself, was disarmed and used as a depot ship before being scrapped in 1949. In this image hundreds of copper pipes are removed from the condensers of *Emperor of India* when she was broken up at Rosyth in May 1932. *Benbow* and *Marlborough* met a similar fate and all three ships were gone by the end of the year. *[TT]*

The army were making full use of Carden Loyd tankettes by August 1930. This group were taking part in the 2nd Division's manoeuvres fought out in the Surrey countryside by *Northland* forces, who had the advantage of mechanised elements against *Southland*, who did not. *Bill Warhurst [TT]*

Manoeuvres taking place the following year saw press interest in the new 6-ton light tank produced by Vickers from a Carden Loyd design. This Mk IIA saw improvements in just about all departments and impressed *The Times* caption writer; 'They are speedy machines, and their general efficiency has been a feature of the exercises.' *William Horton [TT]*

Other units would have some time to wait for their introduction to armoured vehicles. These lads of the 5th Royal Inniskilling Dragoon Guards perfect the finer points of using the Pattern 1908 Cavalry Trooper's Sword. The *Skins* would keep their horses until 1938. *Ernest Barton [KN]*

In September 1931 *The Times* began regular coverage of French army exercises, beginning with one based on Neufchatel-sur-Aisne. This image shows an elderly White TBC armoured car dating from 1918 seen in the village of Tagnon. There were upwards of eleven squadrons of the type still in service with the French army at the time and a number were used in the defence of France in 1940. *Jack Barker [TT]*

This image shows an artillery column of the 'red' army halted near Neufchatel-sur-Aisne. A number of Citroën Kégresse P17 half-tracks are seen passing by.
Jack Barker [TT]

Even as the military kept busy, other pillars of society were seeking divine intervention in pursuit of peace for all mankind. Ramsay MacDonald and Stanley Baldwin are seen arriving for the national service of prayer held on 15 December 1931 in advance of the World Disarmament Conference in Geneva the following year. Archbishop Cosmo Lang warned his congregation, 'The civilised world is approaching one of the turning points in its history… The claim of the old evil maxim, "If you wish for peace you must prepare for war" has been forever shattered. The lesson of the Great War has been written large – literally in letters of blood – that great armaments can only lead to war.' He went on: 'The spirit of fear is still haunting the nations. It is this that makes them cling nervously to their armaments… Armaments are but the symptom of a disease. It is well, indeed, to attack the symptom, but it is the disease itself which must ultimately be reached and healed. And that disease is Fear.' Despite the best efforts of MacDonald and others, no substantive agreement was reached at Geneva over years of fruitless discussions.
Robert Chandler [KN]

While men such as André Maginot had reason to keep a wary eye on the Germans, others were attracted to the aims of National Socialism. Although anti-Semitism and racism in general formed a big part of that, Nazi hostility to communism found favour in all levels of British society, including men like Norman Baillie-Stewart, a Seaforth Highlander who passed military secrets to Berlin. He was found to have supplied the Nazis with details of the Vickers A1E1 Independent tank. A one-off prototype, seen here, in 1926, dwarfs a diminutive Carden Loyd Mk I tankette. The Independent can be seen at the Tank Museum, Bovington. *Cathal O'Gorman [TT]*

The kilted Lieutenant Norman Baillie-Stewart is seen chatting with his defence team during his court-martial in March 1933, where he was found guilty of seven charges and imprisoned for five years. *William Field [KN]*

Baillie-Stewart was held in the Tower of London during his court-martial and greatly enjoyed his notoriety as 'the Officer in the Tower'. He was the last British person to be imprisoned there and was the subject of much curiosity. William Field used a small plate camera to snatch this image of him arriving there prior to his conviction. Baillie-Stewart left Britain for Austria upon his release in 1937 and found his way to Germany, where he made propaganda broadcasts. Although William Joyce is commonly associated with the pseudonym Lord Haw-Haw, it was, in fact, the drawl of Baillie-Stewart that may have influenced Jonah Barrington of the *Daily Express* to come up with the name. Norman Baillie-Stewart fell out of favour with the Nazis, helped by his bitter rivalry with Joyce. He was imprisoned by the British again in 1946 and eventually moved to Ireland, where he died twenty years later. *William Field [KN]*

The fact not many leading Nazis came to Britain was hardly mourned by the establishment or the man in the street. One exception was Alfred Rosenberg, the influential theorist and ideologue who is credited with dreaming up some of the key elements of National Socialism in respect of the Jews, rejection of Christianity, and a yearning for Lebensraum. He came to London in May 1933 in an unsuccessful attempt to gain approval from influential Britons but went away empty-handed. He autographed this portrait of himself for Allan Sinclair, editor of the *Daily Sketch*, who quickly passed it into the care of the picture library. Despite his influence, Rosenberg was unable to make serious headway in the snakes and ladders of the Nazi hierarchy but he held the post of Reich Minister for the Occupied Eastern Territories, where he proved to be typically lazy in a role way beyond his abilities. Tried at Nuremberg, he was hanged for his part in genocide along with other leading Nazis in 1946. We will see senior German military figures on visits to the UK later. *Bertram Wilson [KN]*

Other exotic fascists were creating publicity for themselves in the British Isles in July 1933. General Italo Balbo led a flight of twenty-four Savoia-Marchetti S.55 flying boats – the 'Italian Air Armada' – from Orbetello in Italy to Chicago. Their destination was reached in stages and the stop at Lough Foyle in Northern Ireland gave Charles Maxwell the chance to impress with his aviation photography skills. Two of the aircraft are seen landing. *Charles Maxwell [KN]*

The man himself was photographed at Hendon being greeted by Air Vice Marshal Francis Scarlett on an earlier visit in 1926. Balbo was a leading fascist but was dismayed by Mussolini's friendship with the Nazis and not ashamed to say so, observing that the Germans would dominate the relationship. He was killed by friendly fire over Tobruk in June 1940, thus saving him from seeing his prediction come true. *Alfred Abrahams [KN]*

Home-grown fascism was on the rise. Sir Oswald Mosley's career in mainstream politics might be described as mercurial for throughout the period he failed to settle on a party who reflected his frustrations with post-war realities. He founded the New Party in 1930 and initially attracted support from a few MPs who quit the Labour Party with him, but his increasingly authoritarian style and growing belief in a centralised government wielding extensive powers drew him towards the example of Benito Mussolini. The dismal showing of the New Party in the 1931 general election only acted as an accelerant. He is seen on the left retreating from Glasgow Green on 21 September 1931 after a stone hit him as left-wingers disrupted his address to a gathering where a number of others were slashed with razors. Mosley's future activities were set to attract similar levels of hostility. [KN]

Responsibility for the Reichstag fire of 27 February 1933 remains disputed, although a lengthy trial in Leipzig led to the execution of the Dutch communist Marinus van der Lubbe. Suspicions that the Nazis had orchestrated the fire were real enough to see a number of prominent international legal figures forming a commission of inquiry to investigate the case. *The Times* described the openly left-leaning commission meeting in London in September 1933 as a 'parallel trial' mirroring ongoing events in Leipzig. The week-long proceedings ended with blame for the fire being placed firmly at the feet of Herman Goering and other Nazis. The American civil liberties lawyer Arthur Garfield Hays had assisted in the successful defence of one of the accused in Leipzig (three others were also acquitted) and came to London to contribute to the inquiry. It was all positive PR for German communists, in particular, but Hitler had cemented his grip on power in the wake of the fire and fine words in London would offer no protection to his political enemies.
Herbert Muggeridge [KN]

Nonetheless, protests at the brutality of the Nazis found fertile ground both in print and in the theatre. The Progressive Players' production of *Take Heed* by Leslie Reade in January 1934 impressed the theatre critic of *The Times* with its tragic tale of the persecution suffered by a professor married to a Jewish woman. In this scene Alan Napier as 'Professor Opal' and Selma Vaz Dias as his wife 'Sophie' fall foul of the Brownshirts.
Charles Maxwell [KN]

Sir Oswald Mosley's party had attracted 40,000 paid-up members by the summer of 1934. Twelve thousand people, including many of his prominent backers and a good few intent on disrupting proceedings, attended the British Union of Fascists (BUF) rally at London's Olympia on 7 June. While descriptions of the event vary depending on the sympathies of the source, it is generally agreed that attempts to mimic the theatrics of similar German and Italian rallies were hit and miss. Protestors continuously disrupted Mosley's two-hour monologue that was itself hampered by the erratic public address system. Running fights occurred throughout and the violence between Blackshirts, left-wingers and Jewish agitators caused sections of the media and some erstwhile Mosley supporters to review their positions. Patrick Brown's photograph of Mosley does much to capture the atmosphere. *Patrick Brown [KN]*

The defiantly cheery menace of these Blackshirts is evident, as are signs of recent battle damage. *Patrick Brown [KN]*

The Left were able to turn out in large numbers to disrupt further British Union of Facists events. These people are making their loyalties clear during the rally in London's Hyde Park on 9 September 1934 where there were clashes between fascists, left-wingers and the police, who were attempting to keep order. *Geoffrey Keating [KN]*

For Winston Churchill, only France could stand up to the threat posed by Hitler, but the French army was struggling to shake off its recent past. This image from Jack Barker's coverage of French army exercises on the Swiss border in 1934 suggests half-tracks had superseded the horses we saw earlier, but appearances are deceptive. Although the French continued to both mechanise and motorise there was still plenty of work for horses to do. As with their friends across the Channel, the French struggled to find the money to modernise and a lot of what might have been achieved was, in any case, set aside in favour of financing the system of fortifications championed by André Maginot. *Jack Barker [TT]*

The Great War vintage Renault FT tanks we saw previously were still in service twelve years later and those remaining in use would find themselves utterly outclassed when the Germans invaded France on 10 May 1940. *Jack Barker [TT]*

Nieuport-Delage NiD 622 C1 fighter planes of 4 Escadrille/2EC painted in special green and white 'Defence of Paris' livery for the 1934 air defence manoeuvres held by the Armee de l'Air. *Jack Barker [TT]*

Air defences were one thing but what would the authorities do if, as Stanley Baldwin had predicted, the bombers got through? The fear of gas attacks saw the creation of units with specialised equipment to deal with the menace. Jack Barker's photo of one group on a training exercise in Paris at the beginning of December 1934 conveys much of the fear generated by the spectre of chemical warfare. *Jack Barker [TT]*

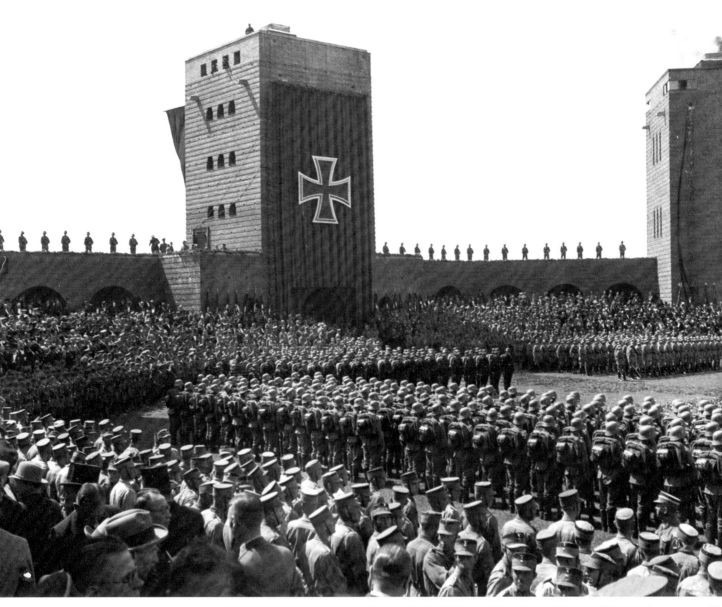

The death of President Paul von
Hindenburg on 2 August 1934 gave Adolf
Hitler the opportunity to conduct a lavish
funeral ceremony for the old man at
Tannenberg, the scene of his great victory
over the Russians in 1914. Bill Warhurst
flew out from London to cover the event
and found himself in a less than ideal
spot to record Hitler paying tribute to the
wily old field marshal. This is the scene
at the imposing Tannenberg Memorial,
now in modern-day Poland, where
Hindenburg was interred much against
his wishes. His remains were moved
west as the Russians closed in during
January 1945, when the site was partially
demolished. The Poles levelled the whole
site after the Second World War and only
odd bits of rubble remain.
Bill Warhurst [TT]

SA standard bearers provide default
setting imagery of mid-1930s Germany.
Bill Warhurst [TT]

As a contemporary of Hindenburg, the elderly Field Marshal August von Mackensen was a prominent mourner, seen here receiving salutes from some of his old comrades. One of Germany's most respected living field commanders, he was just the sort of figure the Nazis were anxious to court, but Mackensen wasn't much keen on them. He was angered by the murders of two generals, the former Chancellor Kurt von Schleicher and his right-hand man Ferdinand von Bredow, during the purge dubbed the Night of the Long Knives that took place in the month before Hindenburg's death. Mackensen was an avowed monarchist and considered disloyal to the Nazi regime, but he avoided the worst of their attentions and died of old age in November 1945. *Bill Warhurst [TT]*

The event gave Bill Warhurst the chance to photograph men wearing the black uniform of the SS, in this case an honour guard of men from *Leibstandarte* SS Adolf Hitler (LSSAH), the Führer's bodyguard commanded by Sepp Dietrich. Members of the unit had taken part in the Night of the Long Knives murdering a number of SA men and other officials, allowing Hitler to consolidate power. The LSSAH would go on to become a leading SS *Panzer* division notorious for excesses in Poland, Italy and Russia, in addition to the murders of American prisoners during the Battle of the Bulge in 1944. *Bill Warhurst [TT]*

The Treaty of Versailles had awarded the entire yield of coal from the Saarland for a period of fifteen years to France to compensate her for the devastation of French coalfields. At the end of that period there was to be a plebiscite to decide whether the region would return to Germany, become a state in its own right, or join in union with France. There was never any doubt what the people's decision would be but, in the summer of 1934, the political enemies of the Nazis embarked on a doomed campaign to keep Hitler and his supporters out of power in the region. They organised a huge rally at Sulzbach on 26 August 1934 to voice their opposition to fascism. Here some of Hitler's opponents call for support on the streets of Saarbrücken. *F.R. Donovan [KN]*

Sixty thousand people attended the rally at Sulzbach, an event commemorated on its 75th anniversary by the *Saarbrücker Zeitung* at the time a memorial was unveiled to recall the people who had much to lose when Hitler came to power. F.R. Donovan's picture is one of two survivors that don't do much to inspire but it is an important reminder that there were alternative voices to the Nazis. *F.R. Donovan [KN]*

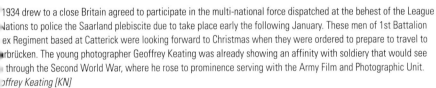

1934 drew to a close Britain agreed to participate in the multi-national force dispatched at the behest of the League [N]ations to police the Saarland plebiscite due to take place early the following January. These men of 1st Battalion [ex] Regiment based at Catterick were looking forward to Christmas when they were ordered to prepare to travel to [Saa]rbrücken. The young photographer Geoffrey Keating was already showing an affinity with soldiery that would see [him] through the Second World War, where he rose to prominence serving with the Army Film and Photographic Unit. [Ge]offrey Keating [KN]

Nazi propaganda material was bold and forthright. This postcard promoting a rally at the Niederwald Monument calls for Saarlanders to pledge allegiance to the Third Reich. 'Swear and say right stays right, true stays true. The Saar is German.' News UK Archive

The regimental band leads men of 1st Battalion East Lancashire Regiment as they march into Saarbrücken. There is no mistaking who had assumed leadership of the campaign for reunification with the Fatherland. Geoffrey Keating [KN]

Another typically inventive image from Geoffrey Keating shows men from the 1st East Lancs writing Christmas messages home. It was published on 23 December 1934. *Geoffrey Keating [KN]*

A Lancashire lad met with the approval of local boys who no doubt found themselves in uniform just a few years later. *Geoffrey Keating [KN]*

Intimidation and sleight of hand were the Nazi stock-in-trade but a fear of a violent reaction from France was ever-present during the plebiscite campaign, causing the Nazis to tone down some of their activities. An obvious move was to ban the wearing of political uniforms in the area; despite this, the allure of flags and ceremony was just too strong and old habits died hard. In this image the Nazi chief in the Saar, Jakob Pirro, and Hitler's commissioner, Josef Bürckel, salute a line of flag bearers whose choice of dress is uniform-like to say the least. Bürckel was an ardent Nazi involved in deporting Jews from Vienna after the *Anschluss*, which he did with relish. While there he developed expensive tastes and took to appropriating Jewish money and property for himself, but he was eventually caught with his hand in the till and removed from his post.
Jack Barker [TT]

Italians formed the second largest contingent of the multi-national force after the British.
Jack Barker [TT]

The East Lancs were soon sharing duties with their Italian colleagues. In this image neither the Italian grenadier nor the Tommy seems overjoyed to receive the attention of a warrant officer. *Geoffrey Keating [KN]*

The plebiscite was held on 13 January 1935. Voters queue up in the snow so they can express their preference. *Jack Barker [TT]*

Goodbye and good riddance to the status quo. These Saarlanders use symbolism to make their wishes clear. A knife stuck in the doll and little boys shooting it with toy guns add to the imagery. Only reunification would do. *Jack Barker [TT]*

Security was tight to avoid any foul play with the ballot. Lanchester armoured cars of D Squadron 12th Royal Lancers make their presence felt. *Jack Barker [TT]*

Although he had been well and truly shafted by Hitler and, unlike several friends and colleagues, been extremely fortunate to avoid death during the Night of the Long Knives, former Chancellor Franz von Papen had managed to retain his position of Vice-Chancellor under the Führer until August 1934, when he was shunted off to be ambassador to Austria. He found time to lead the activities of the Nazis' Deutsche Front in the Saar and is reported to have been a ruthless campaigner for reunification. He is seen here leaving a polling station on the day of the ballot. *Jack Barker [TT]*

Relations between the locals and the British had been warm. Here two members of the Corps of Military Police are shouldered by the delighted crowd in Saarbrücken on the announcement of a landslide result in favour of reunion with Germany. The Brits were practically all back in Blighty by the end of January, many having passed through Reims and the Great War battlefields on the journey west. *Geoffrey Keating [KN]*

Jack Barker continued his coverage of French military exercises in the summer of 1935. This awkward-looking Schneider P16 of the Reims Mechanised Brigade is pictured not far from the city in early September. The P16 dated from 1928 and was designated as a combat armoured car. It was armed with an elderly 37mm gun unlikely to make much of a dent in modern opposition and was due to be replaced by new light tanks considered much more fit for purpose. *Jack Barker [TT]*

French army nomenclature could be confusing. This light tank was designated as an armoured car under the Automitrailleuse de Type Reconnaissance programme. The two-man AMR 33 Renault VM was yet another thinly armoured machine-gun-armed vehicle that would struggle against weightier opposition. *Jack Barker [TT]*

The bulk of the French defence budget was being spent on the Maginot Line. While it is easy to write it off as an enormous folly, the concept of the line in harness with France's alliance with Belgium can be seen as making sense, but once the Belgians pulled out of the arrangement the reality would become ominous. *Jack Barker [TT]*

King Leopold III of Belgium remains a divisive figure for his actions during the Second World War, for which he had to spend some years in exile. He was deeply affected by causing the death of his wife, Queen Astrid, in a car accident in 1935 and his subsequent decision-making would have severe ramifications for France. Belgium withdrew from the Franco-Belgian Military Accord of 1920 and the Locarno Treaty to seek a path of neutrality in 1936, meaning the French Army would not be able to deploy into the country should hostilities break out with Germany. The fact Belgium had been a handy battlefield for her neighbours for centuries was not lost on Brussels. The Belgians elected to seek security behind their own network of fortifications. German heavy artillery had pummelled similar defences into submission in 1914 and modern weapons and tactics employed by Germany would provide an equally tough lesson for Belgian policy makers in 1940. Leopold III is shown on a visit to Paris in 1934. *Jack Barker [TT]*

The Battle of Cable Street took place in London's East End on 4 October 1936. A proposed march through a predominantly Jewish neighbourhood by Sir Oswald Mosley and his supporters could only ever have been seen as provocative, prompting the Left to stage a counter-demonstration. The violence that followed between the different factions and the police helped usher in the Public Order Act of 1936, banning the wearing of political uniforms in public places or at public meetings. The Act received its royal assent on 18 December 1936 and became law on 1 January 1937. Mosley's Blackshirts had involved themselves in disputes over rents in big cities and tithes in rural communities but at all stages uniforms were an important part of their persona. This picture shows Mosley taking the salute from supporters in Royal Mint Street just before violence broke out. Banning uniforms did not kill off support for the BUF entirely or end political violence, but the decline in fortunes of Mosley and his party proved to be a distraction from more serious matters and attention had moved south to Rome and Italian adventures in East Africa. *Alfred Harris [KN]*

The Times' photographic coverage of the Second Italo-Abyssinian War falls into two distinct camps. On the one hand there is the striking work of George Steer leaving us to admire the captivating quality of his photographs of the people fighting against the Italians. His pictures have a warmth and something much more personal about them than those by the experienced professional Bill Warhurst, however pleasing his images may be. Warhurst sailed with the Italians from Naples, accompanying Italian officers pictured relaxing aboard the handsome liner MS *Saturnia* on their way to war. Bill has taken great care with arranging his subjects. *Bill Warhurst [TT]*

Meanwhile, J.W. Eggitt of the *Daily Sketch* based himself in Port Said to photograph the Italian ships transit down the Suez Canal. One of the fine vessels he caught on camera was the elegant SS *Conte Biancamano*. Seized at Panama in 1940, she went on to serve throughout much of the Second World War with the Americans who renamed her USS *Hermitage* in 1941. The ship supported campaigns in Europe, North Africa and the Pacific, in addition to transporting thousands of servicemen and refugees home in 1945. A substantial part of her can be seen in the Leonardo da Vinci Museum in Milan. *J.W. Eggitt [KN]*

Eggitt's colleague Fred Roper had been in Addis Ababa since the Ethiopian New Year in September, when he photographed festivities and military parades using a Leica and a press camera fitted with a film back. He went on to snap warlords and warriors rallying to the cause of Emperor Haile Selassie, including the ceremonial beating of the *Menelik* war drum and the proclamation of mobilisation on 3 October 1935. *F.G. Roper [KN]*

Although several caption sheets typed on the back of imperial government telegram forms have survived, some of Roper's Leica films have not, but what remains offers us a remarkable glimpse of dramatic events. These images show elements of the Imperial Guard, the *Kebur Zabagna*, perhaps the best-equipped unit in Haile Selassie's army, complete with new Czech-designed machine guns. *F.G. Roper [KN]*

As invasion forces began to build up in Eritrea, George Steer was busy meeting and photographing the men who would oppose the Italians. On a tour of the Ogaden he met Balambaras Ali Nur, commander of forces along the border with British Somaliland. He is pictured on the left accompanied by his machine gunner, Ato Wolde. *George Steer [TT]*

The Ethiopians set to digging trenches. Steer photographed local commander Kenyasmatch Malio and his men at a 'challenge post' on the Daggah Bur to Jijiga road at the end of September 1935. Malio was a grandson of Tewodros II, who had reigned as emperor from 1855 to 1868. *George Steer [TT]*

George Steer infused his photographs with a great deal of atmosphere, giving them a modern, informal feel. This image of fighters on the road in the Ogaden at the beginning of October is a case in point. *George Steer [TT]*

Somali troops under the command of Ali Nur man defensive positions at Jijiga. *George Steer [TT]*

A month later Bill Warhurst was busy following the Italian advance. These Blackshirts accompanied by an askari were under the command of General Mantagea and are seen taking pot shots at the enemy in the hills of Amba Bati-Falase near Adigrat. *Bill Warhurst [TT]*

More hot work on the plain beyond Adagamus as gunners go through drills with Cannone da 149/35A howitzers, artillery pieces of Great War vintage. The plates fitted to the wheels were intended to help with traction and to absorb some of the gun's fearsome recoil. *Bill Warhurst [TT]*

On a wholly different scale these askari gunners are practicing with even older 75mm mountain guns. *Bill Warhurst [TT]*

The Abyssinian army was only in possession of four Great War era tanks of dubious reliability and there were no engagements between them and Italian armour. The campaign offered the Italians the opportunity to put some of their new equipment through its paces in challenging conditions and things did not go brilliantly. Bill Warhurst described these diminutive Carro Veloce CV-35s as tanks when in fact they are another example of all but useless two-man tankettes based on a Carden Loyd design. The CV-35, also known as a L3/35, had a disappointing war in Ethiopia and the type would prove to be hopelessly outclassed in the Second World War. *Bill Warhurst [TT]*

Four-wheeled transport was often much less reliable. An OM Autocaretta 32 light truck has come to grief near Makale. *Bill Warhurst [TT]*

This Pavesi P4/100 Mod 30a artillery tractor seems to find the going much easier. The gun is another piece of Great War vintage weaponry, a Cannone de 77/28 modello 05 captured from the Austrians in 1918.
Bill Warhurst [TT]

The name askari comes from the Arabic for soldier. All but France among colonial powers in Africa acknowledged the presence of askaris in the ranks of their armies. Italy's askaris were recruited in Italian Somaliland and Eritrea. Their uniform included a tall fez and a colourful waistband denoting a particular unit. Most Europeans who encountered them gained a healthy respect for the fighting qualities of askaris and this Italian appears to be of a similar mind. Perhaps the most distinguished were those led by Paul von Lettow-Vorbeck against the British and Portuguese in East Africa during the Great War.
Bill Warhurst [TT]

Traditional weapons and dress mix with rifles, bayonets and revolvers as these men dance in celebration after church in their home village near Asmara at the end of November 1935. *Bill Warhurst [TT]*

The commander of the 2nd Eritrean Brigade was Brigadier General Renzo Dalmazzo, seen here with some of his staff enjoying a break during the campaign on the Northern Front as part of General Ruggero Santini's 1st Corps. Dalmazzo fell out with his boss Marshal Rodolfo Graziani during the campaign against the British in the Western Desert in 1940. He was more successful during the conflict in Yugoslavia where he was instrumental in forging an alliance with the royalist Cetniks to fight against Tito's partisans. *Bill Warhurst [TT]*

Two people looking for a pragmatic solution to the war that would keep Mussolini onside amid growing concerns over the ambitions of Nazi Germany were the British Foreign Secretary, Sir Samuel Hoare (right) and the French Prime Minister, Pierre Laval (left). The Hoare-Laval Pact offered Italy freedom of action in Abyssinia but while hostility from the left was only to be expected, there was angry opposition, too, from influential sections on the right. Hoare and Laval were brought down by their plan and were quickly out of office, if only temporarily. They are pictured with Britain's ambassador to Paris, Sir George Clerk, on 8 December 1935. Hoare made a quick return to government and was a key member of Chamberlain's inner circle during the Munich Crisis. Churchill was less enamoured but made him Britain's ambassador to Spain in 1940. Pierre Laval's subsequent history remains contentious. He was at the centre of the Vichy regime after the fall of France and was executed for treason in October 1945. *F.R. Donovan [KN]*

Although eventual victory was increasingly beyond doubt, the Italians struggled to make headway in the prevailing conditions. The invaders were desperate to improve their mobility and the little Fiat 508 truck proved useful, although it seems a far from ideal troop carrier with four men squashed into the cargo bay and two more up front. Significant numbers were used in Ethiopia. Bill Warhurst *[TT]*

The Italians enjoyed complete air superiority and took full advantage to fly bombing and strafing missions virtually unmolested by anti-aircraft defences. Two flights of the 4th Bomber Squadron, the 14th *Hic Sunt Leones* and 15th *La Desperata*, operated on the Eritrean front using tri-motor Caproni Ca.101 D2 aircraft to drop bombs and mustard gas from their base at Asmara. The bombers are seen lined up for an inspection. The aircraft nearest the camera are from the 14th flight. *Bill Warhurst [TT]*

Two pilots enjoying themselves were 17-year-old Bruno Mussolini and his brother Vittorio, who was just two years older. They are seen here at Asmara where they took part in bombing missions that Vittorio particularly enjoyed. Both went on to fly combat missions during the Spanish Civil War and to participate in the Second World War. Of the two, Bruno was the more accomplished pilot who treated his job seriously. He was killed testing a prototype Piaggio bomber in 1941. Vittorio went into exile in Argentina for some years and became a successful film producer and critic. He died in 1997. *Bill Warhurst [TT]*

An air gunner poses for Bill Warhurst in his gun position on a Ca.101 of the 15th *La Desperata*. This type of aircraft was converted from an airliner and proved adequate for operations in Ethiopia, but was unsuited to more dangerous skies over Spain.
Bill Warhurst [TT]

Bombing up.
Bill Warhurst [TT]

Maintenance work under a clear sky had its lighter moments. *Bill Warhurst [TT]*

Although the Italians would not lose any aircraft to enemy action, there were plenty of hazards to catch out the unwary. This Meridionali Ro.37 Lynx of 103rd Reconnaissance Flight came to grief in a landing accident at Dessie in April 1936. *[TT]*

These boys are members of the Opera Nazionale Balilla paramilitary youth organisation; a form of armed Scout movement. This group appear to be the children of settlers from Eritrea. Balillas were named after a Genoese boy who is said to have started the 1746 revolt against the Habsburgs by throwing stones at an official. These kids, however, are armed with a Moschetto Balilla, a scaled-down version of the rifle used by Italian troops. *Bill Warhurst [TT]*

The pleasures of campaigning seem lost on Bill Warhurst, seated second from left in this jolly gathering of Italian officers and correspondents. *[TT]*

With an Italian victory seemingly inevitable while Britain and France stumbled over ways to keep Mussolini on side in dealing with the growing menace of Adolf Hitler, it was unsurprising that *The Times* would scale back coverage of the conflict. George Steer stayed on until the end, and even got married at the British Embassy as Italian troops entered Addis Ababa. Perhaps the best-known picture of Steer shows him enjoying a spot of hunting from his *The Times* lorry before hostilities got under way. He was killed in Burma on Christmas Day 1944. *[TT]*

The former Ras Tafari Makonnen took the title Lion of the Tribe of Judah, His Imperial Majesty Haile Selassie I, King of Kings of Ethiopia, Elect of God when he took the throne in 1930. He went into exile on the defeat of his army and found his way to Britain, where he is seen posing outside his home from home at Fairfield House in Bath. He returned to his country in 1941, taking part in the campaign led by Orde Wingate to defeat the Italians. Victory was sealed five years to the day after the Italians conquered Addis Ababa. His prescient warning that Ethiopia would not be the last place to witness fascist aggression and his support for the League of Nations earned him many admirers. He died in 1975 while in confinement following a Soviet sponsored coup d'etat. *Patrick Brown [KN]*

The Spanish Civil War offers up a range of images taken by staff photographers and a mixed bunch of correspondents sending in their material. A shooting war had started when Gerald Cook of the *Daily Sketch* was at Oyarzun near San Sebastian a month later when Government forces bombarded the town with artillery. His picture shows people killed and wounded by shell fragments. Unfortunately, all his negatives were lost when a German bomb struck Kemsley House in September 1940 and we have to rely on surviving prints to appreciate his work. *Gerald Cook [KN]*

The conflict began on 17 July 1936, a week after a crucial episode involving a number of Britons had taken place. Francisco Franco had been identified as a key opponent of the elected government some time earlier and was languishing in the Canary Islands when he was flown to Tetuán in Spanish Morocco where units of the Army of Africa, including the Spanish Legion, were preparing to mutiny. His pilot was Captain C.W.H. 'Cecil' Bebb, who flew out from Croydon accompanied by his friend Major Hugh Pollard in a De Havilland Dragon Rapide. Pollard's daughter and a friend flew with them, pretending to be tourists. Franco was delivered to Tetuán on 19 July and was soon in command of troops loyal to the cause. It was all something of an adventure for Bebb, who was awarded the Grand Cross of the Imperial Order of the Yoke and Arrows for his pains. He is pictured with Gordon Olley, an airline operator and Great War ace who is credited with being the first pilot to log a million miles of flying. *Robert Chandler [KN]*

Cook speculated on the names of a group of British pilots flying with the Nationalists. One of them is shown ahead of a raid on Madrid in September 1936.
The identities of the Brits were masked with a number of aliases and it has not proved possible to say who actually flew the Breguet 19 shown.
Gerald Cook [KN]

Jack Barker of *The Times* was there to see government soldiers on the receiving end, although not all the shells fired by the Nationalists had the desired effect.
This huge dud is the object of cautious scrutiny. *Jack Barker [TT]*

A little while later Gerald Cook photographed German sailors from the torpedo boat *Seeadler* landing refugees from San Sebastian at St Jean de Luz just up the coast in France on the 17th. *Gerald Cook [KN]*

Female fighters keep watch at a Nationalist barricade.
Jack Barker [TT]

This armoured lorry used by government troops at San Sebastian betrays the chronic shortage of modern weaponry in Spain. While the Germans and Italians would eventually provide a steady stream of hardware to the Nationalists, their opponents were not so fortunate and things would only improve once the Soviet Union was provoked enough by fascist successes to begin supplying munitions and equipment. *Jack Barker [TT]*

The Nationalists enjoyed a qualitative advantage by having units of the Spanish Legion in their army. The Legion was raised to form part of the Spanish Army of Africa and had many hardened veterans of the brutal Rif War, including Franco himself, in its ranks. Although modelled on the French Foreign Legion, the Spanish version did not recruit anything like as many foreign nationals, the majority coming from settler communities in Morocco and elsewhere. Men like these would give the Nationalists a decisive edge during the conflict and individual regiments would be spread around the army as a whole to provide shock troops to take tough objectives. *Jack Barker [TT]*

Guernica 26 April 1937: George Steer cut through pro-Nationalist fake news by identifying German made bomb components to incriminate the Condor Legion, but the denials continued. His revelations created ripples in London as the government's efforts to foster relations with Hitler and Mussolini were supported at Printing House Square. Although he had suffered immense personal tragedy when his wife and infant baby had died during childbirth, he threw himself into his work and was increasingly sympathetic with the Basque people and their aspirations for independence. He was pleased with his scoop and wrote to The Times' foreign editor. Ralph Deakin, "I think we are working up for a grand story here. I'm enjoying this job immensely." *George Steer [TT]*

Four thousand Basque children came to Britain as refugees and were housed in a large camp at Eastleigh in Hampshire. This image shows some of them arriving on 23 May 1937. *William Horton [TT]*

The attack on Guernica caused outrage and the great and the good, including Basil Liddell Hart, no less, signed letters calling for an end to the bombing of open towns. Franco's friends were unmoved. Undoubtedly the best-known image of the atrocity at Guernica comes to us from the hand of Pablo Picasso, whose mural, completed in June 1937, has come to exemplify the horrors of the Spanish Civil War. A *Daily Sketch* critic was unimpressed when the painting was exhibited in London in October 1938: 'Picasso's 250-foot-square painting of the bombing of Guernica is, appropriately, a horror… Wantonly childish drawing gives the picture an unsatisfactorily fragmented appearance. There is more to be admired in some of the preliminary sketches hung around the wall of the gallery.' Alfred Harris exposed a single half plate negative to make the image seen here. The painting went on to be exhibited in Leeds, Manchester and elsewhere in Britain. *Alfred Harris [KN]*

The war came its closest to the British Isles on 2 November 1938 when the SS *Cantabria*, a Spanish government freighter en route from London to Leningrad, was overhauled and shelled by the Nationalist auxiliary cruiser *Nadir* 12 miles off the Norfolk seaside town of Cromer. German agents in Denmark had passed on reports of shipping movements to the Nationalists. *Cantabria* had taken several hits and was in clear danger when the Cromer lifeboat, the *HF Bailey*, arrived on the scene. Coxwain Henry Blogg and his crew rescued the *Cantabria*'s captain, his family and one other man. The lifeboat crew are pictured when they were presented to the media. The remarkable Henry Blogg (1876–1954) is the most decorated lifeboatman in RNLI history. Over a lifetime of service he amassed the George Cross, British Empire Medal, three RNLI gold medals and four silver medals, in addition to a number of other awards. *Clifford Davies [KN]*

Another ship, the *Pattersonian*, got between *Cantabria* and *Nadir* and rescued eleven people, but the Nationalist ship picked up the remainder. One man went down with the ship. Captain Manuel Argüelles is pictured with his wife Trinidad and their children, 8-year-old Begoña and 6-year-old Ramón, while they were staying in London. They left for Mexico some time later. Both Ramón and Begoña returned to Cromer in 2006 to pay tribute to Henry Blogg at the museum set up in his honour. *Edward Taylor [KN]*

The League of Nations sponsored a non-intervention agreement to stop armaments reaching Spain. Both Germany and Italy sent warships along with Britain to monitor the conflict and, as we have seen, naval forces were regularly involved in evacuating civilians from trouble spots. Stopping arms proliferation was another matter, given the reality of the practical support for Franco from Berlin and Rome. While it is fair to treat German and Italian charades with a hefty dollop of cynicism, there were occasions when the harsh reality of the ideological struggle in Spain gave them cause for regret. Republican aircraft had attacked international naval vessels at Palma in May but at the end of the month the German heavy cruiser *Deutschland* had moved to Ibiza, where she was hit by a pair of Soviet-built Tupolev bombers with Russian crews. Thirty-one sailors were killed and over seventy injured. Hitler was furious and had the dead who had been buried at Gibraltar exhumed and brought home to Germany. The incident caused enough friction for Stalin to bar any further attacks on German or Italian warships. *Deutschland* is pictured on a visit to British waters in 1935. *Bill Warhurst [TT]*

Submarine warfare was also an issue, with a number of neutral vessels attacked while going about their business. The British agreed to send aircraft to deter similar events. This Short Singapore III flying boat of 209 Squadron is seen preparing to depart from Felixtowe for Algeria to begin anti-submarine patrols. 16 September 1937. *Stanley Kessell [TT]*

Jack Barker made a number of trips up into the Pyrenees to photograph Republican troops 'fleeing' across the border into France. This image shows men handing in their rifles to gendarmes near Bagnéres-de-Luchon at the beginning of April 1938. *Jack Barker [TT]*

Climbing higher up, he was able to record gendarmes on patrol looking out for gunrunners and other people attempting to slip across the border. *Jack Barker [TT]*

A picture that sums up the tragedy of the Spanish Civil War shows a column of Nationalist armour in Barcelona after the city fell to Franco's forces in January 1939. The mixture of German Panzer I and Russian T26 light tanks illustrates perfectly how the country had become a battlefield for competing ideologies. *The Times* correspondent Kim Philby's Russian handlers ordered him to discover details of the panzers. Ironically, he was considered loyal enough to be awarded a medal by Franco. At one point he was fortunate to narrowly escape death from a Soviet-manufactured artillery shell that killed three other journalists. *[TT]*

Refugee children get a helping hand at Le Boulou.
Jack Barker [TT]

International support for the Republican cause was as fervent as it was hopeless, even in the last months of the war. This couple were detained during the Arms for Spain demo in London's Leicester Square on 31 January 1939.
William Field [KN]

Defeated Republican troops cross into France. A fair number of men like these went on to serve in the French Army. The graves of some of them can be found in war cemeteries on the Belgian border where they died forming the rearguard of the British and French units falling back on Dunkirk in 1940. Others went on to fill the ranks of the French 2nd Armoured Division that liberated Paris in August 1944. *Jack Barker [TT]*

The spirit of defiance lingers on in the voices of these British members of the International Brigades just returned home from a Nationalist prison camp. *Alfred Harris [KN]*

3

THE GOOD MAN

....

TO place all the credit for the rise in fortunes of Germany's armed forces before the Second World War in the hands of Adolf Hitler is a mistake. The Germans had begun a secret policy of revamping the army, the *Reichswehr*, under the tenacious leadership of Hans von Seeckt, an old school general determined to erase the shame of 1918. In April 1922 the Germans met with the Russians at Rapallo in Italy to draw a line under territorial and financial claims arising from the Great War. They saw eye to eye in broad terms over shared hostility to Poland but neither country was prepared to do anything hasty. This was just one consideration that persuaded the Russians to provide training facilities for the Germans in areas far away from prying eyes. Meanwhile, the Germans had also been doing business with the Swedes to develop tanks and gain access to stocks of iron ore.

The Treaty of Versailles forbade Germany from having an air force, armoured vehicles or a general staff. The *Reichswehr* was limited to 100,000 men, but Seeckt manipulated these numbers to ensure the vast majority of serving soldiers were made of up of a large officer corps and junior leader cadre for future expansion. Exercises with dummy tanks were held in

Russia and an embryonic general staff was in quiet operation. It was only on assumption of complete power that Hitler took steps to accelerate rearmament and the construction of armed forces that would conquer much of Europe and take him to within sight of Moscow in the autumn of 1941.

Ten years after Seeckt retired, the forces he did more than anyone to create were given a first tentative mission on the orders of Adolf Hitler. As we have seen, the Allies had withdrawn their occupation forces from the Rhineland by 1930 while the Treaties of Versailles and Locarno forbade the placing of any forces in the region, but Hitler resolved to put that to the test. While Versailles continued to be viewed by Germany as a diktat, Locarno was a consensual agreement. A demilitarised Rhineland was seen as the buffer for peace guaranteed by the stated intention that if either France or Germany attacked the other, Britain, Italy and Belgium would side with the non-aggressor.

As signatories of the subsequent Kellogg-Briand Pact and as members of the League of Nations, it can be argued that a militarised Rhineland was of no merit to either France or Germany, but Hitler had taken Germany out of the League

The Peace Ballot of 1935. Eleven and a half million people responded to five questions, the second of them being, 'Are you in favour of all-round reduction of armaments by international agreement?' Over ten million answered 'yes'. This was all very worthy, but the ballot failed to ask whether Britain should rearm if other countries were doing so, evading the harsh reality that, however reluctantly, the Baldwin government had little option but to commence with rearmament.
Cathal O'Gorman [TT]

following a referendum in October 1933 and was about to abandon Locarno.

Having reclaimed the Saarland after resounding victory in the plebiscite of January 1935, Hitler then announced his intention to rearm. Conscription was set to return and the spectre of a rejuvenated German war machine sent alarm bells ringing in Paris and Moscow. The two countries had already held discussions over a pact proposed by foreign minister Louis Barthou, but he was mortally wounded during the assassination of King Alexander I of Yugoslavia in Marseilles on 9 October 1934. His successor, Pierre Laval, did not share his enthusiasm for ties with the Soviets amid long-standing grievances over Lenin's repudiation of loans to Tsarist Russia in the aftermath of the October Revolution. Mutual suspicion abounded, but the move by Hitler changed everything. Any doubts the French had about the finer points of a pact with communist Russia were set aside in the knowledge that Germany could ill afford a war on two fronts. The Franco-Soviet Treaty of Mutual Assistance was signed on 2 May 1935.

France had also entered into pacts with Poland, Czechoslovakia, Romania and Yugoslavia, the so-called Cordon Sanitaire. For Paris, this system of alliances was designed to hem in the Germans and this might have worked perfectly but for Hitler's decision to probe for weaknesses. He was able to claim that the Franco-Soviet pact broke the spirit of Locarno. It was an aggressive act that required a response. But German rearmament had barely got up a head of steam and the imposing presence of the French Army could not be ignored. Hitler chose to bide his time and waited for the spring of 1936 to launch his audacious coup.

German units crossed into the Rhineland on 7 March 1936. Despite the drama of the event, the move could hardly be described as unexpected because word of Hitler's intentions had spread throughout the diplomatic community and beyond. The arrival of German soldiers and airmen allows us to bring the photographer Stanley Devon into proceedings. A rising star in the world of press photography, he had moved to the *Daily Sketch* after a frustrating time working for the Associated Press. Teetotal and devoted to his craft, Devon had built a strong reputation based on his skill with a camera and the efforts he made to insure he got the shot. It was in the Rhineland that he captured one of the most iconic images of the interwar years, when women greeted mounted troops with flowers as they rode into Dusseldorf.

The Germans puffed out their feathers and looked purposeful, but in reality, the relatively small force sent into the Rhineland would have been crushed by the French had they chosen to intervene. It was a pivotal moment. Historians tend to agree that had the French retaliated, Hitler would have been swept aside. The French army did not march. Political divisions and anti-war sentiment held sway. An emboldened Hitler would soon be looking for new opportunities to expand the Reich.

Steps towards rearmament were also under way in Britain despite opposition in parliament and widespread pacifism across the country. In 1933 Labour won the Fulham East by-election on a peace ticket and that same year an Oxford Union debate ruffled feathers when students passed the motion that they would not fight for king and country. *The Times* poured scorn on the debate with a leader entitled 'The Children's Hour', but the pursuit of peace was seen as a noble cause. The Peace Ballot held in 1934–35 was a much more significant survey of public opinion. It sought to affirm the popularity of the League of Nations and gauge support for banning military aviation.

The ballot confirmed hostility towards the armaments industry but it failed to measure attitudes towards Britain needing to rearm in response to developments abroad. Eleven million voters took part and the result was a substantial boost to enthusiasm for collective security and diplomacy. Photographic coverage of the ballot by *The Times* and *Daily Sketch* was muted to say the least. The finale, a celebration at the Royal Albert Hall attended by the Archbishop of Canterbury and other worthies, was ignored.

Regardless of the ballot, the government of Stanley Baldwin had reluctantly decided to begin rearmament. Someone strongly in favour of this was Winston Churchill. *The Times* reported on his radio broadcast of 16 November 1934 where he called on Britain to not delay in making itself the strongest air power in Europe. He mocked those who deluded themselves that precipitous events on the continent could be ignored, telling his audience, 'If only we could unfasten the British islands from their rock foundations and could tow them 3,000 miles across the Atlantic Ocean to the smiling coasts of Canada.' Churchill reluctantly concluded that Britain would have to make the best of it, but it would be foolish to underrate the risks. The country could not detach itself from Europe, and for its own safety and self-preservation was bound to make exertions and run risks for the sake of keeping the peace. Britain should prepare for the worst with the country facing the 'old grim choice' whether to submit or to prepare. Possession of a powerful air force would 'Recover to a very large extent the safety which we formerly enjoyed through our Navy and through our being an island.' But there was a lot to do.

Despite the Peace Ballot's negativity towards arms sales for profit, what we now think of as the military industrial complex was actually in a very poor state. The intention to rearm was fine on paper but in practical terms there was an awful lot to do before a single artillery shell could be produced. Only very few firms – such as Edward Curran & Co of Cardiff – were capable of manufacturing munitions in significant volume. In January 1936 Baldwin created the position of Minister for Co-ordination of Defence to oversee the rearmament process and Winston Churchill was tipped as the ideal candidate for the job. But no fan of Churchill, the cautious Baldwin gave the role to Sir Thomas Inskip, the Attorney General, a move the spurned Churchill described as 'The most cynical appointment since Caligula made his horse a consul.' Inskip shared none of Winston's fervour.

But there was progress of a kind. Development of what would become the eight-gun monoplane fighters that won the Battle of Britain dovetailed with the decision by Rolls-Royce to progress with the Merlin engine without government funding. There would be teething problems but it would all come right in the end. A new twin-engined light bomber, faster than the RAF's in-service biplane fighters, was born out of a challenge to the British aircraft industry made by Lord Rothermere, in 1934, to build a modern passenger aircraft. The Bristol Blenheim would do vital work during the early years of the war to come. But the RAF's heavy night bomber was the awkward-looking Handley Page Heyford, a biplane totally unsuited to the modern warfare that would be seen in Spain.

The British Army was slowly putting its horses out to grass as motorisation progressed. A large standing army was never a British tradition and there was no form of conscription.

The army continued with weapons of Great War vintage but rearmament would see gradual improvements. The British had no submachine guns and eschewed developing automatic rifles in favour of retaining the trusty Lee-Enfield, the bolt-action rifle all the king's men had carried since 1911. Upwards of fifteen million models were made and the rifle would soldier on in British service until the late 1950s. Fixation on tankettes and infantry support tanks armed with machine guns would cause problems further down the line. Effective anti-tank weapons were thin on the ground but the new 2-pdr (40mm) gun was imminent. Perhaps the most significant weapon to join the British arsenal was the 3.7in heavy anti-aircraft gun. The only question was whether enough to defend Britain could be built in time.

The Royal Navy was still pre-eminent but there were clouds on the horizon. The 1930 London Naval Conference followed up on Washington and inserted more limitations on naval shipbuilding, this time on cruisers, destroyers and submarines. Once again, the latest agreement secured the primacy of British sea power and follow-up discussions maintained the status quo. Britain stunned her erstwhile allies by concluding a naval agreement with Germany in the summer of 1935 without consulting either France or Italy. Here again the treaty ensured the dominance of the Royal Navy, but both parties had different expectations on what the treaty would lead to. To the British it was all about maintaining their numerical advantage. For the Germans it confirmed Britain as master of the seaways while Germany could dominate continental Europe. Little wonder the French and Italians were miffed! Continued German support for the agreement was high on the shopping list of the British Prime Minister when he went to Munich in September 1938.

1935 saw London as the venue for the major naval powers to discuss a new agreement to move on from much of what had been achieved in Washington over a decade earlier. While France and Italy were at the table, the meaty stuff involved Britain, Japan and the United States. The Japanese were serious enough to send a senior naval officer to London for preliminary talks in October 1934. Rear-Admiral Isoroku Yamamoto explained his country's position to the British and *The Times* reported that Tokyo felt intimidated by the wealth and power of the British Empire, and it was apparent the Japanese were seeking to justify naval expansion as a response to the threat from Britain and the United States. Bill Warhurst photographed Yamamoto on the steps of No 10 Downing Street, the one occasion his name went into the picture library card index at Printing House Square.

The Second London Naval Treaty was eventually signed in March 1936, but by then the Japanese had walked, frustrated with the continued failure to gain recognition from her former ally that Japan was well within its rights to seek naval equality in the Pacific. Yamamoto talked of submarines as defensive weapons and aircraft carriers as offensive, an echo of the kind of semantics that helped stall the World Disarmament Conference in Geneva after more than two years of discussions. Yamamoto stated his country had wanted to see the complete removal of offensive weapons for the good of all nations, but with Japan's withdrawal from London the stage was set for him to direct a fleet of aircraft carriers in the most devastating manner at Pearl Harbor in 1941. Italy had also withdrawn as a result of sanctions imposed by the League of Nations over the Abyssinian War. The immediate effect of London was yet more restrictions on the Royal Navy at the most inopportune moment, with the imposition of more limitations on the size and armament of various classes of ship the British would sorely need in 1939.

On 20 September 1930 the Member of Parliament for Birmingham Edgbaston spoke on the subject of Conservative policy at a gathering of the Junior Imperial League held at the Crystal Palace. He told his audience:

Before very long, the Conservative Party may well be entrusted with one of the most responsible missions which any Party has ever been given: the restoration to our country of its self-respect and of that confidence which has been so lamentably shaken by the maladministration of the present Government.

The speaker's name was Arthur Neville Chamberlain. He went on:

Let us see to it that by loyalty to one another – by remembering that as our country comes before Party, so Party should come before self – by fearlessness in the face of opposition, by determining to overcome all obstacles which may stand in our way, we bind ourselves to serve our country and the Empire of which it is still the heart and centre.

Any notion that Neville Chamberlain was a weak man who chose to appease dictators instead of confronting them is far from reality. He was a steely politician with a powerful brain, careful in his choice of friends and allies, and, as Prime Minister, surrounded himself with a coterie of staunch supporters of his policies. He could rely on near unanimous backing from the parliamentary party policed by a formidable Chief Whip and ruthless machinery keeping Tory constituency affairs in check. (Chamberlain would make good use of the services of Sir Joseph Ball, a one-time MI5 figure with fingers in many pies. Best described as 'shadowy', Ball used eavesdropping and all manner of clandestine manipulations against Chamberlain's domestic opponents.) Anyone who was 'off message' would become isolated. Men who stood against his methods of dealing with dictatorships had no place in his Cabinet, much less his inner circle. A significant casualty was Anthony Eden, who was undermined by Chamberlain over dealings with the Italians and resigned his post as Foreign Secretary in February 1938.

Chamberlain was utterly opposed to another ruinous war and was prepared to do almost anything to prevent it. In the case of Czechoslovakia his pragmatism told him that sacrificing the sovereignty of what he termed a 'faraway country' was a price worth paying. He was quite ruthless in this respect and while he well understood there was a point when Britain would have to fight, he remained determined to hold out for peace to the bitter end. Perceptions of how much honour there was for Britain as a result of this has been debated ever since Munich.

To a great extent hindsight has propelled established thinking to agree a duplicitous Adolf Hitler was always one step ahead of Chamberlain and that he made a fool of him. Consider March 1936 when Chamberlain asserted his 'personal belief' in Hitler's peaceful intentions, prompting a cautiously optimistic Herbert Sidebotham writing as 'Scrutator' in *The Sunday Times* to enthuse 'The chances of a settled peace in Europe owe much to Mr Chamberlain.'

Indeed, if Chamberlain had a weakness it was his taking delight in receiving just this sort of praise and adulation. Perhaps he began to believe in his own infallibility, allowing an operator like Hitler to massage his ego just enough to deflect him from the Nazis' long game. We have to ask ourselves how any principled democratic politician was expected to horse trade with a man like Hitler?

Born in 1869, Neville Chamberlain came late to Parliament after a career in business and Birmingham city politics, where he followed in the footsteps of his father Joseph and half-brother Austen. As Lord Mayor of Birmingham, he led strong demands for improved air defences in the wake of several deadly Zeppelin raids on the West Midlands in 1916. David Lloyd George made him Director of National Service that same year, but his tenure was marked by poor relations with Lloyd George, descending into lifelong mutual loathing. Elected to Westminster in 1918 he remained a backbencher until 1922, when he began his rise as Minister of Health and then Chancellor of the Exchequer under Stanley Baldwin. Chamberlain returned to Cabinet politics in 1923 after the short life of Britain's first Labour government, when he served as Baldwin's Health Minister for a second time. Labour returned to power in 1929 but deepening financial crisis led to a budgetary mess.

The circumstances of the creation of the coalition National Government in August 1931 and the expulsion of Ramsay MacDonald from the Labour Party are not part of our story, but he led the coalition through a succession of heated arguments over tariffs and free trade as the economy sank. There were deep cuts in public expenditure, fuelling the mutiny of the Atlantic Fleet at Invergordon in September 1931 when sharp pay cuts for sailors were announced. The impact was immediate as jitters in the markets caused a run on the pound and Britain's subsequent withdrawal from the Gold Standard, but MacDonald's National Government won a landslide victory in the October 1931 general election and he stayed in power until declining health led to his retirement in June 1935.

The mantle passed to Stanley Baldwin, who won the general election in the November of that year on a ticket that made much of support for the League of Nations and the importance of collective security. Britain's relations with Italy had plummeted following Mussolini's invasion of Abyssinia, but attempts to implement meaningful sanctions were hampered by Paris where Pierre Laval fixated on the growing threat from Nazi Germany. He was baffled by Britain's high-minded approach to a country in far-off Africa when the real danger lay just beyond the Rhine. European relations had become a labyrinth of pacts, alliances and grievances that showed no sign of healing.

Little wonder, then, that Baldwin decided to retire after the bruising events of the Abdication Crisis of December 1936 had added to his load. His anointed replacement was Neville Chamberlain, who had reprised the role of Chancellor of the Exchequer since 1931. He became Prime Minister following the coronation of King George VI in May 1937. The new premier was not the sole architect of Britain's appeasement policy but he took it to the limit in his dealings with Nazi Germany.

In early 1938 Adolf Hitler was able to remove two senior army officers as a result of scandals manufactured by their rivals. Field Marshal Werner von Blomberg was head of the German armed forces and had enjoyed a distinguished career. It was he who altered the oath of allegiance in favour of Hitler rather than the German state. Leading Nazis coveted his position and the opportunity to remove him came when Blomberg, a widower, remarried. His unfortunate choice of bride was a much younger woman who had a dubious past with alleged links to the vice trade. It was a gift for leading rivals Goering and Himmler, who moved swiftly to scandalise Hitler with details of Blomberg's apparent folly. But the field marshal stuck by his bride and in doing so was forced to resign for the sake of the armed forces. Cast adrift, Blomberg died while in detention at Nuremberg in 1946.

This left his obvious replacement, the army commander Colonel-General Werner von Fritsch, open to similar treatment. Fritsch's position as a lifelong bachelor left him open to suspicion of homosexuality within the highly moralistic Nazi establishment. Reinhard Heydrich had kept details of unproven allegations against Fritsch on file despite Hitler's demand for them to be destroyed. So when a new opportunity to bring Fritsch down with similar allegations arose, Heydrich was quick to resurrect the old lies. The latest claims proved to be entirely false and although a court of honour acquitted Fritsch, his position was deemed to be untenable. Remarkably, he remained loyal to Hitler despite his torrid experience, professing the strongest support for the struggle against Jewry. He was mortally wounded in Poland on 22 September 1939.

As a result of the scandals, Hitler was free to assume supreme command of the armed forces and dissolve the Ministry of War. He created the *Oberkommando der Wermacht* in its place, led by a compliant Field Marshal Wilhelm Keitel. Hitler had consolidated his power over the armed forces in time to resolve his burning ambition to absorb his homeland into the Third Reich.

Although Austria had made progress as a republic, there were marked differences across the political spectrum. Identification with the spirit of Pan-Germanism was prevalent in much of the population and the desire for unification with Germany was strong. The country sat in the benevolent shadow of Mussolini's Italy and his brand of fascism seemed likely to take hold when the relatively inexperienced Engelbert Dollfuss assumed power in 1932. He took up an increasingly authoritarian position backed by his party, the Fatherland Front. The Nazis and socialists were banned as political violence spread.

The patriotic Dollfuss branded his ideology as Austrofascism, but German Nazis and their many allies within Austria were determined to see the two countries as one. *The Times* reported on a succession of Nazi outrages as Dollfuss maintained his grip on power, including an attempt on his life. A brief civil war broke out in February 1934, but government forces quickly supressed opposition groups and Dollfuss took the opportunity to ban the last of Austria's democratic parties. He engineered a new constitution giving him dictatorial powers, but it was not to last. Things came to a head the following July when Austrian Nazis made a coup attempt, breaking into Dollfuss' office and killing him. Violence broke out across the country but Italian forces intervened to stop German Nazis seizing power in the state of Carinthia. Conflict between Germany and Italy was entirely possible, but Hitler backed off because his forces were unready for war.

Mussolini made much of his grief for the death of his friend Dollfuss and the coup conspirators were hanged, gifting martyrs to the Nazi cause. The new chancellor was Kurt Schuschnigg, who continued the cause of Austrofascsim amid increased opposition on both sides of the German border.

He managed to retain power for four years, by which time Mussolini had lost interest in his role as guardian of Austrian security. The failure to rein in Nazi expansionism by the Stresa Front, an understanding between Britain, France and Italy, drew Mussolini ever more towards friendship with Hitler and the Nazis in a shared opposition to communism.

With Berlin and Rome seeing eye to eye, the power of the Austrian Nazis grew as Hitler pushed to absorb his homeland into the Third Reich. Paramilitary violence was a fact of life and Schuschnigg was forced into appeasing Berlin, releasing Nazis from prison while attempting to retain the façade of a separate Austrian identity. Without support from Rome, Schuschniggs's hopes of finding protection in the west were dashed when it became clear the British would never intervene to prevent unification with Germany.

A disastrous summit with Hitler took place at Berchtesgaden on 12 February 1938 when Hitler browbeat Schuschnigg into including Austrian Nazis in his government. The Führer handpicked people for key positions and demanded the reinstatement of Nazi supporters sacked from the police and security forces. Hitler accused Schuschnigg of persecuting those who desired unification, assuming the role of saviour of the Austrian people.

A shaken but defiant Schuschnigg opted to hold a plebiscite to resolve the question of Austrian statehood once and for all. But voting restrictions disbarred a large proportion of the pro-Nazi vote. For Hitler it was a provocation too far. He insisted the vote be cancelled and demanded the resignation of a faltering Schuschnigg, who caved in on 11 March 1938. He was to be replaced as chancellor by Arthur Seyss-Inquart, a devout Nazi, but the president of Austria, Wilhelm Miklas, refused to appoint him on the principle that no foreigner should appoint Austrian ministers. It was the signal for German forces to enter the country greeted by jubilant crowds. The passage of Hitler himself to Vienna was met with scenes of wild adulation when he arrived on 15 March. The *Anschluss*, the formal annexation of Austria into the Third Reich, was complete. The SS took rapid action to round up political opponents and the suppression of the Jews was under way. *The Times* of 17 March reported the 'Growing roll of suicides' as harassed Jews and other enemies of the Nazis took their own lives, including Emil Fey, Vice-Chancellor under Dollfuss, who killed his wife, son and dog before shooting himself. Further deaths were reported on 22 March. On 19 July a letter from a group of notable interested parties including Violet Bonham Carter and Victor Cazalet claimed that 7,000 Viennese Jews alone had taken their own lives.

Britain made a forceful protest, but accepted that direct intervention by the United Kingdom was impossible. In a speech to Parliament, Chamberlain alluded to the state of Britain's armed forces. Rearmament had become an urgent priority. There was barely a murmur from the United States or at the League of Nations, where only Mexico lodged a protest. Kurt Schuschnigg, an avowed Austrian patriot, spent time in Dachau and Sachsenhausen. He survived the war and died in 1977. His successor, Arthur Seyss-Inquart, was tried for war crimes at Nuremberg and hanged in 1946.

Hitler was encouraged by the failure of the West to offer tangible opposition to his actions. The British, in particular, were seen as dilettante; an image promoted by the Nazi foreign minister Joachim von Ribbentrop, a friend of the Führer reviled by other leading Nazis for his conceit and incompetence. Hitler had referred to the oppression of millions of Germans living beyond the Reich before the *Anschluss*. Now he looked towards the Sudetenland, the strategic border region of Czechoslovakia, where the largely ethnic German population grew increasingly restive.

The collapse of the Austro-Hungarian Empire led to the creation of Czechoslovakia on 28 October 1918, but by the early 1930s it had become a state with significant minorities led by over three million Germans. Both Hungary and Poland had eyes on reclaiming their own minorities, while the Ruthenes, ethnic Ukrainians, and even the modest number of Romanians harboured ideas of carving out their regions from a country heartily resented by its neighbours. Hitler loathed the Czechs and held a deep desire to wipe their country from the map. He wanted control of the Czech armaments industry, dominated by the Škoda Works, and saw the country as a potential vassal state for the Third Reich.

Successive failures by Britain and France to stand up to his adventures took place as the governments of both countries made plain their anxiousness to avoid another European conflict. They chose to appease Hitler, offering concessions in the belief his supposedly limited ambitions could be met without the recourse to war. Neither party were anything like prepared for such a conflict, but Germany was militarising rapidly with a large proportion of its GDP set aside for the armed forces. The new *Luftwaffe* had more front-line combat aircraft available than Britain and France combined. The German army – the Heer, better known in the west as the *Wehrmacht*, was on a path to reach the capability it would enjoy a year after Munich, while the *Kriegsmarine* was building submarines and heavy cruisers dubbed 'pocket battleships' at an alarming rate.

It is a fact that Sudeten Germans faced discrimination within Czechoslovakia. The more moderate German politicians sought greater equality for their people, but it was Berlin, operating covertly through the auspices of the Sudeten German Party who began demanding full autonomy through the so-called Carlsbad Program. This was quite unacceptable to the Czechs, but they came under pressure from London and Paris to reach an accommodation. The alliances Poland and Czechoslovakia had with France were negated by the Poles decision not to support France or its neighbour in the face of German aggression. Any action against Germany relied heavily on the support of Soviet Russia and the Poles made it crystal clear they would never sanction Soviet forces passing through their territory. Prague was already facing difficulties before the *Anschluss* rendered the Czech system of fortifications facing Germany useless. In acquiring Austria, Hitler had outflanked his irritant neighbour without firing a shot.

The Sudeten Germans played a clever game of cat and mouse with the Czech government. Directed by Berlin, they were able to ratchet up tensions and manufacture provocations with relative ease. Money and weapons flowed in from the Reich. Provocateurs were inserted to make trouble. Clumsy and heavy-handed responses from the Czech authorities were a gift. Neville Chamberlain and most of his Cabinet were sympathetic to Sudeten demands for greater autonomy amid long-standing belief in the iniquity in the Treaties of Versailles and Saint-Germain-en-laye. The Czech president, Edvard Beneš, was bullied by the British into requesting the services of a mediator to resolve the Sudeten question. The man chosen for the job was the veteran Liberal politician Lord Runciman. He arrived in Prague on 2 August, showing evident signs of preference for the Sudeten German position.

Runciman negotiated with the Sudeten German Party leader Konrad Henlein without ever realising he was an agent of the Third Reich. Henlein also managed to convince a number of British politicians, including Winston Churchill, of his sincerity over the permanent place of the Sudetenland within Czechoslovakia. He received positive publicity in the British press while the Czechs received no such warmth. Berlin had Henlein use the traditional Nazi tactic of increasing his demands just as the previous set were about to be met. The Nazis ensured the Runciman Mission was doomed to fail but the peer's efforts dragged on until he left the country on the 16th of September.

Matters took another dramatic turn on 7 September when *The Times* published a leader giving tacit support to the transfer of the Sudetenland to Germany, talking up the advantages of Czechoslovakia becoming a homogenous state 'by the secession of that fringe of alien populations who are contiguous to the nation with which they are united by race.' It was later explained that Geoffrey Dawson had reviewed a draft piece written by Leo Kennedy, the diplomatic correspondent who was sympathetic to the Sudeten position, when he somehow added parts of it to the leader he was editing to appear on the 7th. The fallout was immediate. Both the British government and *The Times* were left to deny claims that the paper represented the Chamberlain government position. Official or not, the leader said what a lot of people within the British establishment were thinking.

The Czechs were quite reasonably exasperated. Having waited a lifetime for independence, they found themselves presented with the proposed dismemberment of their country and refused to budge. While they had no alliance with Britain, their pact with France encouraged the assumption the United Kingdom would support the French if the Germans did anything precipitous. To the utter dismay and incredulity of the Czechs, Paris then signalled it was unable to honour the alliance. Prague was on its own.

Hitler chose the moment to denounce the Czech regime as levels of violence rose in the Sudetenland. He presented himself as champion of an oppressed people and went further by including ethnic Poles, the Ruthenes and the Hungarians in his argument for self-determination. He found an appreciative audience for his denunciation, not just within the countries he mentioned. He sought to drive an even deeper wedge between Czechoslovakia and its faltering protector, France, by painting a false picture of French plans to use the country as a base for attacks on Germany. It was at this point that Neville Chamberlain made his decisive intervention when he offered to fly to Germany for a personal meeting with Adolf Hitler.

Their first meeting took place at the Berghof on 15 September 1938. Hitler demanded that the Sudeten Germans have the right of self-determination and unity with the Reich. He hectored Chamberlain over alleged British aggression when all he wanted was to be friends with England. A frustrated Chamberlain denied any hostility and stood up to Hitler questioning whether the meeting was a waste of time. Hitler agreed they could discuss improving Anglo-German relations if the Sudeten issue could be resolved. Chamberlain returned to London, where he met with the French Prime Minister Édouard Daladier the following day. As a result of their discussions the British and French agreed with Lord Runciman's conclusions when they called for the Czechs to cede areas with more than 50 per cent German populations to the Third Reich. Once this was done, they promised to guarantee the security of the remainder of Czechoslovakia. Anti-appeasers in Britain were appalled and the Czechs refused to even consider the proposals. That same day the Czechs sought the arrest of Konrad Henlein.

Chamberlain and his aides flew back to Germany on the 22nd. He was given a lavish welcome when he arrived at Cologne and made something of a triumphalist journey to Bad Godesberg, where the Nazis pulled out all the stops in flattering to deceive the British party. It was there that Bill Warhurst of *The Times* found himself briefly in the company of the Führer as they awaited Chamberlain at the Hotel Dreesen, where Hitler had plotted the Night of the Long Knives in the summer of 1934. His photograph of the two leaders standing awkwardly in the company of Hitler's interpreter, Paul Schmidt, and the British ambassador, Sir Nevile Henderson, is a priceless moment from an outstanding career.

Chamberlain must have felt he was close to success when he announced his acceptance of the demands Hitler had made at the Berghof, but Hitler stunned him by saying they were now out of date. He demanded the complete dissolution of the Czechoslovakian state. He wanted ethnic areas returned to their neighbouring countries, a stance fully supported by the opportunistic Poles and Hungarians who were ready for a land grab.

The Sudetenland was to be ceded to the Reich and the Czech population was to be removed, leaving everything behind. The evacuation was to start no later than 26 September. It was an impossible set of demands for the Czechs to accept and Hitler knew it, but he left Chamberlain with little room for manoeuvre. The Germans set out to deceive the British by inserting false reports of serious violence against Sudeten Germans, but it was the reverse that was true. Hitler's pent-up rage made an impression on Chamberlain but he did not roll over. He succeeded in gaining a concession, pushing back Hitler's deadline for the evacuation to 1 October; the date Hitler had secretly ordered his generals to launch the invasion of Czechoslovakia.

Hitler issued his Godesberg Memorandum on 24 September, demanding the Czechs cede the Sudetenland by the 28th. He called for plebiscites to be held in areas where ethnic German populations fell below the 50 per cent mark and insisted the territorial demands of Poland and Hungary be satisfied. The consequence for failing to comply would be war. In Prague, the government ordered the Czech army to mobilize, but on the 25th they signalled they were prepared to agree to Hitler's original demands, but his tail was up and he widened the goalposts, drawing in the ethnic Germans living in Poland and Hungary. In doing so, he manufactured an impasse that took brinkmanship to the hilt.

A timely letter from Churchill's ally Leo Amery was published in *The Times* on the 26th asking a searching question:

> The issue has become very simple. Are we to surrender to ruthless brutality a free people whose cause we have espoused but are now to throw to the wolves to save our own skins, or are we still able to stand up to a bully? It is not Czechoslovakia but our own soul that is at stake.

However, it was crystal clear that Hitler's latest demands were unacceptable. Chamberlain dispatched his advisor Sir Horace Wilson to personally relay the fact to Hitler. In addition to this, he also had to warn that France would, after all, stand with the Czechs if they were attacked and if it should happen that conflict broke out between France and Germany, Britain would side with her ally. Wilson spent an uncomfortable hour trapped in a room with a furious Hitler who worked himself into a frenzy over the news from London. The situation had become critical and the clock was running.

Meanwhile, there was deep consternation in London and Paris where war fears gathered. The British fleet was mobilized on the 28th and even the Corps of British Speedway Riders offered its services during the 'national emergency'. Upwards of a million French soldiers had begun to mobilize. In Britain, people were issued with gasmasks and efforts to evacuate children from London and elsewhere were in hand. Barrage balloons and anti-aircraft guns were deployed and trenches dug.

With a resolution before Hitler's deadline looking extremely doubtful, Chamberlain proposed that Italy be brought in to mediate. Mussolini agreed, enjoying the theatrics of asking his friends in Berlin to put back the deadline of the ultimatum for the secession. A four-power meeting was convened in Munich on the 29th where Britain, France, Germany and Italy were set to agree the future of Czechoslovakia. Hearing news of the summit, Franklin D. Roosevelt contacted Chamberlain to express his approval. 'Good man,' he said.

Chamberlain left for Munich taking with him the heartfelt wishes of millions of Britons that he did his utmost to avoid war. With a large section of the press behind him, he was presented as a peacemaker on a solemn mission. Mussolini played his part, proffering the German-prepared agenda as his own. There was no contribution from the Czechs. The four leaders concluded the Munich Agreement during the early hours of 30 September. Hitler had got everything he wanted. But Chamberlain needed something to show for his efforts and had little difficulty persuading Hitler to co-sign the document he famously waved to the waiting press and public when he stepped off his plane at Heston later that day. A tired but jubilant Chamberlain expressed his relief at the resolution to the crisis:

> I have received an immense number of letters during all these anxious times... Letters of support, and approval, and gratitude and I can't tell you what an encouragement that has been to me. I want to thank the British people for what they have done...

> The settlement of the Czechoslovakian problem, which has now been achieved is, in my view, only the prelude to a larger settlement in which all Europe may find peace. This morning I had another talk with the German Chancellor, Herr Hitler, and here is the paper which bears his name upon it as well as mine. Some of you, perhaps, have already heard what it contains but I would just like to read it to you:

> *'We, the German Führer and Chancellor, and the British Prime Minister, have had a further meeting today and are agreed in recognising that the question of Anglo-German relations is of the first importance for the two countries and for Europe. We regard the agreement signed last night and the Anglo-German Naval Agreement as symbolic of the desire of our two peoples never to go to war with one another again.'*

There were cheers as Chamberlain reached this point. But he continued:

> *'We are resolved that the method of consultation shall be the method adopted to deal with any other questions that may concern our two countries and we are determined to continue our efforts to remove possible sources of difference and thus to contribute to assure the peace of Europe.'*

The Prime Minister was whisked back to London through streets lined with cheering crowds for an audience with the king, who invited him to step out on to the balcony of Buckingham Palace to receive the adulation from the masses gathered around the Victoria memorial. Later that evening Chamberlain was encouraged to speak again, this time from an upstairs window at No 10 Downing Street, where he invoked the achievement of Benjamin Disraeli at the Berlin Congress of 1878: 'My good friends, this is the second time in our history that there has come back from Germany to Downing Street peace with honour. I believe it is peace for our time.'

In Prague, Stanley Devon of the *Daily Sketch* met up with Jack Barker of *The Times* as they attempted to record events, but they were met with a wave of anti-British sentiment as the Czechs sense of betrayal set in. Both men were sympathetic. They photographed a number of refugees who Devon assumed were displaced Czechs, but they turned out to be ethnic German opponents of the Nazi regime fleeing the Sudetenland. Devon made a hasty retreat back to London, where he had his first chance to catch up with events in Munich. He was convinced there would be war, telling his boss, Tom Noble, that Chamberlain was 'mad' and 'a fool'.

The threat of war was lifted and Britons released a collective sigh of relief. Military and civil defence preparations were stood down, but long-term improvements to Britain's defences continued. Chamberlain enjoyed the acclaim he received. His image appeared on ceramics and special coins. Streets were named after him in foreign cities. Over 90,000 *Daily Sketch* readers sent in the three pence worth of stamps required to receive an 8 by 10-inch glossy portrait of their hero.

For the Russians the agreement led to a shift in policy towards finding some sort of understanding with Nazi Germany. Excluded from the discussions, Stalin felt his French allies had let him down. The door leading to the German-Soviet non-aggression pact of August 1939 had been opened.

Chamberlain rested before the week-long debate on the agreement took place in both the Lords and the Commons. The noted peace activist Lord Ponsonby of Shulbrede was pleased to cut to the chase when he said, 'Apart from questions of this concession or that, the fact remained that Mr Chamberlain stopped a war.' Amid much laughter in the chamber he went on to assess the loudest voice against Chamberlain's policy, Winston Churchill. Although he much admired his literary and artistic skills, 'He had always felt that in a crisis Mr Churchill was one of the first people who should be interned.'

In parliament on 5 October, the man himself rose to cast a despondent view of events at Munich: 'I will begin by saying what everybody would like to ignore or forget but which must nevertheless be stated, namely, that we have sustained a total and unmitigated defeat.'

Later in the speech Churchill turned to his concerns for the state of Britain's defences:

> It is the most grievous consequence of what we have done and of what we have left undone in the last five years; five

years of futile good intentions, five years of eager search for the line of least resistance, five years of uninterrupted retreat of British power, five years of neglect of our air defences.

He bemoaned British attempts to suck up to the Nazis who had spurned Christian ethics and who followed a course governed by what he termed a 'barbarous paganism'.

Churchill finished in style, confirming the image we retain of a voice in the wilderness. Although he was far from being the only dissenter, his role as successor to Chamberlain has fixed his reputation as a prophet of despair awaiting the opportunity to set things right. His warning to the appeasers had not gone without some interruption but he did not mince his words:

> Do not let them suppose that this was the end. This was only the beginning of the reckoning, only the first sip, the first foretaste of a bitter cup which would be proffered to us year by year unless by a supreme recovery of moral health and martial vigour we arose again and took our stand for freedom as in the olden time.

Labour leader Clement Attlee agreed:

> The events of these last few days constitute one of the greatest diplomatic defeats that this country and France have ever sustained. There can be no doubt that it is a tremendous victory for Herr Hitler. Without firing a shot, by the mere display of military force, he has achieved a dominating position in Europe which Germany failed to win after four years of war. He has overturned the balance of power in Europe. He has destroyed the last fortress of democracy in Eastern Europe which stood in the way of his ambition. He has opened his way to the food, the oil and the resources which he requires in order to consolidate his military power, and he has successfully defeated and reduced to impotence the forces that might have stood against the rule of violence.

German troops consolidated the Sudetenland into the Reich at the beginning of October. The usual pattern of arrests of political undesirables soon followed. The plebiscites in marginal areas never took place and the resultant gain in territory amounted to 11,000 square miles. It was a disaster for Czech infrastructure, let alone Prague's defence strategy. The new German frontier was just 40 miles from the Czech capital.

Nevertheless, Chamberlain's stock was at an all-time high and with it his grip on power was assured. His unshakable belief in the need to secure peace at almost any price had paid off for the time being. Hitler drove triumphantly into the Sudetenland just a few days later. On the surface, his assurance to Chamberlain that he had reached the limit of his territorial ambitions appeared to be true. But plans for the conquest of the rump of Czechoslovakia were well advanced.

Stanley Baldwin had heaped praise on his successor during his maiden speech in the House of Lords on 4 October, asserting that it was Chamberlain's courage in recognising he had to go toe-to-toe with Hitler that had saved Europe from disaster. *The Times* regular leader writer Dermot Morrah used Baldwin's statement as a means of criticising the viewpoint of Labour's Herbert Morrison, who believed more would have been achieved by appealing directly to the hopes for peace of Germany's seventy million people rather than dealing with one man.

The paper continued to report on political reaction in the House of Commons where 'The Women's View' was of some interest. Florence Horsbrugh, the Unionist MP for Dundee, enthused that:

> The women of the whole world were thanking God that the means of averting the disaster was found and that men and women of good will had been given once again the chance of working for peace. British mothers about to send their children away to the uncertainty of evacuation where they might never see them again were also thinking of mothers and children in Germany and Czechoslovakia. They realised that war was not worth the price.

The resolutely anti-fascist Ellen Wilkinson admired Horsbrugh's passion for peace but remained critical of Chamberlain. She objected to the personal policy of the Prime Minister which had 'Landed this country in a position where only some dramatic improvisation in the last five minutes and the throwing away of practically everything the country cared for, could rescue us.' She suspected the motives of people in high places behind the Prime Minister who were 'Playing the game of the Fascist Powers against our national interests.' She was particularly suspicious of the malign influence of a 'prominent American airman', Charles Lindbergh (although she did not name him), who claimed the *Luftwaffe* was stronger than the combined air power of Britain, France and Russia, although 'He could not give facts to back up his opinion, but the mischief was done. It was the organisation of defeatism behind the scenes of which this country should take notice.'

Chamberlain could afford to take all this in his stride, but Adolf Hitler never hid his contempt for the 'silly old man' who had briefly stolen his thunder.

Germany now completely dominated Czech affairs. President Edvard Beneš was forced into exile in October and his successor, Emil Hácha, was beset with constant demands from Berlin. Hitler began to undermine the Czech state even further by encouraging the Slovakian region to demand a split. Hácha was powerless and the Slovakian leader, Father Jozef Tiso, a practicing Roman Catholic priest, played his part to the letter. He declared autonomy on 6 October, leading to the renaming of the country as Czecho-Slovakia, a simple but marked shift in perceptions that was illegal just a few months earlier.

Czech weakness was so pronounced the country ceased to be a haven for those seeking to escape the long arm of Nazi justice. The death of a guard at Buchenwald in May 1938 attracted interest from *The Times* who reported the killing of SS *Rottenführer* Albert Kallweit, who was beaten to death with a shovel by a career thief named Emil Bargetsky and left-wing activist Peter Forster as they made their escape. Bargetsky was caught fairly quickly and hanged in June. Forster fled to Czechoslovakia but had cause to regret his choice of sanctuary when his attempts to achieve political asylum failed the following December. He was extradited back to face a show trial and execution at Buchenwald on the 21st of that month.

But, amid all the drama there was room for a little bit of light to penetrate the all-pervading darkness. 'The Lambeth Walk' had become such a popular song and dance that even the crusty old *Thunderer* felt able to enthuse. Even the Nazis liked it. *The Times* commentary of 18 October 1938 noted that had the international crisis descended into conflict 'It would have been the first war in history in which the armies of both sides would have been dancing to the same tune.'

Meanwhile the Nazi pogrom against German Jews known as the *Kristallnacht* took place over the 9th and 10th of November. The true death toll remains unknown. In October the Reverend R.W. Thompson had used his speech to the Autumnal Assembly of the Congregational Union of England and Wales to warn of a 'tyranny of paganism', although the bestiality of the Nazis had yet to do its worst.

This changed when a Jewish man, Herschel Grynszpan, murdered Ernst vom Rath, the Third Secretary, at the German Embassy in Paris over what may have been a lovers' quarrel. It gave the Nazis the opportunity they were looking for to unleash the *Sturmabteilung* (SA) on Jewish businesses, private citizens and the synagogues. That the death of the diplomat was a crime of passion between homosexuals was an inconvenient truth the Nazis would avoid. They connected the murderer with Germany's public enemy, Winston Churchill; the *Angriff* newspaper claiming 'The murder weapon spat in the hands of a Jewish lout and destroyed the last measurable remnants of credibility in the assertion that agitation for war and murder against the Third Reich had never been carried on or contemplated.'

The assault on German Jewry would include a fine of a billion marks levied on the community at large. Thousands of people were rounded up and sent to concentration camps.

The Times gave some prominence to reporting the reaction of British religious leaders. Rabbi Maurice Perlzweig of the World Jewish Congress gave Adolf Hitler and his adherents short shrift on 12 November when he spoke at the North Western (Reform) Synagogue in Golders Green. 'Schooled in adversity, the Jews knew that they would outlive the Nazi tyranny, which was destined to break under the weight of its own follies and iniquities.' True enough, but he went on to ask a serious question:

The problem of the Jew in Germany was a Christian one. What had Christendom to say to an international system which placed those gangsters among the powers and principalities of the earth? The Christian world was

beginning to apprehend the challenge of this system to its own soul.

Perhaps Rabbi Perlzweig noted concerns over Nazi hostility towards Christianity reported in the same edition of *The Times*. Coverage of the Durham Diocesan Conference appeared under the headline 'Brutal repression of Jews' where recent outrages in Germany received the strongest condemnation from Dr Herbert Hensley Henson, the Bishop of Durham. He reminded Adolf Hitler 'The most formidable hindrance to his wish for better relations with Britain arose from the feeling of moral repugnance his racial and religious policy created in British minds.' Dr Henson was equally concerned about the German state's attacks on his own faith, citing a speech made by Alfred Rosenberg on 5 November 1938 when the Nazi ideologue crowed at progress made towards the eradication of Christianity under the Third Reich. 'The curriculum of all categories in our schools has already been so far reformed in an anti-Christian and anti-Jewish spirit that the generation which is growing up will be protected from the black swindle.'

The Bishop of Chichester, Dr George Bell, claimed the pace of the attack on Christianity in Germany was 'Increasing and becoming more terrifying.' The Church was in danger of falling under total state control where 'prayers were censored' and where the Church would find itself 'in a corner, or a ghetto with a subway', or facing 'ruthless destruction.'

Perhaps these grim predictions did little to bolster the strength of purpose of a man like Maurice Perlzweig, but it is possible he drew a little comfort from the Diocesan Conference's unanimous adoption of a resolution expressing horror at the anti-Semitic outrages in Germany, assuring the Jewish community of their deepest sympathy in their terrible trials.

A Christmas filled with uncertainty beckoned. Fine words and good intentions counted for nothing. Britain and France had shown themselves impotent in the face of Nazi aggression. Hitler held the initiative as Europe limped into 1939.

The growing menace of Japan made occasional photo opportunities for our group of photographers. The Japanese claimed the power of the British and American navies was a threat. They would no longer accept the status quo whereby Japan was prohibited from achieving anything like parity with the British and Americans. Rear Admiral Isoroku Yamamoto came to London in October 1934 to explain the Japanese position almost a full year before the London Naval Conference of 1935 began.
He would go on to lead naval strategy for war against the European colonial powers and the United States, exemplified by his direction of the stunning attack on Pearl Harbor. He is pictured (left) at 10 Downing Street with Japanese ambassador Tsuneo Matsudaira.
Bill Warhurst [TT]

Above and below: Cordial relations between the Royal Navy and the *Kriegsmarine* in 1934 were evident. These images of German cruisers paying a goodwill visit to Portsmouth will have disappointed the French, but there was a further nasty surprise to come for Britain's ally. *Leipzig* (shown above) and the warm welcome for the crew of *Konigsberg* made for a fine photo opportunity. *Herbert Muggeridge [KN]*

Britain's hope of limiting the threat of German sea power dovetailed with Hitler's long-standing dream of an alliance with the United Kingdom. The two sides came together in March 1935 to discuss a bilateral naval agreement that sent alarm bells ringing in Paris and served to create a dangerous misconception in Germany that the agreement was, indeed, a precursor to an alliance. For the British, the agreement was seen as an opportunity to guarantee the primacy of the Royal Navy over the *Kreigsmarine*. Hitler's dream appeared to be coming closer to reality and he described the day the agreement was signed on 18 June 1935 as 'the happiest day of his life'. For France it was nothing short of treachery, with Britain implicitly supporting German contravention of the Treaty of Versailles by building capital ships and submarines. The French had a fair point, but whether the British were appeasing Hitler, as Paris believed, or just being realistic was a matter of opinion. *The Times* photographers missed the meeting Sir John Simon and Anthony Eden held with Hitler that kick-started the talks but Stanley Kessell managed to snatch this shot of Joachim von Ribbentrop leaving the Foreign Office on 4 June after events had moved on to London. *Stanley Kessell [TT]*

King George V celebrated his Silver Jubilee in 1935. Special events included the fleet review held at Spithead, where the might of Britain's mercantile and naval sea power was there for all to see. William Horton's spectacular photograph of a searchlight display on HMS *Hood* is the standout image of event coverage the author had to choose from. *William Horton [TT]*

We last saw the fleet moored in the River Thames for peace celebrations in 1919. The Silver Jubilee offered a similar photo opportunity as some of the best-known ships in the Royal Navy dropped anchor off Southend. Passengers on the paddle steamer *Royal Eagle* get up close to admire HMS *Furious*. *Jack Kirby [KN]*

The other fighting services were doing their bit for the Silver Jubilee. Press photographers were invited to record rehearsals for the air pageant that would show off the might of the RAF. Eddie Taylor took this gem when he went aloft with aircrew of No 15 Squadron to film them practicing formation flying with their Hawker Hart bombers at Upper Heyford in June 1935. *Edward Taylor [KN]*

But there was a blot on the horizon. Recent developments in aircraft design showed that the RAF was falling alarmingly behind as it continued with a succession of biplanes quite inadequate for the modern warfare around the corner. Similar issues faced civil aviation so Lord Rothermere challenged the industry to build a modern passenger aeroplane to prove the British could construct up-to-date aircraft. The resulting Bristol 142, seen here in November 1935, was a revelation. It was given the name *Britain First* after flight tests had shown it was faster than the RAF's in-service fighters. Something would have to change very quickly. Rothermere gifted his aircraft to the nation and the Air Ministry wasted little time in adapting the 142 into the light bomber that would become the Bristol Blenheim. *Cathal O'Gorman [TT]*

The RAF had been alive to the challenge of finding new aircraft for some time and 1935 would see the first flight of the Hawker Hurricane. The big problem remained the lack of money and the inertia encouraged by Churchill's Ten Year Rule. The Air Ministry looked at a wide range of designs, some of them clearly unsuitable, and the process inevitably smacks of desperation. A display of new types was shown to the press at Martlesham Heath in the summer of 1934 just as Lord Rothermere was making his historic intervention. The Aeroplane & Armament Experimental Establishment eventually rejected this Northrop Gamma 2E light bomber given the RAF serial number K5053. It is included here because the next number in the sequence was given to a much more promising prototype – the Supermarine Spitfire. *Cathal O'Gorman [TT]*

The army was just as busy struggling with modernisation. These Vickers light tanks have come to an embarrassing halt during manoeuvres in the Avon valley in September 1935. *Stanley Kessell [TT]*

It would be interesting to know what one of the Second World War's leading panzer generals made of all this. Leo Geyr von Schweppenburg would probably put it down to experience. He led panzer forces against Poland, France and the Soviet Union and commanded *Panzergruppe West* when the Allies landed in Normandy in 1944. He is seen observing events at Stockbridge in Hampshire. *William Horton [TT]*

Whether it was the similar sounding but quite different motorisation or mechanisation, the army was modernising. There was still time to experience the idyll of soldiering on horseback for these men of the Inns of Court Regiment enjoying a pint at the Stag Inn at Balls Cross in Sussex. *William Horton [TT]*

But carefully guarded traditions continued. Guardsmen and their families enjoy 'At Home Day' on a fine afternoon at Caterham in August 1935. *Herbert Muggeridge [KN]*

Britain's unpreparedness for war was about to be further exposed by Hitler who had been planning to remilitarise the Rhineland in yet another contravention of the Treaty of Versailles and the spirit of Locarno, although the Germans would argue forcefully that the latter had already been broken by the French entering into a pact with the Soviet Union in May 1935. Britain and France were divided over Abyssinia with the French premier Pierre Laval baffled that London could take a stand against Italy while the real threat to peace was just over the Rhine. Britain's stance had enraged Mussolini, propelling him towards greater understanding with Hitler. The man himself advanced his plans by as much as a year and although rumours of his intentions were rife, the arrival of German troops in Dusseldorf sent shock waves around the world. Stanley Devon had only recently joined the *Daily Sketch* from the Associated Press and was there to film German forces entering the city. His photo of women offering flowers to mounted troops taken on 7 March 1936 became a defining image of the times. *Stanley Devon [KN]*

Right: This lesser known image from the same location has similar elements but has received much less recognition. *Stanley Devon [KN]*

Below: The Luftwaffe played its part. Airmen sing a marching song as they progress along a street lined with people. *Stanley Devon [KN]*

The army were not to be outdone. A mounted kettle drummer is pictured in full flow. *Stanley Devon [KN]*

With an admittedly modest number of troops on the march creating an appearance exaggerating the true state of German military power, Hitler chose the moment to announce his decision to ignore Versailles and rearm. Conscription would be introduced. He took the opportunity to repudiate the Locarno treaties, ending the collective security cherished in London, Paris and beyond. The *Daily Sketch* created a novel way of illustrating how Locarno had been 'torn up' by Hitler. *Jack Kirby [KN]*

The world held its breath waiting for a military response from Paris but the failure of France to act is seen as a lost opportunity to snuff out Hitler while he remained weak militarily. French soldiers moving into positions close to the Rhine buy newspapers to keep up with events. *Jack Barker [TT]*

Stanley Devon stayed on in Germany to record the appearance of Herman Goering sweeping into Cologne, where he was met by a huge number of people delighted with the recent turn of events. Devon's vantage point doesn't give us a close up of the Luftwaffe supremo and founder of the Gestapo but the image goes some way to convey the magnetism of leading Nazis in a reinvigorated Germany. This image is the sole survivor from the set, the rest having fallen victim to the men Goering sent to bomb London four years after this photograph was taken. *Stanley Devon [KN]*

It seems fitting that the workings of the League of Nations should seem somewhat anonymous in this narrative, but this is largely governed by a lack of photo coverage of the organisation in action by the sources for this book. The remilitarisation of the Rhineland provides a glimpse of the League Council at work during a meeting in London on 19 March 1936 where the Germans sought to justify their position by claiming the Franco-Soviet pact of 1935 had given them little option but to act in self-defence. An interpreter reads while von Ribbentrop listens. To his right is Hans-Heinrich Dieckhoff, set to enjoy a brief spell as German ambassador in Washington DC.
William Horton [TT]

The climax of the London Naval Conference was set against the backdrop of events in the Rhineland but despite this, a treaty was signed on 25 March 1936. By this point both Japan and Italy had walked away, but while their absence was a detriment to the end result, the fact is the treaty created yet more hurdles for the Royal Navy, setting further limitations on types, armaments and gross tonnages. Decisions made in London did little or nothing to halt German ambitions and the Japanese withdrawal was a steppingstone to the Pacific War in 1941. *JW Eggitt [KN]*

New vessels were coming to the Royal Navy. Cammell Laird shipyard workers watch as the S-class submarine HMS *Spearfish* is launched at Birkenhead on 21 April 1936. The highlight of her sadly brief war service came when she wrecked the stern of the German heavy cruiser *Lützow* on 11 April 1940. The ship we saw earlier as the *Deutschland* was supposedly renamed on the order of Adolf Hitler, who feared adverse imagery of a ship named for his country being sunk. However, the Germans had sold a new Lützow, then under construction, to the Soviet Union and needed to cover their tracks. *Spearfish* was lost on 1 August 1940. *[KN]*

A stunning montage showing Bristol Bulldogs of No 54 Squadron getting airborne from RAF Hornchurch made in February 1936. Time was being called on the era of the biplane fighter but No 54 would be equipped with Gloster Gauntlets and Gladiators before the arrival into service of the Sptifire, still some way off. *Edward Taylor [KN]*

But the British were keeping pace with developments elsewhere. The new Fairey Battle light bomber was unveiled in March 1936. It had a retractable undercarriage and was powered by a Rolls-Royce Merlin engine and impressed the *Daily Sketch* a great deal: 'It could leave the Fairey aerodrome at Hayes, Middlesex and be over the South Coast in just over 10 minutes.' This image is scanned from an annotated print that has lost most of its caption labels eighty years later. The Battle would have a torrid time over France and Belgium in 1940. *Edward Taylor [KN]*

NIGHT LANDING LIGHT

The Times were just as interested in the performance of the Battle but noted its top speed had not been revealed. *Stanley Kessell [TT]*

The prototype Handley Page HP.52 bomber gets airborne at Radlett in Hertfordshire on 21 June 1936 with Chief Test Pilot Major James Cordes at the controls. The aircraft would go through some revisions before it entered service and we shall see it again later. *Bill Warhurst [TT]*

The prototype Vickers Type 271 *K4049* was flown for the first time by 'Mutt' Summers at Brooklands on 15 June 1936 and is seen being shown to the press a fortnight later. Although this particular aircraft was lost within a year, the development programme of the type progressed at pace and it morphed into one of the best-known and most successful aircraft of the Second World War. But a name had to be agreed upon first and the initial choice of Crecy was soon passed over in favour of Wellington. *Cathal O'Gorman [TT]*

Another aircraft shown at the same time was a million miles away from the Bristol Bulldogs we saw earlier. R.J. Mitchell's prototype Supermarine Spitfire K5054 first flew on 5 March 1936 with 'Mutt' Summers doing the honours. He is reputed to have said 'Don't touch anything' after landing, he was so impressed. Sadly, the sole surviving print of Cathal O'Gorman's pictures of the aircraft from the day does not do it much justice. *Cathal O'Gorman [TT]*

There were some silver linings despite the dense clouds caused by German rearmament. Building the new Luftwaffe was a massive task hindered by having a man like Erhard Milch making many of the important decisions. He carried out a vendetta against key aircraft manufacturers, not least Hugo Junkers and Willy Messerschmitt. In fact, Milch was so bitter towards Messerschmitt he barred him from entering a design for a new fighter plane, but the Bf 109 would prove too good to ignore. Milch's behaviour was not untypical and this nonsense between senior figures in the German aviation hierarchy would have a significant impact on the future of the Luftwaffe. Major-General Karl Bodenschatz and General Ralph Wenninger flank Milch in this image taken during an exhibition of new aircraft at Hatfield in June 1936. Karl Bodenschatz was seriously injured when the bomb placed by Claus von Stauffenberg nearly killed Adolf Hitler on 20 July 1944. Erhard Milch was tried for war crimes in 1947 and although sentenced to life imprisonment he was released in 1954. *William Horton [TT]*

Another year on for the British Army and the sturdy but dated Vickers Medium tank was still leading the line. This image was taken during an exercise at Lulworth in May 1936. *William Horton [TT]*

The time seems to have stood still since 1914 in this view of men of the Wiltshire Regiment on exercise at Corfe Castle the following August. *Cathal O'Gorman [TT]*

The travails of imperial policing were the army's lot in the years before the Second World War, like this scene in Palestine where Arab disaffection had boiled over into violence. J.W. Eggitt was sent out by the *Daily Sketch* to record events using a mixture of nitrate and 35mm films. This frame shows men of the Royal Scots Fusiliers taking over the security of a convoy from the Cameron Highlanders on a road near Nablus in June 1936. *J.W. Eggitt [KN]*

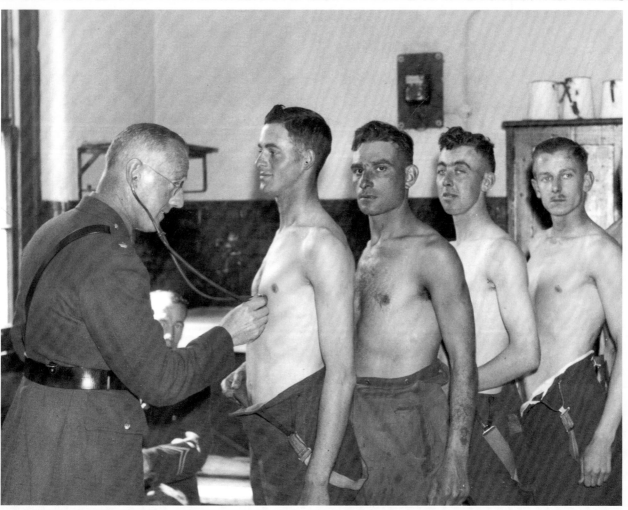

These guardsmen are having check-ups at Aldershot before deployment to Palestine in September 1936. *Robert Chandler [KN]*

A trumpeter of the Life Guards helps his mate affix the royal cypher of King Edward VIII to his dress uniform in November 1936. They would need to make a further change by Christmas. *Edward Taylor [KN]*

While photographs of battleships sailing line astern have come to be synonymous with our image of British sea power, we do well to remember that the reality of this strength came in all shapes and sizes. Bill Warhurst's dramatic view of a naval exercise in the Atlantic in March 1937 shows ships of the 2nd Destroyer Flotilla shepherding HMS *Queen Elizabeth* in robust weather. HMS *Hyperion* is nearest the camera. Completed in 1936, she had a typically busy service life that came to a sad end when she struck a mine in December 1940. *Bill Warhurst [TT]*

The aircraft carrier HMS *Ark Royal* was launched on 13 April 1937. The London Naval Treaty came too late to hinder her construction at Cammell Laird on the River Mersey. She was laid down in September 1935 and completed at a cost of £3 million (by contrast the aircraft carrier HMS *Queen Elizabeth* has cost £3 billion). In the event *Ark Royal* weighed in with a displacement of 22,000 tons, the precise limit for aircraft carriers set by the treaty. She took part in many major engagements during the early years of the war, including the sinking of the *Bismarck* in 1941 before she was, herself, lost in the November of that year. *[KN]*

The Coronation Naval Review at Spithead in May 1937 was another huge occasion. A number of warships were sent to represent foreign powers and one to cause a stir was the German heavy cruiser *Admiral Graf Spee*, which the British dubbed a 'pocket battleship'. The *Daily Sketch* printed a guide to the ships taking part and some of the prints used for it retain the caption numbers stuck on by the art desk. The visit of *Graf Spee* gave the British the chance to get a proper look at a ship they would have to take on in the year war was declared. She was scuttled famously at the mouth of the River Plate following her battle with a number of British cruisers in December 1939. *Stanley Devon [KN]*

The First Sea Lord, Admiral Ernle Chatfield, recognised the deficiencies caused by years of low investment in new ships and called for more cruisers to bolster the ranks of the fleet. The new Town class was intended to fill that gap. Ten would eventually be built and of them four would be lost during the war. HMS *Southampton* was built by John Brown on the Clyde and launched in March 1936. She was commissioned just two months before the Coronation Review and looks brand new in this image. *Southampton* was lost in 1941. There is one survivor of the Town class afloat today in the shape of HMS *Belfast*, nowadays a popular attraction in London. *Stanley Devon [KN]*

'The fleet's lit up!' Apologies to the BBC's Thomas Woodrooffe for recalling his oft-repeated broadcast from Spithead, but to be fair, it most definitely is! This superb image is a 'join-up' made from two negatives for use across the full width of a page. *William Horton [TT]*

Left: 28 May 1937: The Abdication Crisis had taken its toll on Stanley Baldwin and he declared his intention to step down after the coronation of King George VI. His successor was Neville Chamberlain, seen smiling for the cameras on that historic Friday when he assumed the roles of Prime Minister and First Lord of the Treasury. *Stanley Kessell [TT]*

Above: He was immediately compelled to make serious decisions on rearmament as the threat of German military expansion loomed. Chamberlain's predecessor had said 'The bomber will always get through' but men like these from 16 (Bhurtpore) Anti-Aircraft Battery Royal Artillery were expected to try and stop them in the summer of 1937. *Edward Taylor [KN]*

Handley-Page Heyford bombers provide targets during an air-raid defence exercise. This remarkable image is the only survivor from this set. No details of how it came to be taken are known. *[KN]*

Preparing the general public for war would take considerable care and energy and would cost yet more money. Gas masks were set to be at the centre of imagery of the late 1930s as fears of the use of chemical warfare against cities rose. *Edward Taylor [KN]*

These officer cadets passing through the RAF College at Cranwell in Lincolnshire would bear the brunt of the war to come. *Geoffrey Keating [KN]*

But anti-war sentiments remained strong across the spectrum of British society, offering some comfort to Neville Chamberlain, who was about to face a series of crises threatening peace in Europe. The Co-Operative Women's Guild had their say on 20 September 1937. *Herbert Muggeridge [KN]*

The bulwark that was the French army continued to offer reassurance. A march-past follows the conclusion of exercises at Alençon. *Jack Barker [TT]*

France had not escaped the tankette fad but saw the type to have more potential as a light armoured transport system with a special trailer rather than as a fighting vehicle. Interest in Carden Loyd's machines was strong but Renault, who won the competition to build the *Chenillette*, opted to make something very similar rather than agree a licencing arrangement with Vickers. Five thousand of the resultant UE and follow-up designs were built in France and under licence in Romania. *Jack Barker [TT]*

The French had taken note of developments in the Soviet Union and began to create airborne forces in 1937. These men parading through Paris on Bastille Day are true pioneers serving with Groupe de l'infanterie de l'air 601 based at Reims. Unfortunately, the performance of the unit on exercise failed to inspire the high command, but German observers were quietly impressed and took careful note of what they were witnessing. *Jack Barker [TT]*

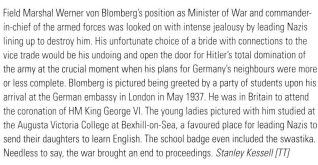

Field Marshal Werner von Blomberg's position as Minister of War and commander-in-chief of the armed forces was looked on with intense jealousy by leading Nazis lining up to destroy him. His unfortunate choice of a bride with connections to the vice trade would be his undoing and open the door for Hitler's total domination of the army at the crucial moment when his plans for Germany's neighbours were more or less complete. Blomberg is pictured being greeted by a party of students upon his arrival at the German embassy in London in May 1937. He was in Britain to attend the coronation of HM King George VI. The young ladies pictured with him studied at the Augusta Victoria College at Bexhill-on-Sea, a favoured place for leading Nazis to send their daughters to learn English. The school badge even included the swastika. Needless to say, the war brought an end to proceedings. *Stanley Kessell [TT]*

Political dramas were set to consume a great deal of public and media attention in Britain. The first of them was the resignation of Foreign Secretary Anthony Eden, who strongly disagreed with Neville Chamberlain over making overtures towards Italy. Although both men were in agreement over the appeasement of Hitler, Eden knew for certain that Mussolini was increasingly hostile towards Britain. But the Prime Minister's quest for improved relations with Italy to act as a counter to the growing understanding between Rome and Berlin led him to undermine Eden by carrying out his own dealings with Mussolini. There could only be one winner in a Chamberlain cabinet. Eden resigned on 20 February 1938, just as Adolf Hitler began putting his plans for his neighbours into effect with the tacit support of fascist Italy. *Alfred Harris [KN]*

Hitler's first target was his homeland Austria, where divisions over unification with Germany had seen a mercifully brief civil war take place in 1934. The diminutive figure of Chancellor Engelbert Dollfuss makes for an unlikely dictator, but his determination to maintain Austrian independence led him to take an increasingly authoritarian stance against both the Nazis and democratic parties. He could rely on support from Italy while Mussolini kept a wary eye on the activities of Adolf Hitler, but this did not stop Austrian Nazis from attempting to force their will on their country as they sought unification with Germany. Dollfuss died after being shot during a failed coup on 25 July 1934 and it was his successor, Kurt Schuschnigg, who would hold on to the reins as Hitler increased the tempo of his demands for unification. Dollfuss is pictured at Croydon Airport in 1933 accompanied by the imposing figure of Georg Freiherr von und zu Franckenstein, the Austrian ambassador to the Court of St James, a leading anti-Nazi who opted to take British citizenship to continue his opposition to Hitler after the Anschluss. *Frederick Ashby [KN]*

Kurt Schuschnigg's visit to London in 1935 gives us the only surviving image of him (centre) in the News UK Archive. He is pictured at Victoria station being met by Sir John Simon and Baron Franckenstein. Second left is Baron Egon Berger-Waldenegg, the Austrian ambassador to Rome. Schuschnigg's attempt to foil Hitler ended in disaster when his call for a plebiscite over unification enraged Nazis on both sides of the border. He capitulated under intense pressure from Hitler and was replaced by the ardent Austrian Nazi Arthur Seyss-Inquart, who promptly invited German forces to enter the country in the interests of 'security' at the behest of his master in Berlin.
Alfred Harris [KN]

The Nazis held a plebiscite to secure approval from the people of Germany and Austria for the union of the two countries. The result was a foregone conclusion because the vast majority were genuinely enthusiastic for the merger. Citizens living abroad were included leading to a marvellous photo opportunity when the brand-new liner MV *Wilhelm Gustloff* sailed up the Thames to Tilbury Docks to embark passengers eager to have their say. The ship sailed out into international waters for the vote to take place on 10 April 1938 before returning to Tilbury. Voters heading for the ship are pictured aboard a special train about to leave St Pancras.
Robert Chandler [KN]

A postcard from Vienna. Accounts of the Anschluss tell of a strong degree of organised chaos as the much-vaunted German war machine lumbered along riding a mixture of requisitioned vehicles and military motors. But once in place the Nazis wasted no time in seeking out undesirables from an extensive list. The imagery here suggests Austria was now secure in the warm glow of unity with its neighbour. It is a fact that a good many Austrians were delighted at the incorporation of their country into the Third Reich, but by then national identity was lost when Austria was renamed the province of Ostmark. *[KN]*

As coverage of the Anschluss had been limited to agency pictures, the Kemsley papers were keen to make the most of the occasion and sent a team of photographers to record events. It was seen as a golden opportunity to do a little sales promotion for the *Sunday Graphic*.
Charles Maxwell [KN]

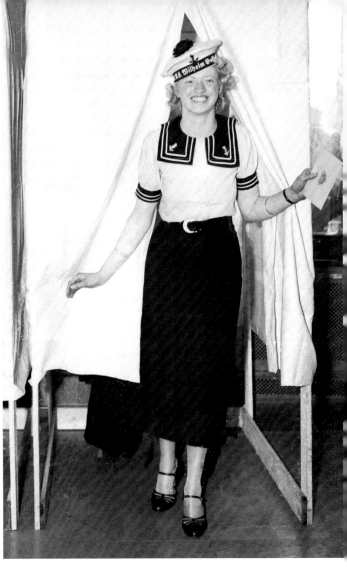

There were dissenting voices. These men are encouraging a 'no' vote in support of freedom, homeland and prosperity. *Robert Chandler [KN]*

The Germans were keen for the electoral process to be fully recorded and some voters happily entered into the mood. *Stanley Devon [KN]*

The ship's band strikes up the German national anthem. *Stanley Devon [KN]*

The *Wilhelm Gustloff* was the pride of the Kraft durch Freude (Strength through Joy) organisation but her time working as a cruise liner for deserving German workers was brief. She performed a number of roles after being requisitioned by the *Kriegsmarine* in September 1939 and is best remembered for the manner of her loss on 30 January 1945 when she was torpedoed by a Soviet submarine. Over 9,000 people died in the incident, the greatest single loss of life in maritime history. *Stanley Devon [KN]*

The Anschluss had ramifications for the neighbours of the much-expanded Third Reich. The *Daily Sketch* dispatched Geoffrey Keating to Budapest to record reactions in Hungary, where interested citizens are seen perusing a map reflecting territorial changes. *Geoffrey Keating [KN]*

Defeat for Hungary in 1918 had seen the humiliating loss of territory to the republics that sprung up in the wake of the Austro-Hungarian Empire. Admiral Miklós Horthy, Regent in the absence of King Charles IV who remained banned from entering the country under terms of the Treaty of Trianon, would soon take the opportunity to recoup some of it. A vehement anti-communist, Horthy saw Nazi Germany as the lesser of two evils and was drawn into doing business with Hitler because he was anxious to redress territorial losses arising from Trianon. But these would prove to be short-term gains.
Geoffrey Keating [KN]

Fascism was on the rise in the country. The *Turul* were named after the mythological bird of prey that remains a national symbol of modern Hungary. Uniformed members took part in demonstrations calling for revisions to Trianon that became ever louder as the events of 1938 unfolded.
Geoffrey Keating [KN]

Geoffrey Keating's picture of troops parading in Budapest offers a hint of the injured pride about to be redressed as a consequence of Adolf Hitler's next move.
Geoffrey Keating [KN]

British military reaction to recent events was muted but messages could be sent through the power of news photography. There are many famous propaganda images from the period that owe their look to careful modification in the darkroom. In this instance the use of a montage helps create a strong impression of naval power. The views of the battleships and the flight of Avro Anson aircraft from No 217 Squadron RAF are separate images filmed on a combined forces exercise. *Stanley Devon [KN]*

But the shock of the Anschluss was felt strongest in Czechoslovakia. The young republic had toiled to defend its existence but soon found that the best of its western defences had been outflanked in one fell swoop as German troops moved up to what had been the Austrian frontier. It was nothing short of a strategic disaster. Hitler's antipathy towards the Czechs was no secret and fears over German invasion were realistic. Geoffrey Keating moved on to Prague and recorded the Czech armed forces preparing for things to come. Czech gunners endure an anti-gas drill during a snowstorm. *Geoffrey Keating [KN]*

The Nazis coveted the Czech armaments industry and much of what it produced was set to be absorbed into the German war machine. Armoured cars such as this Tatra OA vz.30 would find use with police units and several powers allied to Berlin after 1939. *Geoffrey Keating [KN]*

The country's frontline fighter aircraft was the Avia B-534, seen here being prepared by ground staff. The fact the Czechs had not, as yet, introduced a monoplane fighter to match developments elsewhere was academic. The type and its Bk-534 variant equipped twenty-one Czech squadrons but they would not be used in 1938. A good number would see service with Slovak units in 1939 but the type would prove inferior to the majority of its opponents. *Geoffrey Keating [KN]*

Czech pilots parade for the camera. It is interesting to speculate how many of these men would see service with the British and French from 1940 onwards. *Geoffrey Keating [KN]*

Keating spent time photographing some of the leading actors in the drama to come. At the centre of Nazi machinations against the Czechs was Konrad Henlein, a Great War veteran and strong advocate of German nationalism who, like many of his peers, bridled at the fall from grace they had suffered upon the creation of Czechoslovakia where the influence of ethnic Germans had plummeted in the young republic. He had embraced the völkisch cause and was increasingly in favour of Sudeten German autonomy. Henlein maintained the façade of respectability in his political dealings despite accurate suspicions of members of the Czech government that he was in league with Berlin. As leader of the Sudeten German Party he took direct orders from the Nazis, in addition to receiving funding and practical support for his campaign for greater autonomy that quickly became one of incorporation of the Sudetenland into the German Reich. *Geoffrey Keating [KN]*

Opposite him was the dignified presence of Czech president Edvard Beneš, a career politician, leading Czech nationalist, and a man possessed of considerable diplomatic skill and who had many admirers. Beneš was a statesman in every sense of the word and his powers of diplomacy were to be put to the test by the storm about to break over his beloved country. *Geoffrey Keating [KN]*

Below: Jan Masaryk, the Czech ambassador to London, was a popular figure whose father Tomáš had been the first president of an independent Czechoslovakia. The caricature by Eric Gibbs for the *Daily Sketch* is a rare survivor in the News UK collection and is a fare interpretation of the man himself. Masaryk stayed on in London to become foreign minister of the exiled Czech government after the German occupation began in March 1939. He continued in the role after the war when communists were beginning to take control of the country. He died in suspicious circumstances in 1948, having jumped or been thrown from a window that conveniently shut itself afterwards. *Eric Gibbs/William Field [KN]*

Above: The Sudeten question was a springboard on Hitler's mission to snuff out Czechoslovakia. He had ordered Konrad Henlein to call for autonomy, well aware it was unacceptable to Prague. Henlein duly delivered the Carlsbad program on 24 April, demanding equality for ethnic Germans within the Czech state, self-government for German areas, and reparations for financial hardships arising from the punitive Treaty of Saint-Germain-en-Laye in 1919. Henlein stopped off in Berlin to firm up his orders before his key visit to London on 12 May for what we might call a charm offensive, where he sought to assure leading opponents of appeasement that he was sincere in his wish for Sudeten autonomy within the Czechoslovak state and nothing more. That he succeeded to impress this blatant lie on Churchill and others seems remarkable. He is pictured leaving Churchill's London flat. *Alfred Harris [KN]*

Britain's ambassador to Germany would be a key figure in events to come. Sir Nevile Henderson was a career diplomat brought back from Buenos Aires to replace Sir Eric Phipps, who was seen as obstructive to Chamberlain's appeasement policy. Henderson's memoir *A Mission Failed* is typically diplomatic in the way it skirts around the nitty-gritty of Munich and is seen as self-serving. Henderson is pictured enjoying the trappings of his position on an earlier posting to Belgrade in 1933, where he was Envoy Extraordinary and Minister Plenipotentiary to the Kingdom of Yugoslavia. *Patrick Brown [KN]*

Hitler had ordered maximum effort to destabilise the Sudetenland. Numerous agents-provocateurs slipped into the country to make trouble and Berlin began to circulate stories of atrocities by the Czech police and military. This combined with fears in Prague that the German army was about to invade. Having been given false assurances during the Anschluss, Mason-MacFarlane had to go out and see for himself, causing ruffled feathers in Ribbentrop's ministry. He now had to repeat the exercise but was unable to find any significant movement of German forces along the Czech border. Nevertheless, the Czechs mobilised and prepared for war. This image shows a pair of Škoda PA-II Želva armoured cars on the move. *[KN]*

A Czech anti-aircraft battery prepares for the worst. *[KN]*

Right: In Britain, opposition to the Third Reich continued to take varied forms while the Sudeten crisis percolated. An exhibition of modern German art labelled as degenerate by the Nazis was put on at the New Burlington Galleries in July 1938 and opened by Augustus John, seen here chatting with H.G. Wells at the launch. The chairman of the organising committee, Herbert Read, told *The Times* that the exhibition was a response to the Nazi clampdown on the arts they deemed degenerate. The organisers felt that a response 'Was not a question of politics, but simply of justice.' Any profits from the exhibition would go to a fund for distressed exiled artists. *Robert Chandler [KN]*

Below: Nazi pressure on Czechoslovakia intensified. After much handwringing, Georges Bonnet, the French Foreign Minister, delivered a nasty surprise to Prague on 10 July. While they would continue to express public support for the Czechs, the French would not honour their long-standing undertaking to take up arms if Germany were to attack. The very basis of Czech strategy was built on military support from France, and by extension, Britain. Although the British had no agreement with Prague, there was an assumption that Britain would go to war in support of her closest ally, France. The Czechs were on their own, but for France the threat of war could not be ignored and annual army exercises continued throughout August and September, giving an indication of how prepared France actually was. *Jack Barker [TT]*

The French public could take comfort in the might of their army. Hotchkiss H35 light tanks fill the Champs-Élysées on Bastille Day. *Jack Barker [TT]*

Men of the 21st Infantry Regiment prepare to let slip the dogs of war during an exercise at Camp du Valdahon. *Jack Barker [TT]*

The British insisted that the Czechs appoint a mediator to address the crisis, putting Edvard Beneš in the awkward position of having to accept so as not to damage ties with Britain and France. The man nominated for the job was Lord Runciman, a Liberal peer with a long career in politics, who set out on 2 August 1938. There seems little argument that he headed off to Prague already in favour of the Sudeten German position and he never took to the Czechs. To be fair to Runciman it was recognised that the Czechs did not treat their ethnic German minority particularly fairly and that many of the injustices claimed by Konrad Henlein and his followers were genuine. Unfortunately for Runciman, Henlein followed Hitler's orders to string him along and never reach agreement on anything. The Runciman Mission was doomed in every sense of the word but he would stay on for over a month in the vain hope of achieving something meaningful. *Alfred Harris [KN]*

Our image of opposition to appeasement tends to fix on Winston Churchill. He wrote to David Lloyd George on 13 August: 'I think we shall have to choose in the next few weeks between war and shame, and I have very little doubt what the decision will be.' *[KN]*

Someone with Churchill's reputation could choose to ignore the strictures of party machinery but lesser lights at Westminster needed to take care not to incur the wrath of the Tory Chief Whip, Captain David Margesson. Best described as uncompromising in his maintenance of parliamentary discipline, Margesson ran a tight ship and was quite content to humiliate MPs deemed disloyal. It might seem remarkable that, despite their differences of opinion, Churchill and Margesson enjoyed a cordial relationship. As Prime Minister, Churchill was astute enough to keep him on as Chief Whip at a time when the Conservatives in parliament held divided loyalties. Churchill elevated Margesson to the role of War Minister on 22 December 1940. *[KN]*

Sir Nevile Henderson was recalled from Berlin as the crisis developed. He is pictured with Sir Robert Vansittart and Lord Halifax in Downing Street. A career diplomat, Vansittart served for eight years as Permanent Under-Secretary for Foreign Affairs and was a firm anti-appeaser but, curiously, he was a friend of Konrad Henlein and had introduced him to Churchill earlier in the year. Although well connected and influential, his opposition to Hitler and appeasement led to him being moved sideways to become Chief Diplomatic Advisor to Chamberlain's cabinet. *William Field [KN]*

Uncertainty was beginning to have an impact. French reservists head off to the Maginot Line. *M Fryszman [KN]*

It was business as usual for the British Army. These Bren Gun Carriers used by the Durham Light Infantry on a night exercise near Winchester were early incarnations of the most successful design borne out of Carden and Loyd's tankettes. Over 110,000 Universal and other variants were built in the UK and elsewhere before the last one rolled off the production line. *Geoffrey Keating [KN]*

Come daylight it was time for the Durhams to enjoy an inspection by Brigadier Arthur Percival at Hackwood Park. The men are wearing a combination of 1937 Pattern battledress with Great War era web equipment, showing that modernisation was gradually happening. Percival was on the General Staff of Aldershot Command and had, until recently, been Chief of Staff to General William Dobbie, the commander of British forces in Malaya. Percival's knowledge would see him replace Dobbie as GOC in April 1941, where he would preside over the defence of Malaya and Singapore that ended in abject defeat on 15 February 1942. *Geoffrey Keating [KN]*

In London it became quite normal for crowds anxious for news to gather at the top of Downing Street hoping to hear something positive, as in this image from 12 September.
William Horton [TT]

Lord Runciman returned that same day and would take a little time preparing his report for the government. He is pictured with his senior government advisor Frank Ashton-Gwatkin, who advocated Britain should find an accommodation with Germany to secure trade links.
William Horton [TT]

There was always room for irreverent British humour despite the deepening crisis. Penguins at London Zoo appear eager for news on 13 September 1938. *Alfred Harris [KN]*

It was a torrid time for the stock market. These brokers are having a busy time of it. *Robert Field [KN]*

Neville Chamberlain made his critical intervention that same day, asking for a face-to-face meeting with Hitler to try and resolve the crisis. Hitler agreed to a meeting at Berchtesgaden, giving Chamberlain a day to prepare for the challenge ahead. This image of the Prime Minister speaking to the BBC on the morning of the 15th when he flew out to Germany from Heston suggests how low key the trip appeared. This would change. *Bill Warhurst [TT]*

Neither *The Times* or Kemsley photographers travelled to Berchtesgaden to record the meeting, but the British Airways Lockheed 10A Electra used by Chamberlain was followed for some of the journey by an aircraft with Cathal O'Gorman aboard. He took a couple of plates and this is the best of them. *Cathal O'Gorman [TT]*

Media interest had increased considerably by the time Chamberlain returned to Heston later that day. To his credit, Chamberlain confronted Hitler at Berchtesgaden where the Führer attempted to dominate proceedings, demanding self-determination for the Sudeten Germans. He claimed Britain was threatening Germany but Chamberlain stood his ground, saying he had issued no such threats and asked why Hitler had wasted his time inviting him to Germany if they were not to have a meaningful discussion.
With tempers diffused the two men then held three hours of talks to resolve the crisis, but Hitler was not by any means finished with his plan to force the issue in his favour.
William Horton [TT]

Édouard Daladier, Georges Bonnet and Andre-Charles Corbin flew into Croydon the next day to discuss their next moves with Chamberlain and Lord Halifax. They agreed with Runciman's view that the Sudeten Germans had a case and called on the Czechs to cede areas with German populations higher than 50 per cent, after which they would guarantee Czech security. The Czechs, unsurprisingly, refused and sought the arrest of Konrad Henlein.
William Horton [TT]

Above and below: Jack Barker and Stanley Devon travelled separately to Prague to record events in the country during the weeks of crisis. Devon tells of how they met up after the Munich Agreement had been signed, but it is clear from their work that they often attended the same photo opportunities. Refugees housed at the Masaryk stadium in Prague are a case in point. Stan roamed the grounds for his subject matter but Jack went inside, where he found kids being fed and given medical check-ups. Stan recorded his surprise that the refugees were actually the families of left-wing Germans fleeing the Nazis. Their tragedy was far from over. *Jack Barker [TT]*

Czech military preparations were an obvious source of interest. Stan's image of artillerymen galloping into action is virtually identical to Jack's. Contact prints of Barker's work tell us the gunners were from the 1st Prague Regiment taking up positions at Motol as part of the 1st Infantry Division's defence of the Prague Fortified Area. *Stanley Devon [KN]*

Gunners go through their drills. *Stanley Devon [KN]*

Time for a well-earned smoke. *Stanley Devon [KN]*

Below: It was exhausting work for this machine gunner. *Stanley Devon [KN]*

These men seem quite relaxed given the menace descending on their country. *Stanley Devon [KN]*

Jack Barker headed to Eger in the Sudetenland where he photographed Jewish and Czech business premises damaged during disturbances and Czech police going about their duties. Violence escalated as Sudeten Germans supported by infiltrators from across the border began to attack Czech security forces and institutions. While people were killed and injured, the Germans also put their propaganda machine to work manufacturing all manner of lurid stories claiming barbarous attacks by Czech police and gendarmes. The Czechs, meanwhile, used a mixture of clumsy and occasionally deft measures to keep a lid on things but they were under attack from well-armed cells determined to make trouble. A captured German arms cache that includes MP 18 submachine guns is examined. *Jack Barker [TT]*

The image shows confiscated weapons being taken to Eger police station. *Jack Barker [TT]*

With London and Paris in agreement, it fell to Neville Chamberlain to return to Germany to settle the matter with Adolf Hitler. He flew out to Cologne from Heston on 22 September. As he waited to board his plane Chamberlain took time for a quick chat with the bowler hatted Geoffrey Dawson, editor of *The Times*, a friend and loyal supporter of his appeasement policy. A mistake by Dawson when editing a leader column had seen the paper drawn into the drama on 7 September when *The Times* appeared to voice support for the Sudetenland being ceded to Germany. It was assumed in many capitals that the paper spoke for the British government and although this was denied, Chamberlain's acceptance of the transfer of the Sudetenland to the German Reich in his next meeting with Hitler made such a denial difficult to accept. Chamberlain's close advisor Sir Horace Wilson stands behind him while German embassy official Theodor Kordt stands next to the bobby on the left. *Bill Warhurst [TT]*

The Prime Minister takes a moment for reflection. *J.W. Eggitt [KN]*

Chamberlain carried with him the broad-based support of the British public. *William Horton [TT]*

Upon their arrival in Cologne, Chamberlain and Wilson were given an outwardly warm greeting from an utterly insincere Joachim von Ribbentrop. *Bill Warhurst [TT]*

The meeting with Hitler was to take place at the Hotel Dreesen on the banks of the Rhine at Bad Godesberg, a favourite of Hitler's where he had plotted the Night of the Long Knives when Ernst Rohm and other rivals were purged in 1934. *Bill Warhurst [TT]*

Chamberlain was known to enjoy all the fuss. The motorcade taking him to his hotel took a circuitous route through cheering crowds to heap carefully orchestrated flattery on the Prime Minister, all part of the deception organised by the Nazis to seduce him into believing his intervention in the crisis would alter Hitler's plans. Bill Warhurst had gone ahead and missed the charade, but he took time to photograph the long line of Mercedes-Benz 200 W21 limousines used for the summit. *Bill Warhurst [TT]*

The Nazis pulled out all the stops at Godesberg. A Luftwaffe band marches past the SS guard of honour. *Bill Warhurst [TT]*

Photography did not always go smoothly for Bill Warhurst. His attempt to get a shot of Hitler saluting as he rode past did not go well, but he would have another opportunity to photograph the Führer later in the day.
Bill Warhurst [TT]

Chamberlain and Sir Nevile Henderson take a few moments on the veranda of the Hotel Petersberg to take in the panoramic view of Godesberg.
Bill Warhurst [TT]

A moment in history: Neville Chamberlain and Adolf Hitler pose for Bill Warhurst's camera in the Hotel Dreesen. Sir Nevile Henderson stands on the left and behind him is Hitler's interpreter Paul Schmidt. At the back is the British diplomat Ivone Kirkpatrick. Bill Warhurst was an intensely modest man who made light of situations like this, but he was amused by the fact he found himself alone in the room with Hitler waiting for Chamberlain to arrive. No words passed between them. More serious matters occurred in the meeting when Chamberlain announced his acceptance of the terms demanded by Hitler at Berchtesgaden only for the Führer to tell him it was too late as he presented a new set of demands designed to turn the screw even further.
Bill Warhurst [TT]

Neville Chamberlain returned to England with Hitler's threats ringing in his ears. The Führer had called for the dismemberment of Czechoslovakia. But he appeared to falter later in the day, toning down his demands. The Czechs would have to begin the evacuation of areas with a German majority by 2000hrs on 26 September. Chamberlain pushed for a later date, allowing Hitler to offer the concession that the Czechs could begin their evacuation on 1 October – the same date he had set his generals for the invasion of Czechoslovakia. Once the Czechs were gone, he would enter into an agreement to guarantee the new border between the two countries. *Bill Warhurst [TT]*

Britain's military attaché in Berlin was one of the most colourful characters involved in the crisis. Some diplomats and politicians assessed Colonel Noel Mason-MacFarlane, MC & Two Bars, to be temperamental, but 'Mason-Mac' had a critical part to play, slipping into Czechoslovakia from Germany to deliver a map of disputed territories drawn up during the second meeting between Chamberlain and Hitler at Bad Godesberg. A keen shot, Mason-MacFarlane loathed Hitler, offering to 'pick the bastard off' from the bathroom window of his home as the Führer took the salute at his 50th birthday parade in April 1939. It was a pragmatic solution to a problem his political masters would not countenance. He was awarded the DSO for his leadership during the retreat to Dunkirk in 1940 and rose to be a lieutenant general, serving on the British Military Mission to Moscow and as Governor of Gibraltar. This is the only image of him to survive in the News UK picture archive. He is seen in a distant February 1917 on the day he received the Military Cross.
Thomas Houlding [KN]

There were angry scenes in Prague as news of Hitler's demands hit home. *Jack Barker [TT]*

Czech Prime Minister Milan Hodža and his government resigned in protest on 23 September, leaving Edvard Beneš looking for someone who would cooperate with Britain and France. General Jan Syrový, a hero of the Great War and head of the army, was reluctant to accept the role but he had little choice. One of his first acts was to order mobilization, but his subsequent acceptance of the terms of the Munich Agreement left him between a rock and a hard place. He was swept up in the storm of retribution in 1945 and found guilty of collaboration at a show trial in 1947. Syrový was released from prison in 1960 but refused a pension and barred from finding employment, causing great hardship. He died in 1970. *Geoffrey Keating [KN]*

Refugee children get a helping hand at Le Boulou. Jack Barker [TT]

Czech troops were soon on the streets of Prague and something like a million men rushed to join the colours to defend their country. *Jack Barker [TT]*

Others enjoyed a quick meal before heading off to the frontier. *Jack Barker [TT]*

There was just time for a parting moment of reassurance. *Jack Barker [TT]*

People were on the move. The fall of the Habsburgs and the glimmer of a safe and secure homeland would prove to be just episodes in the tragedy of Central Europe in the lifetime of this lady and many like her. *Jack Barker [TT]*

Above and below: There was anger elsewhere. The idea that the Czechs were being sold out was too much for those who recognised that the only way to meet with the threat of force was to stand up to Hitler. Demonstrators in London clashed with police as tempers ran high. Years of defence cuts had made the likelihood of a British military response to Nazi aggression difficult to implement. The chickens were coming home to roost. *Jack Kirby/Alfred Harris [KN]*

Stanley Baldwin had handed the poison chalice of responsibility for rearmament to Sir Thomas Inskip, whose background was in law not weapons. We have to balance deciding if he was an ideal choice by asking whether the parlous state of Britain's military industrial complex could have been invigorated by anyone with the resources available to them. That a dynamic character like Winston Churchill had been mooted for the role tends to make final analysis black and white long after the event, but things were not so straightforward. Anyone in the post of Minister for Co-ordination of Defence had a mountain to climb. *Geoffrey Keating [KN]*

War fears grew. Although the Czechs reluctantly agreed to the conditions accepted by Britain and France after Berchtesgaden, Hitler's latest demands went too far. Hitler had released his Godesberg Memorandum on the 24th, calling for Prague to cede the Sudetenland and hold plebiscites in other areas with large German communities. Both Poland and Romania had blocked a Russian offer of support provided Soviet forces could pass through their countries. Old enmities made this impossible for Warsaw and Bucharest to accept. Hitler set a deadline of 28 September for the Czechs to accept his demands or he would invade the Sudetenland. Jack Barker and Stanley Devon photographed worried citizens besieging a shop selling gasmasks in Prague. The sign promises the shop had everything people needed to protect them from gas and air attack. *Jack Barker [TT]*

Business was brisk. *Stanley Devon [KN]*

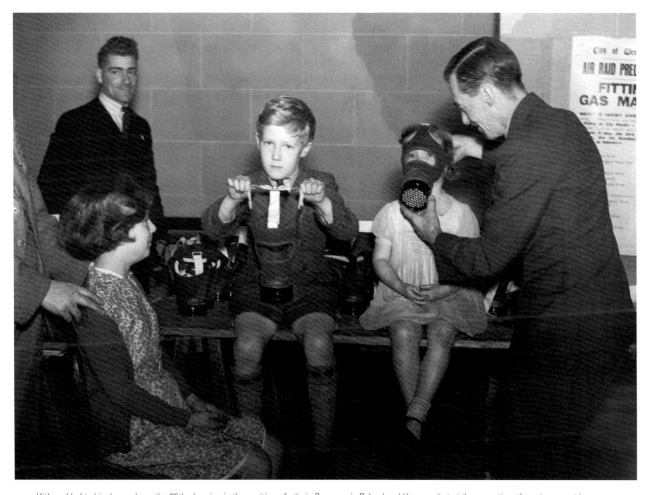

Hitler added to his demands on the 25th, drawing in the position of ethnic Germans in Poland and Hungary, but at the same time those two countries were following events with interest because of their own territorial claims against Czechoslovakia. The worsening situation caused fear of impending disaster to carry to London, where children were pictured being fitted with gasmasks in Piccadilly on the 26th of September. *Alfred Abrahams*

Meanwhile, a critically important decision had been made in Downing Street where the British and French had discussed their next move. Chamberlain dispatched his close advisor Sir Horace Wilson to Berlin to deliver a letter to Adolf Hitler. He found the Führer in poor temper as he wound himself up for his speech to be broadcasted from the Sportpalast later that evening. The hapless Wilson, dubbed the 'Office Boy' by detractors, had little choice but to deliver Chamberlain's message but news that the Godesberg Memorandum had been poorly received in Britain left Hitler feeling the time for talk was over. It wasn't so much Hitler's demands but the timetable that had caused concern in London. Wilson had only been able to deliver the first part of Chamberlain's letter as a raging Hitler continuously interrupted before the meeting was brought to a close. This image of a shaken Wilson on his return to London retains the typical masking used by newspapers of the period to make a 'cut-out'. *Alfred Harris [KN]*

Hitler had worked himself into a typical frenzy at the Sportpalast and the next day Wilson was ushered back in to continue with his task, although Hitler's demeanour had barely improved. Wilson finally managed to get to the crux of the matter, telling Hitler that if he attacked Czechoslovakia, causing France to honour her treaty obligations, then Britain would have to side with the French. Hitler was unmoved. He would 'smash' the Czechs and take on Britain and France too, if need be. Wilson was sure there would be war. Back in London workers began digging trenches in Kensington Gardens on 28 September. *Alfred Abrahams [KN]*

Stanley Devon had returned from Prague, where he had been met with open hostility amid perceptions of betrayal by Britain. He had little time to sort himself out before he was out earning his keep again. Mobilisation was in hand. Cheerful naval reservists head to Portsmouth from Waterloo. *Stanley Devon [KN]*

But Jack Barker had travelled to the Sudetenland and he was already busy. The Sudeten Freikorps had declared the Free State of Asch and taken control of a Czech gendarmerie building. This image was published on the 27th. *Jack Barker [TT]*

The renaming of streets had begun. *Jack Barker [TT]*

There was the prospect of a bright future under the umbrella of the Third Reich for enthusiastic youngsters like these. *Jack Barker [TT]*

Jack managed to get a snap of him mixing with local Hitler Youth. He stands second on the right. [TT]

Territorial Army units were also preparing for war. These men of 39th (the Lancashire Fusiliers) Anti-Aircraft Battalion, Royal Engineers gather for drinks and a snack at Cross Lane Barracks in Salford. The complicated name of the unit reflects the re-tasking of former infantry battalions into specialised roles after the Great War. [KN]

While preparations for war continued in Britain, Neville Chamberlain made representations to Benito Mussolini to intervene as the hour of Hitler's deadline drew near. The Duce contacted Berlin and asked for 24 hours grace while he came up with a solution to the crisis, although he made it clear he was in full support of Hitler's position. Hitler agreed but the truth is it did not alter his longstanding plan to begin his invasion on 1 October. A four-power summit between Britain, France, Germany and Italy was to be held in Munich on 29 September, where the fate of Czechoslovakia would be decided. Chamberlain set off from Heston once again with a large crowd there to wave him off. *William Field [KN]*

Bill Warhurst returned to Germany with Chamberlain and his party, where they were met by Joachim von Ribbentrop and other leading Nazis. To the left of Chamberlain are Adolf Wagner, the Gauleiter of Munich and the highly decorated ex-soldier Franz Ritter von Epp, *Reichskomissar* for Bavaria. Reynhard Heidrich is behind them. *Bill Warhurst [TT]*

Édouard Daladier received similar courtesies on his arrival, after which he drove to the summit accompanied by von Ribbentrop. *Bill Warhurst [TT]*

The summit was to take place at the Führerhaus. The building was suitably decorated for the occasion with large British and French flags. *Bill Warhurst [TT]*

Neville Chamberlain strode past the *Leibstandarte* SS honour guard ready to do business. *Bill Warhurst [TT]*

We are used to the modern era
of cameras that can take
multiple frames in seconds but
the two pictures Bill Warhurst
managed to take of Hitler in
the daytime at Munich were
hit and miss, reflecting the
difficult nature of timing the
use of a plate camera. It is
easy to see why operators like
Stanley Devon were so
contemptuous of the younger
photographers working around
the time he was nearing
retirement at the end of the
1960s. To compound the
problem with glass plates, the
better of the two frames was
broken at Printing House
Square. Imaging software
makes a repair relatively easy.
Bill Warhurst [TT]

Back in Britain the evacuation of children was well under way. Mealtime away from the threat of danger for these evacuee kids from London staying in the Ashdown Forest was an excellent photo opportunity. *William Field [KN]*

Anti-aircraft guns were deployed in the capital, perhaps most strikingly on Westminster Bridge in the shadow of the Houses of Parliament. This QF 3in 20cwt gun mounted on an elderly Peerless lorry were virtually obsolete but its presence was likely to offer some assurance to a nervous public. *William Field [KN]*

In a few short hours Chamberlain and Daladier did what they thought was right and averted a European war their countries were not fit to fight at the cost of giving Hitler what he wanted. The Sudetenland would be ceded to Germany on 10 October and plebiscites would be held in other areas where German populations were high. The decision was presented to the Czechs as a 'take it or leave it' diktat, giving them little option but to accept. The future of Czechoslovakia was now in the hands of Nazi Germany. Mussolini's charade as an honest broker may have impressed London and Paris, but he and Hitler had choreographed proceedings from the outset and both went away very happy with their days work. *Bill Warhurst [TT]*

Édouard Daladier rarely put on a smile and the events at Munich gave him no grounds to do so, but Chamberlain was ecstatic. He had set out to win peace and had succeeded. *Bill Warhurst [TT]*

We, the German Führer and Chancellor and the British Prime Minister, have had a further meeting today and are agreed in recognising that the question of Anglo-German relations is of the first importance for the two countries and for Europe.

We regard the agreement signed last night and the Anglo-German Naval Agreement as symbolic of the desire of our two peoples never to go to war with one another again.

We are resolved that the method of consultation shall be the method adopted to deal with any other questions that may concern our two countries, and we are determined to continue our efforts to remove possible sources of difference and thus to contribute to assure the peace of Europe.

[signature]

Neville Chamberlain

September 30. 1938.

But Chamberlain needed something tangible to show for his trouble. In a second meeting with Hitler he presented the draft of an understanding between the two countries underpinned by the Anglo-German Naval Agreement he was keen to see continue. Hitler took little time to agree and the document they signed would go down into history as the piece of paper Chamberlain would flourish on his return to Heston. *[TT]*

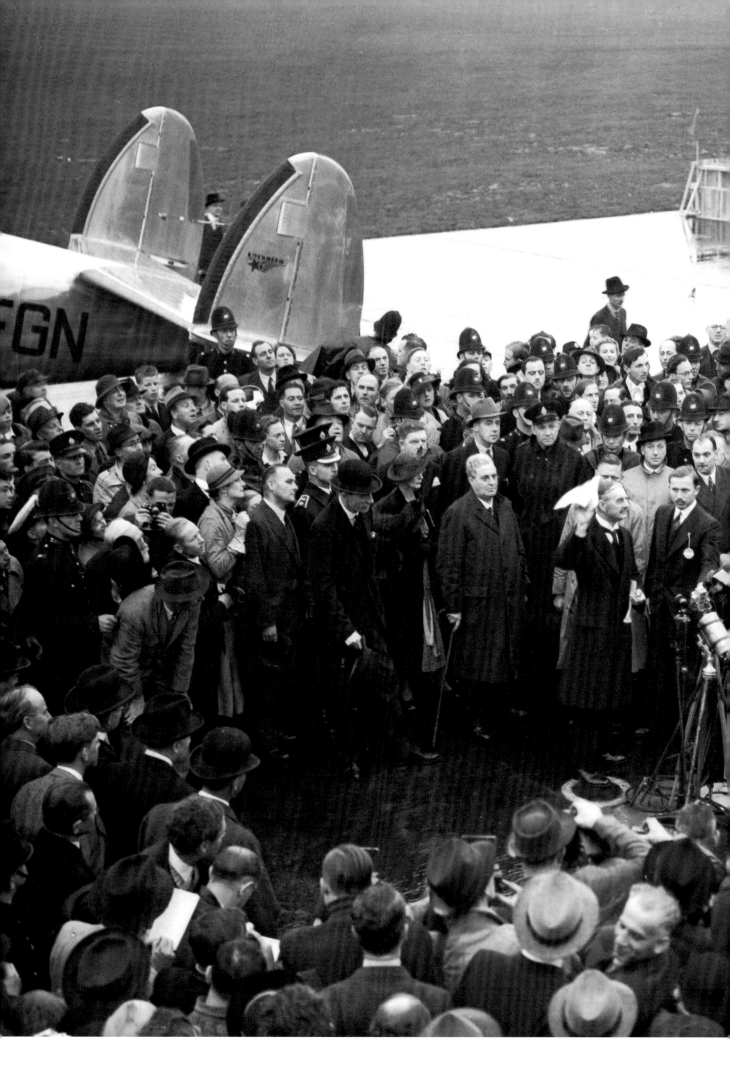

A cheering crowd of government colleagues, pressmen and admirers greeted Chamberlain when his Lockheed Electra touched down at Heston. The speech he gave has come to define his apparent folly in attempting to treat with a man such as Hitler. Not all the plates taken by *The Times* and Kemsley photographers survived the war that followed. Bill Warhurst took the close-up of Chamberlain waving the document but the wide shot has been attributed to him in error – this was taken by an unidentified photographer. Even Bill couldn't have been in two places at once!
Bill Warhurst [TT]

The scene of Chamberlain's moment in history is today a service area on the M4 motorway west of London. *Stanley Devon [KN]*

A large crowd greeted Chamberlain, expressing their joy and relief that war had been averted as his car swept into Downing Street. *Alfred Harris [KN]*

Accompanied by his wife Anne, he went on to Buckingham Palace for an audience with King George VI and Queen Elizabeth. *William Horton [TT]*

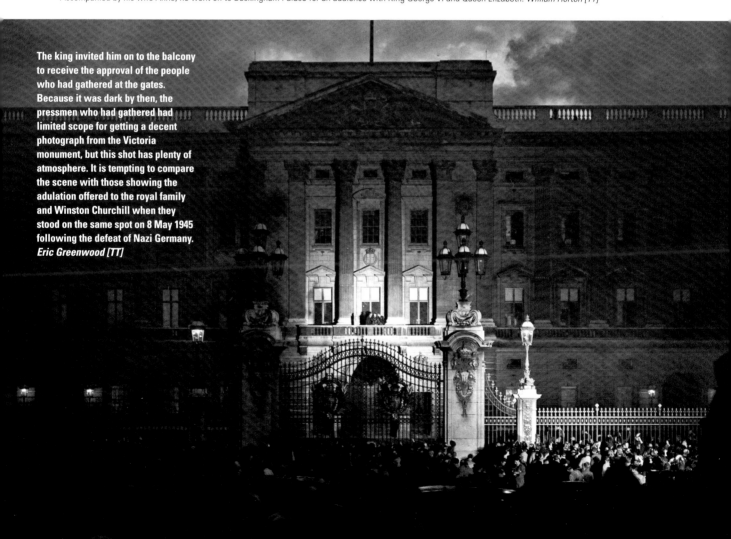

The king invited him on to the balcony to receive the approval of the people who had gathered at the gates. Because it was dark by then, the pressmen who had gathered had limited scope for getting a decent photograph from the Victoria monument, but this shot has plenty of atmosphere. It is tempting to compare the scene with those showing the adulation offered to the royal family and Winston Churchill when they stood on the same spot on 8 May 1945 following the defeat of Nazi Germany. *Eric Greenwood [TT]*

The Chamberlains returned to Downing Street, where the Prime Minister was encouraged to speak from an upstairs window. 'My good friends, this is the second time in our history that there has come back from Germany to Downing Street peace with honour. I believe it is peace for our time. We thank you from the bottom of our hearts… Now I recommend you go home and sleep quietly in your beds.' *Alfred Harris [KN]*

While Chamberlain and his supporters could celebrate what seemed like a victory, opponents like Churchill and the Labour front benches saw nothing but 'unmitigated defeat'. Churchill's prediction of shame rather than war had come to pass.
Charles Maxwell [KN]

The Sudetenland was incorporated into the Reich. Adolf Hitler visited the town of Eger, now known as Cheb, on 3 October. He was greeted by an ecstatic crowd who were equally pleased to see German troops driving through the city and the return of military age men who had slipped over the border into Germany. *Jack Barker [TT]*

There were flowers for these troops and their Zundapp motorcycles. *Jack Barker [TT]*

An *Arbeitsmann* of the Reich Labour
Service appears to have met his match.
Jack Barker [TT]

The crew of an Sd.Kfz.232 armoured car
receive similar attention. The men are
wearing leather helmets covered by a
large black beret that proved to be
impractical and was eventually replaced.
The latticed grid fixed over the vehicle is
an aerial array. *Jack Barker [TT]*

Luftwaffe flak gunners wave to saluting Egerlanders from their prime movers. The mechanised capability of the Germans would soon be put to the test but while vehicles like this Sd.Kfz.7 epitomise the kind of hardware developed in Nazi Germany, it is correct to remember that much of the army relied on horse transport for the entirety of the Second World War. *Jack Barker [TT]*

Back in Britain a volunteer police force formed from over a thousand members of the British Legion were preparing to travel to areas of Czechoslovakia, where plebiscites were due to take place to determine whether they would remain Czech or become German. The men were sworn-in as special constables and issued with a stout walking stick for protection. But the pace of events saw the Legion's police become redundant within days. As we have seen, the Nazis occupied the areas without plebiscites taking place after an international commission in Berlin deemed them unnecessary. These men waiting to board the SS *Naldera* at Tilbury on 11 October would be going nowhere. *Robert Chandler [KN]*

Labour's Ellen Wilkinson was scornful of the pro-Nazi comments made by the famous American aviator Colonel Charles Lindbergh, a prominent isolationist viewed as both Anglophobic and anti-Semitic and no friend of the democracies opposing Hitler. His enthusiasm for the Luftwaffe in particular raised hackles in London and Washington DC, but he would continue to fight the Roosevelt administration's support for the democracies right up until Hitler's declaration of war against the United States in 1941. *[KN]*

Things continued to get worse for Czechoslovakia. On 6 October Slovakia declared autonomy, with Father Jozef Tiso taking the role of Prime Minister. These events were supported by Hungary, for whom the chance to recoup territory taken away by the Treaty of Trianon in 1919 was too good to miss. A protracted dispute ensued but a weakened Czech state was in poor shape to stand up to Hungarian demands while Poland, too, was getting in on the act. Things were no better for the isolated Slovakian leadership facing anger from Prague and their powerful neighbours. In acting as supposedly neutral arbitrators, Germany and Italy were keen to rubber stamp the Hungarian claims and so on 2 November the treaty known as the First Vienna Award was signed, giving Hungary control of predominantly Magyar populated areas. Father Tiso is pictured in the disputed border town of Komárno where he negotiated with Hungarian foreign minister Kálmán Kánya. *Jack Barker [TT]*

The plight of Germany's Jews was unimaginable for those who could not believe a civilised country such as Germany could sink so low. The shooting of a German diplomat in Paris triggered the *Kristallnacht* of 9 and 10 November, the beginning of a pogrom where the wanton destruction of synagogues and countless murders shocked the outside world. A mediaeval Talmud was smuggled out from the ruins of a gutted synagogue and brought to Britain. Rabbi Maurice Perlzweig displayed the scrolls for the press on 19 November and read *Isaac's sacrifice* from them as a party from the Jewish Ex-servicemen's Association looked on. The Nazis levied a 1 billion Reichsmark fine on the Jewish community that was to be paid immediately, knowing full well that the international community would assist, bringing in foreign currency. Rabbi Perlzweig was unimpressed: 'Our brethren in Germany will not be bludgeoned into paying a ransom. Self-respecting tradesmen will prevent that method of bringing foreign money into Germany.' Having moved to New York, Perlzweig became a leading advocate of human rights in the post-war world. *William Field [KN]*

Irene Dipper enjoys her moment as Queen of the Lambeth Walk accompanied by an enthusiastic crowd. The dance itself was a product of the musical *Me and My Girl* and it became immensely popular worldwide. *The Times* enjoyed quoting from a poem: 'And while dictators rage and statesmen talk, All Europe dances – to *The Lambeth Walk.*' *Robert Chandler [KN]*

There were contrasting fortunes on Armistice Day 1938. Neville Chamberlain could purchase poppies for himself and his wife in the firm belief he had preserved the peace won at such a cost in 1918. *Jack Kirby [KN]*

It seems likely that former Czech president Edvard Beneš, living in exile in London, was not so sure. *Geoffrey Keating [KN]*

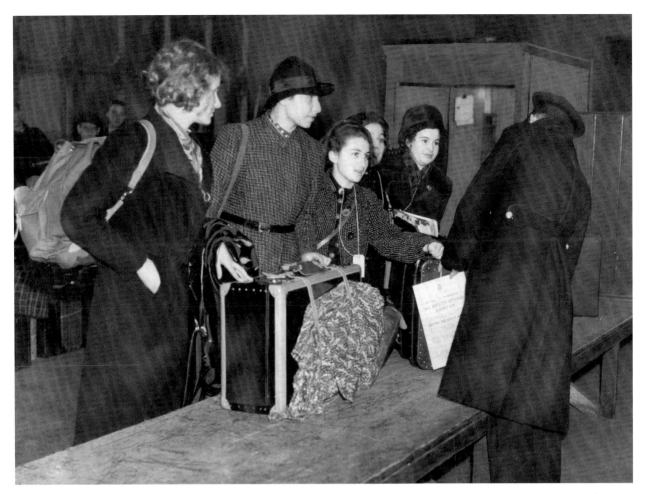

But Britain became a haven for some. The *Daily Sketch* reported the arrival of Jewish refugees at Harwich on 2 December 1938, with Alfred Harris doing the honours in the customs hall at the port where he photographed these girls having their belongings checked. The published caption tells us 'First of 5,000 who are to be given refuge in England. 200 young Jews reached Harwich yesterday from Germany – a rather forlorn party shepherded by eight of their schoolteachers. With only two cases each, the Customs gave them little trouble.' *Alfred Harris [KN]*

Teenaged boys enjoy tea in their sanctuary at Flint Hall, a farm run by George King and his wife at Hambledon in Buckinghamshire. The cinematic feel of this powerful image is tangible. *Herbert Muggeridge [KN]*

It is unclear what good Georges Bonnet hoped to achieve from signing a non-aggression treaty with Joachim von Ribbentrop in Paris on 6 December 1938. The Germans held all the aces and the meeting between the two men led to all manner of difficulties later when Ribbentrop claimed Bonnet had given Germany a free hand in Eastern Europe, undermining the Cordon Sanitaire and confirming that France's pact with the Soviet Union was more or less defunct. Like Chamberlain's piece of paper at Munich, Bonnet needed something to show for all his efforts, but it was short-termism at its best. Hitler held the initiative as the year came to an end. *Jack Barker [TT]*

Those lucky enough to be on the Chamberlain's Christmas card list were in for a treat. Still basking in the apparent success of Munich, the Prime Minister was bold enough to use a photo of the Lockheed Electra that carried him on his historic mission. *[KN]*

4

BREATHING SPACE

....

THE new year heralded with a mixture of words and deeds. In Berlin, Hitler broadcast to the Reich, saying farewell to the old year and offering deep thankfulness to the 'gracious workings of Providence' for the gains made by the country. He demanded, 'Who, after so unprecedented a change in the life of a people, will deny that the powers which were used and the methods which were employed were the right ones?' Amid other restrictions, 1 January 1939 was the day it became illegal for Jews to own or drive a motor vehicle. Hitler concluded by hoping that in the coming year Germany might 'Be able to make our contribution to the general pacification of the world.'

In his own broadcast, the Archbishop of Canterbury seemed unconvinced. 'In Europe restless national ambitions are increasing the widespread sense of insecurity. No wonder that sometimes it seems as if the whole world were going mad.' The Bishop of Carlisle saw 'Ominous signs of new and impending crises.'

Meanwhile, the Bishop of Liverpool concentrated on the evils of unemployment. He sought a unified Christian demand for a national effort to rid the country of the 'plague'. He was right to suspect that the 'plague' would stick around, for, surprisingly, the coming war would be well advanced before large-scale unemployment declined in Britain.

Progress was seemingly everywhere. *The Times* reported that The Southern Railway, operators of the world's largest electrified suburban rail network, were about to expand the system to encompass Virginia Water, Aldershot and Guildford. The tube was also benefitting from modernisation. £14.5 million was being spent to electrify the Central Line eastward beyond Leyton and west from Acton to Ruislip. But it was military expansion that concentrated minds more than infrastructure. Naval developments at home and abroad had

Below: Lord Rothermere's Britain First had morphed into the Bristol Type 142M. Given the name Blenheim, it would be a vital part of the RAF's light bomber fleet during the early years of the war and would also serve as a night-fighter. Halton Brats are getting a good look at a Mk I at the No 1 School of Technical Training, where Lord Trenchard's scheme to provide the RAF's skilled technicians of the future had long since matured since we saw him there earlier in our story.
Reginald Coote [KN]

seen a number of new battleships under construction in France, Germany and Italy. British shipyards were busy, too. On the Tyne the new battleship HMS *King George V* was a month away from being launched. In Birkenhead, the ill-fated *Prince of Wales* was just a few months behind. A further two battleships would be launched in 1940.

There was more. A further six battleships of the Lion class were proposed to counter principally the threat of a bellicose Japan. Class leader *Lion* and her sister *Temeraire* were laid down in the summer of 1939, but along with *Conqueror* and three un-named siblings the ships were cancelled as the Second World War progressed. Britain's very last battleship, *Vanguard*, was launched in November 1944, too late for service during the war.

Neville Chamberlain used his New Year address on the BBC to remind listeners that suggestions that Britain's rearmament programme was faltering were just scaremongering. While conceding there was still much to be done, he asserted that Britain was ready to fulfil obligations to her allies, the empire and at home.

Nevertheless, Sir Thomas Inskip was succeeded as Minister for Co-ordination of Defence by a former Admiral of the Fleet in the shape of Lord Chatfield, a veteran of three naval battles during the Great War. He wasted no time in noting that efforts needed to be stepped up, but his desire to see production put on a war footing met with opposition from the Board of Trade.

Britain's War Minister was Leslie Hore-Belisha, a divisive figure whose combative style and Jewish background attracted varying degrees of antipathy amongst colleagues and more seriously within the army high command, led by Lord Gort, where his name was mud. Hore-Belisha enjoyed the favour of Neville Chamberlain, who, impressed by the writings of Basil Liddell Hart, encouraged his war minister to 'stir up the dry old bones' at the War Office where he duly sacked the Chief of the Imperial General Staff, Field Marshal Cyril Deverell and much of the Army Council, including the tank luminary Hugh Elles. Chamberlain, through Hore-Belisha (aided and abetted by the influential Liddell Hart) sought a strategy for rebooting the army dominated by cost-cutting in precedence to military reality. Liddell Hart's belief in an indirect approach to warfare, termed 'limited liability', eschewed the need for a large traditional field army and an increase in mechanised formations (although Liddell Hart was a supporter of the latter) at a time when the Germans were building theirs up at an alarming rate. Deverell, a realist, quite rightly saw this as nonsense and had to go, but his replacement, the fearless Lord Gort, was hardly likely to be any more enthusiastic towards a dubious shift towards home and imperial defence favoured by the thrifty Chamberlain administration.

The rapid growth of Hitler's legions dictated that the Field Force preferred by Deverell and his peers was a necessity but it's development, particularly the mechanised element, was hampered by the Treasury and it was barely in place by the spring of 1939, just months before it would be needed to fight a continental war. This encouraged an impressionable Hore-Belisha to look towards expanding the Territorial Army to plug the gap in troop numbers when it became apparent the armed forces needed an infusion of albeit reluctant recruits. With this in mind he introduced a form of conscription for young single men who would have six months' training before becoming reservists. To sugar the pill the long since abandoned Militia was invoked, pretty much in name only, to give conscripts a notion of kudos. They were to receive a stylish suit for walking-out dress. The Military Training Act was passed on 27 April 1939, a week after Chamberlain finally relented to pressure from Hore-Belisha to create the Ministry of Supply to control Britain's growing output of armaments and essential equipment. (Chamberlain snubbed Churchill once more, when he chose the undistinguished Leslie Burgin to head it up.)

The author's father was part of the influx of young conscripts getting into uniform. He served with the 7th (Stoke Newington) Battalion of the Royal Berkshire Regiment but had barely started training when the Germans invaded Poland. He was destined for a frustrating war afflicted by disease contracted in India. But he came home, unlike many of the friends he made in the summer of 1939.

While Leslie Hore-Belisha was passionate about his job, both Lord Gort and the Director of Military Operations and Intelligence, Henry Pownall, were exasperated by the abrasive minister chopping and changing policies. It was they who would lead a British Expeditionary Force beset with the legacy of financially inspired meddling in the autumn of 1939, and they would succeed in getting rid of the war minister when his interference in military matters was seen to have gone too far.

Meanwhile, tank production continued to centre on types such as the Vickers Light Tank that would prove next to useless against superior German armour. Of close on a thousand tanks produced in 1939, three quarters would be of this type. A key figure in tank development was Brigadier Giffard Le Quesne Martel, who pioneered the tankette designs. He had risen to the role of Deputy Director of Mechanisation at the War Office and had been instrumental in pushing through the licensing of the tank suspension system designed by the American engineer J. Walter Christie, whose work had also found favour in the Soviet Union. Designs based on the Christie suspension would serve in France in 1940 and throughout the Western Desert campaign but, unlike the Russians, the British never wedded Christie's system to an acknowledged war-winning weapon. Christie-based Cromwell tanks would rub noses with their distant cousin, the legendary T-34, when British and Russian forces linked up in May 1945.

Aside from light and cruiser designs the British Army also had heavily armoured infantry support tanks, the Matilda I and II. The former was a wholly inadequate two-man contraption that was desperately slow and armed with only a machine gun, but its armour could withstand hits from most German anti-tank guns. The Matilda II was a different proposition altogether, but it, too, lacked a truly potent gun, being armed with a 40mm 2-pdr just capable of piercing the armour of the German Panzer III and IV at modest range. Hardly any Matilda IIs had been produced at the start of the war and a hotchpotch of different tanks would go to France with Lord Gort. Elderly Vickers Medium tanks introduced more than a decade earlier were employed at home.

The army had taken up the Boys Anti-Tank Rifle, a bulky 5ft-long brute that weighed over 35lb. It fired a .55in bullet that could penetrate the armour of German light tanks and armoured cars at around a 100 yards range. By far the most significant addition to the British soldier's arsenal in the late 1930s was the Bren light machine gun that was, ironically, based on a Czech design, the ZB vz.26. The weapon was the brainchild of Václav Holek, a noted firearms engineer who epitomised the ingenuity and skill of Czech weapons design coveted by the Nazis. Descendants of the Bren gun would remain in British service until the 1991 Gulf War.

Things were improving for the Royal Air Force where a construction programme of permanent bases with improved living accommodation and facilities was well under way. The decision to separate tasks with the creation of dedicated commands was also paying dividends, particularly at Hugh Dowding's Fighter Command, for whom the Hawker Hurricane and Supermarine Spitfire were set to achieve immortality. Dowding had taken up the role of Commander-in-Chief at the tail end of his career and was approaching retirement just as his system of defence was finding its feet. His efforts had not been made easy and he is best remembered for his no-nonsense approach to problem solving and the kind of single-mindedness that held no concerns over causing offence when he encountered red tape.

Dowding was impressed with the work of Robert Watson-Watt and his colleague Arnold Wilkins who led the development of technology that could locate aircraft using radio beams. A series of experiments proved successful, leading to the construction of an expanding network of Chain Home stations. Watson-Watt's and Wilkins' work was subsequently given the official name Radio Direction Finding, as it was wedded to Dowding's system for reporting and disseminating information on approaching enemy aircraft. It would prove vital in defence of Britain against Axis incursions and seal the fame of Watson-Watt, although the pivotal role of Wilkins should never be understated. An American-derived acronym coined during the Second World War would see radar become universal language for Watson-Watt's and Wilkins' triumph.

Although the Hurricane and Spitfire had shown immediate promise, other designs would not match their success. Fairey Battle light bombers had come into service but their small payload would prove ineffectual and, worse, their poor defensive armament would expose their valiant crews to a torrid experience over France and the Low Countries in 1940. All these aircraft designs relied on the Merlin engine and Rolls-Royce simply could not build enough to go around. The Boulton Paul Defiant was yet another, having won a design competition against the Hawker Hotspur. The Defiant was chosen to a strong degree because Hawker could not meet the requirement for Hurricanes and make the Hotspur as well. It was a sure sign that more resources and facilities were needed as aircraft production was at full stretch.

Bombers were also being produced in ever increasing numbers, including the Handley Page Hampden and Harrow, the Armstrong Whitworth Whitley and the Vickers Wellington. Of the four only the latter could be considered a real success in the role it was designed for. The Secretary of State for Air, Lord Swinton, was confident enough in March 1939 to claim that the bombers coming into service were 'believed to be the best in the world.' Only time would tell. The summer of 1939 would see the first flight of the Short Stirling and the Avro Manchester, an aircraft dogged by its unreliable pair of Rolls-Royce Vulture engines. The new Handley Page Halifax would fly for the first time a little while after the outbreak of the war.

The downward spiral that allowed for all this weaponry to be put to the test had already started by the beginning of 1939. A weakened and newly hyphenated Czecho-Slovakia was ripe for the picking as German strength and menace grew. The First Republic had foundered in the wake of Munich with Edvard Beneš going into exile. The Second Republic did not have long to run.

Slovakia enjoyed the dubious benefit of self-proclaimed autonomy within the republic, but with so much territory lost to Hungary after Munich the opportunist nationalism of Father Jozef Tiso was tempered by his doubts a viable Slovak state would get by. The Slovaks had seen Hungary nibble off chunks of territory rubber stamped by Germany and Italy through the First Vienna Award formalised on 2 November 1938. It was a move by Hungary to redress the loss of lands directed by the victorious Allies in 1920 when the Treaty of Trianon, a sequel to Versailles, was signed under protest by the Hungarians. None of this was of any interest to Hitler but Germany called the shots, encouraging Tiso to further damage the already weakened Czechs by going for full independence. Negotiations with the Nazis began in early 1939 but an outraged government in Prague sent in troops to oust Tiso and consolidate the country.

Hitler's plans for his neighbours were already finalised when he left Tiso and his supporters between a rock and hard place by making it clear he had no sympathy for their ambition for statehood beyond the difficulties they created for Prague. They could have their own country under the Nazi umbrella or be consumed by their neighbours.

Meanwhile Britain and France had offered financial support to the Czechs to the tune of £12 million. Eight million of it would be a loan but the remainder was a gift. The cash was to be used to help resettle the people forced out of areas now absorbed into Germany, Hungary and Poland. But, as we have seen, events outstripped the worthy intentions of London and Paris. Emil Hácha, a good Catholic and a former judge, was picked for president due to his lack of entanglement in recent politics. Born in 1872, he was already in a delicate state of health when the burden of high office was placed upon him. Hácha was thoroughly bullied by a scheming Hitler, who engineered the declaration of independence by Slovakia on 14 March 1939. That same day Hitler summoned the ailing Hácha to Berlin.

Arriving very late in the day he was treated appallingly and did not see the Führer until the early hours of the 15th, by which time the Czech leader was in serious difficulties. Hitler berated Hácha, demanding he sign over his country to German occupation. An already weakened Hácha suffered a heart attack but was revived sufficiently for him to cave in to Hitler's demands. German troops poured across the border that morning, meeting only isolated opposition from Czech units who ignored their president's order to stand down. The Germans set up the Protectorate of Bohemia and Moravia with Hácha as nominal president, but the real power was in the hands of *Reichsprotektor* Konstantin von Neurath, seen as a moderate, and Himmler's SS. The odious Sudeten Nazi Karl Hermann Frank headed up the police. The machinery of Nazi oppression was soon to be unleashed.

The Slovakians got their republic under Nazi protection but a greedy Hungary stepped in to carve out more territory for itself and this would eventually lead to a week of largely inconclusive fighting in March 1939 known as the Little War. A strong degree of coercion by the Nazis does not detract from the ambitions of Father Tiso and his colleagues to achieve statehood, but their subsequent involvement in the invasions of Poland and the Soviet Union were signposts on the road to ruin. The Slovak regime's acquiescence to Nazi plans for the country's Jews damned them even further in the post-1945 quest for justice and retribution. Tiso had enjoyed the trappings of leadership as president of Slovakia and took the title Vodca, an approximation of Führer. He was hanged for treason in

1947. The tragic Emil Hácha was imprisoned in May 1945 and died the following month.

Hitler flexed his muscles again a week after the occupation of Prague when he bullied Lithuania into giving up the contested Baltic port of Memel off the back of the embattled Lithuanians reaching an understanding with Poland over a long-running territorial dispute of their own. Not to be outdone, Benito Mussolini ordered the invasion of Albania, starting on 7 April 1939. The country had enjoyed the long-standing protection of Italy, but the Duce needed to raise his profile on the international stage in response to German expansion.

None of the papers whose archives are featured in this book had photographers in Czechoslovakia during the occupation, and press coverage centres on the reaction in the UK. Hitler's actions were a body blow to Chamberlain. He reminded the House of Commons that Britain had no obligations to the Czechs and, in respect of Munich, he refuted claims that there had been a breach of faith. He went on: 'I am bound to say that I cannot believe that anything of the kind which has now taken place was contemplated by any of the signatories to the Munich Agreement at the time of its signature.' Then, as now, some people were prepared to take his words with a pinch of salt.

In reminding the House of the terms of Munich in respect of the German-Czech border, the clearly disappointed Chamberlain continued, saying of the Germans:

They have now, without so far as I know any communication with the other three signatories to the Munich Agreement, sent their troops beyond the frontier there laid down. But even though it may now be claimed that what has taken place occurred with the acquiescence of the Czech Government, I cannot regard the manner and the method by which these changes have been brought about as in accordance with the spirit of the Munich Agreement.

That fact was that one signatory, Benito Mussolini, knew all about the invasion in advance, but Hitler's perfidy seems to have genuinely shocked Chamberlain.

In reply, Labour's David Rhys Grenfell declared 'This is a day of humiliation and shame for all of us. We have allowed the truth to be set aside, we have allowed violence to take the place of reason and justice, and violence has triumphed.' The Prime Minister's belief that 'what was done at Munich was done in good faith' was incredible. Britain was not looking towards 'A period of peace and security in Europe, but a period fraught with immediate and terrible danger to all of us.'

But it was on his home ground of Birmingham a few days later that Chamberlain let loose his feelings in a speech broadcast in Britain, throughout the empire and the United States. He regretted the failure of his predecessors to resolve the mistakes of Versailles and defended his decision to negotiate with Hitler, but accepted the Munich Agreement had fallen short of his hopes for the Czechs:

Nothing that we could have done … could possibly have saved Czecho-Slovakia from invasion and destruction. Even if we had subsequently gone to war to punish Germany for her actions, and if after the frightful losses which would have been inflicted upon all partakers in the war we had been victorious in the end, never could we have reconstructed Czecho-Slovakia as she was framed by the Treaty of Versailles.

But I had another purpose, too, in going to Munich. That was to further the policy which I have been pursuing ever since I have been in my present position – a policy which is sometimes called European appeasement. I do not think myself that it is a very happy term or one which accurately describes its purpose.

For the policy to succeed there could be no dominant power in Europe. Each nation should be content with its share of resources and trade and improving the lives of its citizens.

… I felt that although that might well mean a clash of interests between different States, nevertheless, by the exercise of mutual good will and understanding of what were the limits of the desires of others, it should be possible to resolve all differences by discussion and without armed conflict. I hoped in going to Munich to find out by personal contact what was in Herr Hitler's mind, and whether it was likely that he would be willing to cooperate in a programme of that kind.

Chamberlain recalled that in his much-publicised speech at the Berlin Sportpalast after the summit at Bad Godesberg, Hitler had declared:

I have assured Mr Chamberlain, and I emphasise it now, that when this problem is solved Germany has no more territorial problems in Europe… I shall not be interested in the Czech State any more, and I can guarantee it. We don't want any Czechs anymore.

Chamberlain had hoped that the Munich Agreement would allow him to 'carry farther' the policy of appeasement:

I am convinced that after Munich the great majority of British people shared my hope, and ardently desired that the policy should be carried further. But today I share their disappointment, their indignation – that those hopes have been so wantonly shattered. How can these events this week be reconciled with those assurances?

Instead of consulting with Britain as the Munich declaration required, Hitler had:

Taken the law into his own hands. Before even the Czech President was received, and confronted with demands which he had no power to resist, the German troops were on the move and within a few hours they were in the Czech capital.

Citing a speech he had made previously, Chamberlain continued with a warning:

Any demand to dominate the world by force was one which the democracies must resist, and… I could not believe that such a challenge was intended, because no Government with the interests of its own people at heart could expose them for such a claim to the horrors of world war… With the lessons of history for all to read, it seems incredible that we should see such a challenge… No greater mistake could be made than to suppose that, because it believes war to be a senseless and cruel thing, this nation has lost its fibre that it will not take part to the utmost of its power resisting such a challenge if ever it were made.

He ended in the same vein:

We need not be downhearted. This is a great and powerful nation – far more powerful than we were even six months ago, and acts of violence and injustice bring with them sooner or later their own reward. Every one of those incursions raises fresh dangers for Germany in the future, and I venture to prophesy that in the end she will bitterly regret what her Government has done.

He was correct, of course, but there was work to be done. Regardless of the position the government presented, or indeed the true situation feared by its critics, it was crystal clear that increased effort would be needed to improve Britain's defences still further. Lord Chatfield, Secretary for Co-ordination of Defence, fought back at the critics and he made a point of lauding the efforts of his predecessor, Sir Thomas Inskip, for whom hindsight has not always been so charitable.

Above and below: Rearmament was picking up pace in Britain and France and this is a good moment to review some of the developments. Vickers-Armstrongs were at the heart of Britain's armaments industry. The company was created when Vickers and Armstrong-Whitworth merged in 1927 with shipbuilding, artillery, aircraft, munitions and armoured vehicle interests coming together to form a giant enterprise. It was inevitable that the merged company would play a major role in the country's rearmament programme and a visit to the home of Vickers in Sheffield gave Geoffrey Keating the opportunity to take these striking images of work in a foundry. *Geoffrey Keating [KN]*

A Defence Loans Bill to raise money for a significant war chest was due to be debated at Westminster. Of the critics, Chatfield had this to say: 'The argument has been used that if the Government had acted differently in the past, and had shown more moral and physical courage, we would not now have reached the appalling position of having to find £580,000,000 for defence.' To say it was appalling was possibly an understatement. He went on: 'Every schoolboy knew that the taunt of cowardice was the worst insult that could be addressed to an Englishman, the one failing which an Englishman considered inexcusable.' While in India he had read reports in the Indian newspapers suggesting that the British government were 'Acting, or had acted, or were about to act in a cowardly manner. Strange as it might seem, those comments came not from other countries but from our own countrymen. Such statements were bound to have an unfortunate effect on the mentality of the world at large.'

Intentionally or otherwise, Chatfield pretty much summed up attitudes to appeasement and the Chamberlain administration ever since.

But he was defiant; such negativity was:

'Eagerly seized upon by those who wished to weaken confidence in the British race or to have it believed that at last, as they had so long hoped, we had become decadent. It was perhaps not always realised abroad how ready we were to criticize ourselves and to express gloomy depreciation of our achievements and qualities, but, of course, if anyone were to assume from this self-criticism that fear was the basis of our actions they would be dangerously deceiving themselves.'

He makes a fair point. Neville Chamberlain had committed himself to averting a disastrous world war at all costs but he was no coward. A good many members of both Houses of Parliament had seen the horrors of the Great War up close and did not want a repeat. The British public at large were shown to be anti-war. The reception Chamberlain had received on his return from Munich illustrated how popular his policy of appeasement was. But in accepting the dismemberment of Czechoslovakia – the 'faraway country' – to satisfy what he believed to be the limited territorial aims of Adolf Hitler, Chamberlain and his Cabinet, supported by influential friends in the media, took what their opponents saw as a dangerous gamble and lost. He had just six months to prepare for the next great trial of his political life.

If the Vickers site was impressive, a visit to the Royal Arsenal at Woolwich was bound to offer Geoffrey Keating the opportunity to take stunning photographs. Shell manufacture was just one facet of the massive site. *Geoffrey Keating [KN]*

Above: Gun production was in full swing. *Geoffrey Keating [KN]*

Below: The Royal Navy was a good customer. This twin mounting of 4.7in QF Mark XII guns is seen aboard the Tribal class destroyer HMS *Eskimo* during a combined Fleet exercise off Gibraltar in March 1939. The destroyer *Wishart* and the aircraft carrier *Courageous* are in the background. *Bill Warhurst [TT]*

The size and number of guns produced at Woolwich was impressive. *Geoffrey Keating [KN]*

Another huge manufacturing centre could be found at Enfield Lock, where the Royal Small Arms Factory had been making firearms and edged weapons since Napoleonic times. Enfield gave all or part of its name to a long list of historic weapons and the Bren gun continued the tradition when the British adopted it in 1935. The gun was designed by Václav Holek at the Zbrojovka Brno factory in Czechoslovakia, as the ZB vz. 26 and had been further developed into the ZGB 33 when agreement was reached to build it under licence in the UK. The gun's name was an amalgam of Brno and Enfield and versions of the weapon would see over fifty years of service with the British armed forces. Over 170 years of weapons manufacture at Enfield came to an end in 1988. *Herbert Muggeridge [KN]*

The Handley Page HP.52 bomber we saw earlier had gone through some modifications by the time the production-standard prototype L4032 first flew at Radlett, when the aircraft was christened Hampden on 24 June 1938. *Herbert Muggeridge [KN]*

Handley Page's Chief Test Pilot Major James Cordes seems very pleased with the Hampden. *Herbert Muggeridge [KN]*

Cordes was the test pilot when the Handley Page Heyford bomber first flew in 1930 and it seems incredible that the type was still in front-line service just before Britain went to war in 1939. Some were still doing odd jobs in 1940. *Edward Taylor [KN]*

But the Heyford has a deserved place in history. In 1935 one had stooged around while the little-known scientists Robert Watson-Watt and Arnold Wilkins tested a device for detecting aircraft using a system called radio direction finding in a field near Daventry in Northamptonshire. Radar was born. Their work would lead to a network of Chain Home stations that would become a vital part of Britain's air defences in the war to come and it would make Watson-Watt one of the best-known scientists of the century. Needless to say, tight security barred press photography of his work, but Watson-Watt was able to pose for the camera in 1941. He was knighted the following year and went to work in the United States. He died in 1973. *Clifford Davies [KN]*

The man who capitalised on Watson-Watt's genius was an RAF officer whose work to build the system of air defence that saved Britain in 1940 earned him plaudits as much as it did the professional jealousy of some of his peers. Hugh Dowding was not the easiest man to get along with but his tenacity in getting what he wanted knew no bounds. At one point he had to forcefully insist on bullet proof glass for the Hurricane and Spitfire, pointing out that if it was good enough for the limousines of Chicago gangsters it must surely be good enough for RAF fighter pilots. He won the argument but his detractors would bring him down after he had won the Battle of Britain in a shameful exercise that did the RAF and the Air Ministry no credit. He is pictured discussing a home defence exercise in August 1937 with Air Chief Marshal Sir John Steel, the first leader of Bomber Command, Under-Secretary of State for Air Lieutenant-Colonel Tony Muirhead and Lord Swinton, Secretary of State for Air. *Edward Taylor [KN]*

Swinton's failure to achieve sufficient progress with aircraft production saw him replaced by Sir Kingsley Wood. The new minister visited aircraft factories in Hampshire on 30 January 1939. He spent time inspecting Airspeed at Portsmouth then on to Woolston, where he saw production of the Supermarine Walrus amphibian. 'But the thrill of his day awaited him at Eastleigh,' wrote a breathless *The Times* reporter. 'There he saw two Supermarine Spitfires… give an exhibition of high-speed flying. Climbing like rockets they shot up to a high altitude, then swooping rapidly down whizzed to and fro across the aerodrome at a speed exceeding 350 miles an hour.' The minister is pictured standing between test pilots Jeffrey Quill and George Pickering after their display.

The legendary Quill was Chief Test Pilot on the Spitfire programme but managed to get himself transferred to No 65 Squadron during the Battle of Britain on the excuse he needed combat experience to improve the aircraft. He shot down a Bf 109 and shared in the destruction of a Heinkel bomber before he was ordered back to Vickers after just nineteen days with the squadron. George Pickering was something of a daredevil pilot much admired for his bravery.

He is said to have barrel rolled a Walrus on one test flight. He was killed in a tragic accident in 1943 when, having made friends with some Irish Guardsmen, he was travelling up a hill with them in a Bren Carrier when it rolled over on top of him. *Cathal O'Gorman [TT]*

The aircraft that would be the lynchpin of Dowding's victory was entering service. This fine air-to-air study of a Hawker Hurricane Mk I was made by Cathal O'Gorman in November 1938. The original caption reported that Hurricanes were being supplied in 'large numbers' and that one had flown from Edinburgh to London at an average speed of 408mph. This was all a long way from the Bristol Bulldogs we saw earlier. *Cathal O'Gorman [TT]*

The pilot on the flight from Edinburgh was Squadron Leader John Woodburn 'Downwind' Gillan, AFC, seen holding maps in the middle of this group of No 111 Squadron pilots. He performed a similar feat by flying to Paris from Northolt in just sixty-six minutes. With him, left to right, are Sergeant William Lawrence Dymond, Pilot Officer Michael Lister Robinson, Pilot Officer James Gilbert 'Sandy' Sanders, Pilot Officer Roy Gilbert Dutton, Pilot Officer Robin Peter Reginald Powell, Pilot Officer Charles S. Darwood and Pilot Officer Stanley Dudley Pierce Connors. Only Sanders, Dutton and Powell would survive the Second World War. *Alfred Harris [KN]*

Below: The Hurricanes of Treble One lined up at Northolt. The squadron was the first to operate the Hurricane. Coincidentally, it was the last to operate the Tornado F3 fighter and was disbanded when the type was withdrawn from service in March 2011. *Alfred Harris [KN]*

The 'large numbers' noted by *The Times* are evident in this image of the Hawker factory at Kingston. *Robert Chandler [KN]*

Below: These ladies applying fabric to a wing were just some of the millions of women who would be vital to Britain's eventual victory in 1945. *Robert Chandler [KN]*

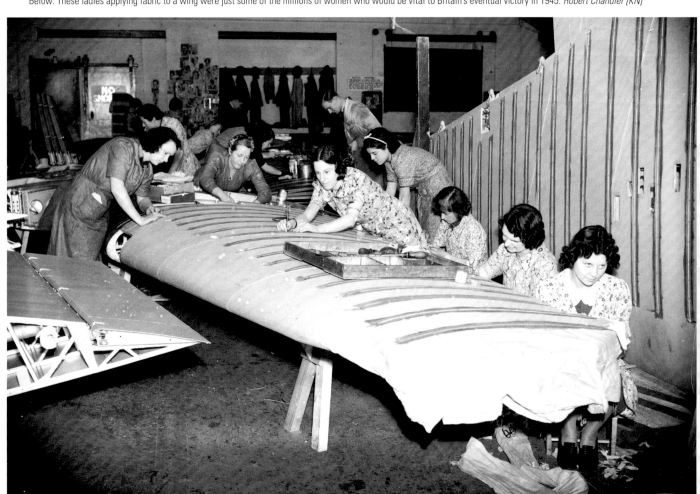

Edward Taylor's impressive air-to-air shot of a No 601 Squadron Blenheim 1F up from RAF Hendon gives us a clear view of the plain white underside camouflage on the starboard wing. The port wing was painted in a colour very close to black which was named 'Night' on Air Military colour charts. Hugh Dowding suggested the colour scheme in 1937 but it was largely replaced by sky blue at the start of the Battle of Britain, by which time the Millionaires Squadron had exchanged its Blenheims for Hurricanes. *Edward Taylor [KN]*

A 1935 proposal to construct shadow factories to build aircraft and aero engines in conjunction with the British motor industry began to bear fruit within a year and new sites were developed after the war had started. The term shadow did not imply anything secret; rather the new factories were in the shadow of established plants operated by some of the best-known motor manufacturers in the country. The scheme would be rolled out to other industries. Permission to photograph these factories might seem to have been out of the question, but a visit to the Rootes Group's new shadow factory under construction at Speke went ahead without any restrictions. *Edward Taylor [KN]*

Charles Maxwell visited the Austin shadow factory, better known as the East Works of the company's vast Longbridge site in January 1939. The production of Fairey Battle light bombers was well under way. *Charles Maxwell [KN]*

The first RAF squadron to receive the Spitfire into service was No 19 at Duxford. They were introduced to the press on 7 May 1939. The early two-blade propellers would soon give way to one more consistent to our imagery of the aircraft. Needless to say, Stanley Devon was able to produce memorable photographs of the occasion. George the squadron mascot sits to attention. *Stanley Devon [KN]*

Pilots had a couple of goes at simulating a 'scramble' for the cameras. This shot doesn't appear to have been reproduced before. *Stanley Devon [KN]*

Other squadrons had received their Spits by the summer of 1939. RAF Hornchurch is seen hosting cadets of the Officer Training Corps where a line-up of No 54 Squadron aircraft must have made quite an impression. The cadets are getting a good look at K9885, an aircraft that would be written-off after an accident in January 1940. *Cathal O'Gorman [TT]*

Imports from the United States would prove critical to the expansion of the wartime RAF. The first of one of the most successful American aircraft to enter British service arrived at the Marine Aircraft Experimental Establishment (MAEE) at Felixstowe in July 1939. This Consolidated Model 28-5 flying boat was put through rigorous testing by the MAEE before it moved on to take part in early long-range recce sorties. It was written-off in a landing accident in February 1940. The type was designated as a PBY in US naval service and it was christened the Catalina by the British. Over 3,000 were built. This particular aircraft retained the US civil aviation prefix 'N' ahead of its British serial number P9630 for the journey from San Diego. *Stanley Devon [KN]*

We saw some of Stanley Devon's 35mm frames of a No 37 Squadron Handley-Page Harrow bomber at RAF Feltwell in the introduction to this book. Stan took a good number of plates in addition to the films and these were used to impress upon *Daily Sketch* readers that modern combat aircraft were coming into service. But the suggestion that the RAF's new bombers were 'believed to be the best in the world' made by Lord Swinton isn't supported by the Harrow. With a modest capacity of 3,000lb (1,400kg) bomb load, it achieved more working as a transport aircraft. Note that an aerial has been painted out on the nearest aircraft in this published image. *Stanley Devon [KN]*

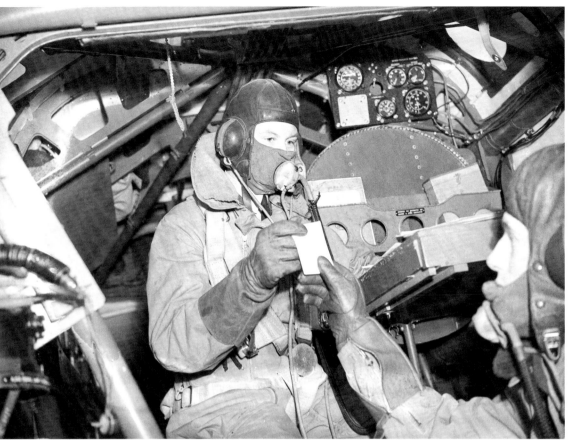

The Harrow had a crew of five. The wireless operator hands a note to the navigator. *Stanley Devon [KN]*

Below: The RAF flew in a large number of aircraft in honour of what would be the last peacetime Bastille Day until 1946. Vickers Wellingtons of No 149 Squadron fill the foreground. Spitfires, Hampdens and other aircraft add to this vista taken at Dugny aerodrome; it would become Le Bourget Airport after the war. *M. Fryszman [KN]*

The Wellingtons were carefully guarded.
M. Fryszman [KN]

Whatever doubts may have arisen from the state of British air power, Britannia most definitely ruled the waves. Bill Warhurst captured an idyllic moment aboard HMS *Rodney* where a keenly fought game of deck hockey took place as the ship kept station with HMS *Hood*. Bill Warhurst [TT]

How could there be any doubt when presented with images like this? *Royal Sovereign*, *Revenge* and *Ramillies* steam into 'battle' during an exercise off Weymouth. *Herbert Muggeridge [KN]*

HMS *Ark Royal* had entered service and was photographed having a busy time on the same exercise off Weymouth, where she is seen turning into the wind to launch some of her aircraft. Giving chase is HMS *Wren*, the designated rescue destroyer in case any aircraft ended up in the drink. *Wren* was launched in 1919 exactly a year after the Armistice and was lost to Stuka dive-bombers off the Suffolk coast in July 1940. *Bill Warhurst [TT]*

Right: The battleship HMS *King George V* was launched on 21 February 1939 at the Walker Naval Yard at Newcastle upon Tyne. The ship was the class leader of five and took part in the sinking of the Bismarck in 1941. She was the product of limitations set by the Washington Naval Treaty and this had consequences for her and her four sisters. 'KG5' suffered from poor seaworthiness in heavy seas when attempts to upgrade her fighting weight reduced her freeboard, leaving her bow prone to flooding. Regardless of this the ship had a busy war, operating in the Atlantic, the Mediterranean and the Pacific. She was scrapped in 1959.
Stanley Devon [KN]

Modern combat aircraft for the navy were making an appearance. The Blackburn Skua dive-bomber holds the distinction of being the first aircraft to sink a major enemy warship when planes from 800 and 803 Naval Air Squadrons flew from Orkney to attack the light cruiser *Konigsberg* at Bergen in Norway on 9 April 1940. Whether any of the German sailors we saw pictured in happier times at Portsmouth in the last chapter were on board when *Konigsberg* capsized is a moot point. *Stanley Devon [KN]*

The haste to rearm is linked to the trivial but lethal blockage of a test cock by enamel paint that led to the loss of the submarine HMS *Thetis* on 1 June 1939. The brand new submarine was carrying out test dives in Liverpool Bay when an error led to flooding of the forward torpedo room, causing the boat to sink by the bow. A blocked test cock is thought to have given the impression a torpedo tube was closed when it was in fact open, allowing tons of water to rush in. The accident was made worse because *Thetis* had 103 people aboard, including expert engineers from Cammell-Laird in addition to the crew and other naval personnel. Only four men managed to escape. The loss of *Thetis* played out with much media interest, with Stanley Devon taking aerial photographs of the stern of the stricken submarine jutting out of the water. *Thetis* was salvaged out of grizzly necessity and rebuilt. The job of removing the remains of ninety-nine unfortunate men cannot have been pleasant. Renamed HMS *Thunderbolt*, the submarine had a busy war until she was sunk with all hands by an Italian warship in 1943, earning her the unwanted distinction of being lost twice. *Stanley Devon [KN]*

We have seen examples of elderly anti-aircraft guns deployed during the Munich Crisis. Happily, the QF 3.7in AA gun was starting to appear in numbers. It was an excellent heavy weapon that would remain in use until the missile age. Guns need gunners and the new weapon arrived as a major reorganisation of the UK's anti-aircraft defences was under way. Expansion was vital but appeared to be lagging behind other schemes. Basil Liddell Hart reported that there were barely a hundred guns covering London as late as October 1938 and time was short. The Territorial Army was key to the plan and units such as the 4th (City of London) Battalion Royal Fusiliers found themselves re-tasked and re-badged to become 60th (City of London) Anti-Aircraft Brigade, RA (TA) based in Catford. Three batteries, 168, 169 and 194, operated from Artillery House on the Bromley Road. Night exercises were an essential part of training for the brigade. *William Field [KN]*

A thrifty Neville Chamberlain had encouraged flirtation with concentrating on home and imperial defence based on the influence of Basil Liddell Hart, but the implementation of a traditional field army for Continental warfare had become imperative by the spring of 1939. Britain's war minister Leslie Hore-Belisha is pictured with General Lord Gort when he installed him as Chief of the Imperial General Staff in December 1937 after sacking Field Marshal Cyril Deverell, who he saw as resistant to the varying policies he sought to impose on a reluctant high command. The embodiment of a straight-up Guards officer, Gort was the recipient of the Victoria Cross, three Distinguished Service Orders and the Military Cross and was not the sort of man to be cowed by a political animal like Hore-Belisha, and their relationship quickly soured.
Alfred Abrahams [KN]

Concepts can be seductive but the wishful-thinking Chamberlain and Hore-Belisha shared based on Basil Liddell Hart's ideas would not stand up to the need for a traditional field army. None of this would dent the image of Liddell Hart (left) and he would further enhance his reputation after the Second World War with successful books benefiting from his access to German generals held prisoner and the papers of Erwin Rommel. How strong an impression his pre-war theories made on their tactical thinking remains open to debate. While some post-mortem assessments play down his importance to German ideas, he remains one of the standout military theorists and commentators of the twentieth century. He is pictured with A.S. Frere of Heinemann in November 1938.
Edward Taylor [KN]

The Territorial Army urgently needed to expand and a call for 300,000 volunteers by Hore-Belisha was met with some enthusiasm. One of the men to answer the call was the photographer Rodney Cockburn of the Daily Sketch, who joined the London Irish Rifles. His colleague Geoffrey Keating was also in uniform. Kemsley Newspapers would see a good many of its staff in uniform as photographers and in fighting roles. *William Field [KN]*

The rush to join up hardly compared to the clamour of 1914 but every man counted. These men are outside the Central London Recruiting Depot in Great Scotland Yard. *Herbert Muggeridge [KN]*

The decision to bring in compulsory military service for young men who met requirements was not taken lightly. The Military Training Act of 26 May 1939 was Britain's first ever piece of peacetime conscription legislation. The title Militia was used as an evocative reminder of the golden age of volunteer soldiering in the nineteenth century, but the men plucked by the scheme might find themselves in any one of the three fighting services. It was, however, the army that took most of them. The Daily Sketch enthused at the new scheme '15th July 1939 will become historic as the day on which our Army of the Twenties came into being. For today 30,000 very fit young men gladly answer the nation's call to military training… They are just the first instalment of Britain's new army of keen, virile youth; 273,000 will be called up during the next few months.' This young man was evidently happy to be chosen. *Stanley Devon [KN]*

"…I will, as in duty bound, honestly and faithfully defend His Majesty, His Heirs and Successors, in Person, Crown and Dignity against all enemies…." Recruits take the Oath of Allegiance at Duke of York's Headquarters in Chelsea. *Stanley Devon [KN]*

The intended provision of distinctive walking out dress for militiamen was expected to give conscription a degree of kudos and the inference at this photocall is it would make the wearer attractive to the opposite sex! Events would overtake the general issue of these fine duds. *F.R. Donovan [KN]*

The army retained a large amount of Great War era artillery for use on the battlefield, but new weapons were coming. Liddell Hart revealed that the government was spending £5 million on the new Ordnance QF 25-pdr field gun. Pending its arrival, a number of existing 18-pdrs were re-bored to the larger calibre and fitted on new carriages. These gunners of 24th Field Regiment Royal Artillery are seen demonstrating their guns during a rehearsal for the annual Tattoo held at Aldershot in June 1939. *Stanley Kessell [TT]*

Anti-tank weapons were a feature of the modern British Army but the effectiveness of the new Ordnance QF 2-pdr would be put through rigorous examination by German tanks in 1940 and later in the Western Desert. This dramatic image by Bill Warhurst reveals none of the deficiencies that presented themselves when the shooting was for real, but the Vickers Medium exposing itself to the gunners helps illustrate how close these guns would often need to get to have any hope of delivering a knockout blow. *Bill Warhurst [TT]*

What of France? Jack Barker and M. Fryszman had covered a number of traditional parades where la gloire was not in doubt, but visits to major exercises did not happen in 1939. France had many colonial units in its armed forces that would play a significant role in the war to come. These Algerian Spahis did not just look magnificent and would gain an enviable reputation for their fighting qualities even after they gave up their horses for armoured vehicles. *M. Fryszman [KN]*

These smart-looking FCM 36 light tanks on show for the Feast Day of Joan of Arc illustrate how the French appeared to have several designs for similar requirements, effectively watering down the value of all this armour. French designers were turning out a wide range of innovative prototypes of self-propelled guns and armoured personnel carriers, in addition to tanks and wheeled armour, but where and when they would ever be built was a serious issue. France simply did not have the capacity, especially in terms of manpower, to build enough of the tanks its army really needed. Further orders of the FCM 36 were cancelled so the company could concentrate on building the heavier Char B1bis. *Jack Barker [TT]*

The Char B1bis was conceived as an infantry tank and considered by many to be the best in the Anglo-French arsenal, combining a hull-mounted 75mm howitzer with a 47mm anti-tank gun in the turret. Production was spread across five manufacturers, with Renault building the most. Less than 800 of the two principal models were built between 1936 and 1940. *Jack Barker [TT]*

Let us be clear, however effective, British tanks were hardly being produced in decent numbers. *The Times* reported on the visit of General Maurice Gamelin, Chief of Staff of the Armed Forces of France, to Aldershot on 7 June 1939. The general got the opportunity to get a look at the tanks in British service including the Tank, Infantry, Mk I Matilda I. Just 140 of these tanks were built. What Gamelin thought of the Matilda is open to question. Awkward looking and slow, the tank possessed excellent armour able to withstand German anti-tank guns in 1940, but armed with just a single Vickers machine gun, it was unable to make a serious impression on the campaign. Lieutenant General Sir John Dill is on the right, while Brigadier Thomas Heywood in the centre will have been well known to Gamelin as he was a former Military Attaché to France.
Bill Warhurst [TT]

Gamelin is pictured on the deck of a Tank, Cruiser, Mk III, the fruit of Britain's dealings with the maverick American engineer J. Walter Christie, a man best described as challenging to deal with; so much so that many officials from his own country would not. One of Christie's champions was Brigadier Giffard Le Quesne Martel, the onetime inventor whose tankette we saw much earlier. The British opted to deal with Christie and a vehicle was acquired for £8,000 through the Nuffield Organisation, where improvements were made leading to the introduction of the tank shown. The Mk III could speed along at 30mph and was armed with the 2-pdr gun. Only sixty-five of this model were built. *Bill Warhurst [TT]*

Efficient Civil Defence would prove to be as vital as anything the armed forces were doing during the first years of the war. These women of the Red Cross Society based at Grosvenor Crescent in London appear to be ready to meet the challenges to come. *Alfred Abrahams [KN]*

The new medium of television was playing its part in preparing the public for what to expect from air raids. A BBC cameraman films anti-aircraft gunners during an outside broadcast from Alexandra Palace. *Charles Maxwell [KN]*

Members of St John Ambulance prove their readiness. *Charles Maxwell [KN]*

Below: In Leicester the volunteer spirit was alive and well. *Herbert Muggeridge [KN]*

But there remained an urgent need for more civil defence volunteers. A parade for East Ham's new May Queen provided an ideal opportunity to get the message home. *Alfred Harris [KN]*

Air raid precautions volunteers at the Stork margarine factory at Purfleet in Essex gather for the camera after presenting a display of anti-gas measures. *Stanley Devon [KN]*

The residents of Tiber Street in Islington take delivery of Anderson shelters to be erected in their gardens. The shelters were issued free to households with an income less than £250 per annum or they could be bought for £7. Around 3.5 million were distributed. Six corrugated iron panels and steel end pieces were assembled within a specially dug pit, which was then covered with earth to complete the shelter.
Alfred Abrahams [KN]

These ladies do not seem so convinced of their value.
Alfred Abrahams [KN]

Workers wearing gasmasks try out the new shelters built for them at the ECKO radio factory in Southend-on-Sea. The company was a vital part of Britain's war effort and, as such, the work done there was considered sufficiently important for it to be dispersed to shadow factories away from the town.
Robert Chandler [KN]

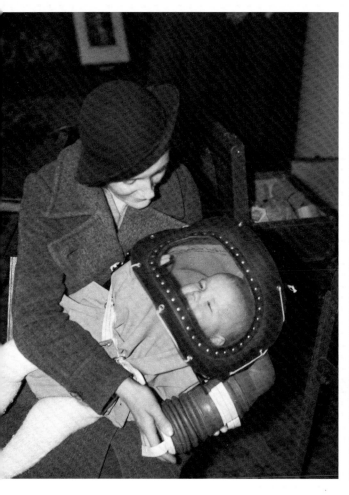

There were also gasmasks for infants under the age of 2. With the child sealed inside it was the job of the parent to pump in air, but the contraption had mixed success during tests and the fact it was lined with asbestos would quite correctly cause health and safety nightmares today. *Robert Chandler [KN]*

Volunteers of the Auxiliary Fire Service gather at County Hall in London after a march from the headquarters of the London Fire Brigade in Lambeth. The service was founded in 1938 and disbanded twenty years later. *Alfred Harris [KN]*

The Special Constabulary had been expanded in police forces across the country. Volunteers such as this un-named gentleman in Nottingham would be kept busy. *Herbert Muggeridge [KN]*

The promotion of National Service was the order of the day and there were many ways women could do their bit. With so many agricultural workers expected to fill the ranks of the armed forces it made good sense for the government to rekindle the Women's Land Army in light of its success during the Great War. These women are being enticed to become Land Girls during a National Service display on Hackney Marshes. *Geoffrey Keating [KN]*

A fleet of French bombers flew over London to emphasise the strength of the alliance between Britain and France, but it also hinted at things to come. Recording the scene proved challenging, if not impossible, for photographers on the ground. The answer was to create a montage of two images in the darkroom at Kemsley House. But even this didn't quite work and the result was not published. The image does, however, give an impression of the fear of bomber fleets extant in 1939. People had seen in Abyssinia, China and Spain that Stanley Baldwin's prophesy that the bomber would always get through had been accurate. Events were unfolding quickly that would bring his nightmare vision to the British Isles. But that horror was a year away and other dramas would have to play out first. *Herbert Muggeridge/William Field [KN]*

In a much-weakened (and now hyphenated) Czecho-Slovakia the Munich Agreement and the First Vienna Award led the fall of the First Republic and the imposition of the Second with the unfortunate Emil Hácha as president. Adolf Hitler had turned his eyes to Poland where the status of Danzig was at the heart of his future plans, but he could not settle scores with Poland until the Czech situation was tidied up. Hitler coerced Father Jozef Tiso to declare Slovakian independence on 13 March 1939, leaving him in no doubt this was a take it or leave it offer. Slovakia could be free under German protection or else it would be swept up into the Third Reich. The Slovak Diet hurriedly agreed to independence the following day. German troops invaded the remaining Czech territories of Bohemia and Moravia on 15 March. Hungarian forces soon crushed any opposition when they took the Czech region of Carpatho-Ukraine. News of the German invasion soon reached Britain. *Alfred Harris [KN]*

The new Reichsprotektor of Bohemia and Moravia was Baron Konstantin von Neurath, pictured here with his wife Marie Auguste at the height of his diplomatic career. Neurath had been foreign minister before Joachim von Ribbentrop but was more of a nationalist than an ardent Nazi, keen to see Germany regain territories lost to Versailles. Nevertheless, he carried out repressive measures in the new protectorate and crushed opposition to Nazi rule. But Neurath was never seen as fully committed to his role and was superseded by the altogether unpleasant Reinhard Heydrich. Neurath was found guilty of war crimes in 1946 and sentenced to fifteen years' imprisonment. He was released from Spandau Prison in November 1954 and died in 1956.
William Horton [TT]

Neville Chamberlain vented his spleen at Adolf Hitler in a speech from Birmingham that was broadcasted around the world on 17 March. He went through the events of the past six months and was shocked at the perfidy of the Nazi regime. His anger was palpable, but Chamberlain finished with reassurance and a prescient warning for his audience at home and abroad: 'We need not be downhearted. This is a great and powerful nation – far more powerful than we were even six months ago, and acts of violence and injustice bring with them sooner or later their own reward. Every one of those incursions raises fresh dangers for Germany in the future, and I venture to prophesy that in the end she will bitterly regret what her Government has done.' Time would tell. The Munich Agreement was dead. *Edward Taylor [KN]*

The German ambassador to the Court of St James's, Herbert von Dirksen, was kept a very busy man shuttling to and fro between London and Berlin as Hitler's plan for the Czechs came to fruition. Dirksen attempted to excuse anti-British rhetoric in the German press but he failed to convince Lord Halifax. The British were at the beginning of making an accommodation with Poland and Halifax sought to convince Dirksen that despite the beliefs of his boss, von Ribbentrop, the British meant business. *Alfred Harris [KN]*

There could be no doubt that German attitudes were hardening. Nazi propaganda was working hard to denigrate the British press. The position of *The Times* as the 'establishment' newspaper caused it to come in for particular attention. This jigsaw was one item from a sustained campaign against the paper, sending a clear message that the Thunderer was part of an international Jewish conspiracy. *News UK Archive*

A young Jewish girl sits on her luggage after arriving at Antwerp aboard the German liner MS St Louis in June 1939. The 937 passengers had attempted to find sanctuary in the USA and Canada without success, although a few were allowed to stay in Cuba before the liner returned to Europe.
The decision to refuse them entry would prove particularly embarrassing for the United States, who made a formal apology in 2012. *M. Fryszman [KN]*

The remainder were found homes in Belgium, France, the Netherlands and Britain. This group pictured at Waterloo station were among 287 who arrived at Southampton aboard the *Rhakotis* on 21 June. Around a quarter of the refugees aboard St Louis died during the Holocaust after the Nazis conquered Western Europe. *Alfred Harris [KN]*

5

A BITTER BLOW

....

THE 1,000-year-old city port of Danzig had witnessed centuries of conflict amid the comings and goings of Poles, Pomeranians and Prussians since it received its charter from the Teutonic Knights in 1263. The city had long enjoyed a special status reflecting its cultural mix of German and Polish citizenry. There had been harmony even after Danzig was absorbed by Prussia following the defeat of Napoleon. But the Poles were determined to build a lasting nation state with Danzig, nowadays Gdańsk, as its primary ocean port. A century later they saw their opportunity fall within their grasp when their aspirations were advanced by the demand for a Polish state listed in Woodrow Wilson's Fourteen Points. The dream became reality when a new republic was founded amid disarray in Germany and Russia at the end of 1918, but there was hard fighting to do before they could secure their infant republic. A succession of conflicts followed with the Poles fighting Ukrainians, Lithuanians, Russians, Germans and Czechs for their independence. Their greatest victory came in 1920 at the Battle of Warsaw when a Soviet army was defeated by Józef Pilsudski, signalling the end of Lenin's plan to deliver Bolshevik revolution across Europe on the bayonets of Russia's armies.

Independence was hard won and to be treasured, but there was a fly in the ointment regarding the status of Danzig. With Germans forming the majority living in the city and its environs, delegates in Paris fudged the issue of sovereignty and agreed to reform Danzig as a Free City separate from the German territory of East Prussia, but in a customs union with Poland. The status of the city was guaranteed by the League of Nations protecting the rights of the German populace while recognising the position of the Poles. It was a far from ideal situation reflecting the muddled decision making incorporated into the Treaty of Versailles. The city would remain a permanent thorn in German-Polish relations, contributing to a sense of belligerence in the Polish establishment. The situation was set to worsen in 1933 when local Nazis came to power in Danzig and began supressing political rivals and Jews. They were a long way from the spirit of the Teutonic Knights whose motto was 'Help, Defend, Heal'. Having long since relinquished their military arm, the knights' charitable wing was banned by a suspicious Hitler in 1938.

Below: The Spitfires of No 65 Squadron at RAF Hornchurch.
Edward Taylor [KN]

The Polish foreign minister Józef Beck had secured a non-aggression pact with Russia, but a similar arrangement with Germany signed in 1934 did not stop the Nazis from pressuring Warsaw for the return of territory lost under the terms of Versailles. Despite Hitler's claims that the acquisition of Czechoslovakia was the last of his territorial demands, he held strong ambitions to recover the lands awarded to Poland and saw the country as a means of providing *lebensraum*, living space for the fast-growing German populace to expand into. While Danzig was very much a German city in terms of its character, Poles were in the ascendant in the all-important Corridor taken away by Versailles after so many Germans had moved west in the aftermath of the Great War. But just as he had been with the Czechs, Hitler was quite unconcerned with such realities and whatever the injustices of Danzig's placement within Poland, the city was no more than a convenient focal point for his wider aims.

Having consolidated their republic after a series of costly wars the Poles refused to roll over. The country continued to endure tricky relations with her other neighbours amid antagonism over the rights of Polish minorities, and these helped encourage the ruling faction to jump on the bandwagon during the dissection of Czechoslovakia in 1938. Being sandwiched between Germany and Russia gave the Poles a strong sense of isolation, but they were not the only country harbouring concerns about powerful neighbours. The Romanian Plenipotentiary in London, Viorel Tilea, claimed the Germans had demanded control of all Romanian exports and were massing forces in preparation to invade. This all proved to be untrue and fears of Hungarian aggression were more pressing, but the claim set hearts fluttering in London and Paris with a sudden rush to set in place guarantees for the security of Greece, Romania and eventually Turkey.

But the real impact was on relations with Poland and Anglo-French commitment to the country in case of war. For the Chamberlain government, the issue of the Danzig Corridor and Polish sovereignty offered the chance to act tough. While the Prime Minister remained committed to coming to an understanding with Hitler, it was clear that a hardening of Britain's stance was necessary and this may well have been encouraged by the efforts of the future *General der Panzertruppe* Gerhard von Schwerin, who used his position in the German Embassy in London to approach the British with the proposition that tangible Anglo-French support for Poland would stimulate support for an anti-Nazi coup within the *Wehrmacht*. With this and much more in mind, Britain and France gave Poland an assurance of their full support in case of a threat to the country's independence on 31 March, and this was confirmed during the visit of Józef Beck to London within the week. The assurance would be followed up by negotiations to secure a formal arrangement between the countries. In response, Hitler tore up the German-Polish Non-Aggression Pact and the 1935 London Naval Agreement which Chamberlain had been so keen to see supported at Munich.

The German dispute with Poland rumbled on and there was no sign of a peaceful solution. Nevertheless, *The Times* of 4 May reminded its readers that the Poles were keen to negotiate but 'The difficulty is that the mere word negotiation has become distasteful to the present leaders of Germany, who are in danger of driving Europe back to the violent methods of earlier epochs.' The paper was firm: 'Danzig is really not worth a war.'

The Chamberlain administration also had to contend with a bellicose Mussolini, who launched his invasion of Albania on 7 April. Although Britain and Italy appeared to have patched up differences over Spain and Abyssinia, amongst other disputes, with the signing of the Anglo-Italian Agreement of April 1938, long-standing tensions powered by Italy's descent into fascism were about to come to a head.

Britain and France had sought to keep Italy onside in their manoeuvring to hem in Nazi Germany and it seemed that Italian interest in the affairs of Austria would keep the former allies together. But Italian grievances were fed by any slight detected by a suspicious leadership who felt they were treated as the poor relation by powerful democracies who had once been equal partners in victory over the Central Powers. Mussolini and his supporters had a chip on their shoulder against Britain and France and were drawn into an alliance with Germany, even though some leading fascists, including Balbo, were convinced Hitler would drag them into a ruinous war.

Germany and Italy formed their alliance, the Pact of Steel, on 22 May 1939. One person celebrating was Count Dino Grandi, the Italian ambassador to London, an ardent fascist (but anti-German) who had been with Mussolini from the beginning. Grandi had enjoyed the influential role he held in London's diplomatic circles, where he had several affairs with aristocratic ladies. But his loathing for the dilettante democracies was thinly disguised and he let rip in a speech when the pact with Germany was signed. He spoke of a 'midsummer madness' in Europe where the democracies – Britain and France – were trying 'to save old injustices by the help of new mistakes and new presumptions' revealing 'the rabid impotence of our adversaries, and betrayed once again the spirit of intentions which guide the political action of the two democracies.'

> Twenty years since Versailles had taught Italians who were their real enemies. Twenty years of presumptuous injustice. Twenty years of obstinate denial of our right to live… The muddling, petty politicians of Versailles and Geneva having defrauded us of our victory in 1919, attempted in 1935 by means of sanctions, by a siege which was supposed to be economic but was in fact a real war to strangle Italy and her future as a nation.

Lines had been drawn.

In Britain spring gave way to summer amid the usual mix of traditional sporting and social events. Portsmouth played up to the Pompey Chimes to thump Wolves four goals to one in the FA Cup Final at Wembley. The promising Blue Peter won the 2,000 Guineas and the Epsom Derby in a stellar year of four major wins but the war ended his career. Sporting glory aside, of far more significance was the month-long tour of Canada and the United States made by King George VI and Queen Elizabeth. The king and queen had been able to put the recent torrid past of the House of Windsor to rest and were proving extremely popular. Their extensive tour emphasised the status of Canada and served to bolster confidence in Britain at a crucial time.

The week spent in the United States was especially important as the royal couple won over hardened American media commentators and influential politicians. Michael Burn of *The Times*, one of the paper's younger talents, held a different perspective to many of his older colleagues and was no fan of Geoffrey Dawson's support for appeasement. His time spent reporting on the tour was an education and he was able to recall the wave of enthusiasm in the USA for the king and queen when he reflected on Munich and the last months of peace from the confinement of Colditz, where he languished after being captured during the commando raid on St Nazaire in 1942. Despite the serious damage caused by Munich, the British were beginning to convince wavering friends abroad that they might just mean business and fight, but attempts to avert disaster continued.

If the position of the Soviet Union appears to be peripheral throughout much of the story told in this book, it is as much a consequence of a total lack of photographic coverage of events in the USSR from *The Times* and Kemsley photographers as it is the state of relations between London and Moscow during the rule of Joseph Stalin. Mutual suspicion abounded between the two countries but they shared a common interest in limiting the ambitions of Nazi Germany.

In April 1939 the British and French began negotiating a mutual assistance agreement with Russia, but the protracted series of discussions were hampered by the inability of the western negotiators to make any independent decisions without the need for constant referral to their political masters at home. There were sticking points relating to Russia's neighbours, the Baltic States and Finland, and how those countries might react to overtures from Berlin. Although the basis for an accord was reached relatively quickly, there was just too much fine print for a rapid settlement. The British and French had different perspectives on what they wanted from an alliance and this, too, impacted on the discussions. To Moscow it suggested a lack of intent and it became increasingly clear an agreement was unlikely to be achieved.

The situation was exacerbated by the fall from grace of Maxim Litvinov, the People's Commissar for Foreign Affairs, at a time when Stalin's heightened paranoia had fuelled a succession of bloody purges of political and military figures. Litvinov was seen as being in favour of improved relations with the West and had secured membership of the League of Nations and recognition of the USSR from the United States. His dismissal on 3 May 1939 saw the appointment of Vyacheslav Molotov, a tough cookie more inclined towards rapprochement with the Nazis than the collective security offered by untrustworthy imperialists. Litvinov also happened to be a Jew, a factor that drew scorn from the Nazis, so his removal opened doors for secret discussions between Moscow and Berlin.

Notions that the USSR could achieve a better deal from the Nazis were encouraged by Berlin. The two countries were no strangers to secret protocols going back to the 1920s, when the Russians offered the Germans military training facilities out of sight of Western powers. So, while Anglo-French military negotiators continued discussions with the Russians, the conditions had arisen for something wholly more precipitous for Europe to take place. In fact, Erich Kordt, Joachim von Ribbentrop's chief-of-staff and a resolute anti-Nazi, used a convenient channel to warn the British negotiations were already under way between Berlin and Moscow. Kordt's equally committed brother, Theodor, was Chargé d'Affaires at the German embassy in London, where he played a vital role in keeping British officials up to date with developments.

Providing a decisive intervention in the crisis could be the making of a political career and there was a brief moment when

Robert Hudson, Britain's Minister for Overseas Trade, must have thought he'd done just that when he briefed selected journalists about a potentially game-changing proposal. Hudson had attended meetings with Dr Helmut Wohlthat from Hermann Goering's Four Year Plan organisation, from which his notes revealed the suggestion Britain would loan the Germans upwards on £100 million in exchange for a commitment to disarm, along with other concessions. Hudson's glee over his coup was short-lived. Disgust that the Chamberlain government would consider such a blatant bribe was not confined to domestic opponents alone and even the Germans were scathing in their response. Chamberlain was forced to tell the House that Hudson's plan was his own and not the policy of His Majesty's Government (*The Times* 25.07.1939). Hudson would do an efficient job serving as agriculture minister during the war to come.

Even as Chamberlain worked for peace, a mixed bag of aristocrats and newspaper proprietors were busy running initiatives of their own. Lord Kemsley, owner of *The Sunday Times* and *Daily Sketch*, amongst others, achieved an audience with Adolf Hitler on 27 July. For someone not afraid of a bit of publicity, Kemsley remained fairly reticent and his papers did not publish any photographs of the meeting. Hitler seemed amenable to Kemsley's suggestion that he should list his demands to remove any doubts, but, of course, the press baron was blissfully unaware that instructions to implement Fall Weiss (Plan White) – the invasion of Poland by no later than 1 September 1939 – had already been issued.

Fears grew that the war Neville Chamberlain had done so much to avert was now imminent. Winston Churchill told his American radio audience on 9 August that 'The hush hanging over Europe was one of suspense – in many lands it was the hush of fear.' But it all depended on the will of one man. 'If Herr Hitler does not make war there will be no war. No one else is going to make war.' But it was right to look ahead to a time when better human relations would 'bring to an end this hideous insanity, which will let the working and creative forces get on with their job, and which will no longer leave the whole life of mankind dependent upon the virtues, the caprice, or the wickedness of a single man.'

In Australia the Minister for External Affairs, Sir Henry Gullett, warned his countrymen that they faced critical days and that war 'on a scale without precedent' could break out at any moment. German pressure on Poland to give up the Danzig Corridor intensified and Mussolini joined in, telling Warsaw 'to come to terms with Germany before it is too late.' Chamberlain and Halifax had escaped to their country retreats for some respite but there was little to be had. In Berlin the British ambassador, Sir Nevile Henderson, reaffirmed that Britain and France would stand by their obligations, but there was bad news to come.

On 22 August, the day after negotiations between Britain, France and Russia had finally broken down, it was announced that the slippery Joachim von Ribbentrop would visit Moscow. Within two days of this revelation the Nazis and Soviet Russia signed a ten-year non-aggression pact. To the outside world it presented the chimera of Soviet neutrality amid growing tensions in Europe. There was no escaping the open hostility between competing ideologies but, on the surface, this was set aside by Berlin and Moscow, who, behind the diplomatic niceties of the pact, had agreed a secret protocol the Soviets only admitted to as late as 1989. The two sides marked out spheres of influence for Stalin and Hitler in Central Europe.

At the heart of this was Poland, which was to be divided between the two countries. Estonia, Latvia and parts of Finland and Romania were to go to the Soviet Union. Lithuania would eventually be shared.

To call the pact a coup for Hitler would be an understatement. In one fell swoop he had removed the spectacle of conflict on two fronts, a deciding factor in the course of the Great War. Adolf Hitler had every intention of waging war on the Russians at a time of his own choosing. The sense of alarm in London and Paris, quite apart from Warsaw, was intense. The news was treated with dismay in Tokyo, where Germany's Japanese allies were still reeling from defeat in a border war with Russia.

There was jubilation in Berlin and all the while the Germans repeated the propaganda methods used against the Czechs, filling the press with make-believe stories of Polish atrocities and showing tearful 'refugees' fleeing the border region. None of it impressed *The Times* but it served to illustrate that Hitler meant business.

While Nazi suspicion of the British press was ever present, the authority of *The Times* gave the paper access to people in the know:

> One matter which must be set aside first, in the German view, and which will be settled within a few days is the future of Poland. It is stated as a bald fact by well-informed Germans that Poland in its present form will have ceased to exist in a short time.

How right they were:

> It is said that a 'conquered Poland' fully independent, but comprising perhaps some 15,000,000 Poles, would be allowed to survive, but Germany will regain all that ever belonged to her from Danzig to Upper Silesia; and there are hints that Russia may also have her share of the spoils.

The well-placed Germans speaking to *The Times* knew their stuff and went further:

> It remains to be seen whether there is a statesman in England strong enough to help inaugurate a new period of peace by admitting Germany's hegemony on the Continent in return for a similar recognition by the Reich of the paramount position of Great Britain in the rest of the world.

The British response to the Nazi-Soviet pact was immediate. Four months since the beginning of discussions, the mutual assistance agreement with Poland was finally concluded on 25 August 1939, guaranteeing British and French military support for Poland if she was attacked by any of her neighbours. German aggression was certain, but the Western powers now also had to consider Stalin. One immediate effect of Britain's pact with Poland was to make Hitler postpone his invasion plans by as much as a week while he considered his options. The British action had been unexpected, but any sort of wobble suffered by Hitler was purely temporary.

However unwelcome news of the agreement between London and Warsaw was for Hitler, current German opinion voiced to *The Times* was fuelled by the consistent misreading of the British by Joachim von Ribbentrop, who made a fateful error of judgement. 'It is firmly believed that England will not fight for such a "lost cause" as Poland is now held to represent.'

Meanwhile, the Swedish businessman Johan Birger Dahlerus was busy attempting to play the middleman between his old acquaintance Hermann Goering and the British. Dahlerus was seen as something of a naïve amateur, while his efforts to convince the Germans that the British really did mean business never sank in. He spoke with a number of British businessmen before meeting with Chamberlain and Lord Halifax as he carried out his own version of shuttle diplomacy.

Dahlerus' efforts foundered on the disastrous misconceptions of Joachim von Ribbentrop, who would not be swayed from his belief that the British would cave in, a view that it appears was not held by a more realistic Hermann Goering. While it was correct to say England had 'never been anxious to go to war', the German belief that Britain would not honour her guarantee to Poland was wide of the mark. For the Germans the guarantee was of no practical help to Poland, and in this respect they were absolutely right, but the longer-term consequences of it would prove ruinous for the Thousand-Year Reich.

Franklin Roosevelt appealed to Hitler to take a step back 'in the hope that the war which impends and the consequent disaster to all peoples may be averted.'

He suggested three courses of action to settle the crisis – direct negotiation, the use of arbitration, or by using the services of a conciliator from one of the neutral American republics with no connection to European politics. He reminded Hitler that the people of the United States were 'opposed to policies of military conquest and domination.' They could not accept the right of 'any ruler or people' to take actions that plunged the world into a disastrous war, bringing 'distress and suffering to every nation of the world.'

> I appeal to you in the name of the people of the United States, and I believe in the name of peace-loving men and women everywhere, to agree to a solution of the controversies existing between your Government and Poland…

Hitler ignored him.

Rudolf Hess went on the radio to describe Neville Chamberlain as a 'blind old idiot bound to an impossible policy and led by the nose by Jewish financiers.' He trotted out typical Nazi rhetoric when he blamed Britain for the crisis by backing Polish aggression. 'She would be sacrificing millions of soldiers if she supported Poland and the international ring of Freemasons.'

Roosevelt tried again, telling the Germans that Poland had agreed to direct negotiations over the fate of the Danzig Corridor. 'All the world prays that Germany, too, will accept.' The French agreed, but on 27 August Hitler rebuffed their efforts to broker negotiations. He blamed Britain and said he:

> Would regret it if fate should decree a conflict between Germany and France. But there would be this difference – that Germany would be fighting for reparation of an injustice, while France would be fighting for its preservation. The severest consequences would have to be borne by Poland, for no matter what the outcome of a war would be the Polish state would be lost either way.

As he had already decided on war, his efforts to blame everyone else for a situation he created can only be seen as a cynical manipulation.

German preparations continued. The pre-dreadnought battleship *Schleswig-Holstein* breezed into the port of Danzig on a goodwill visit during the last week of August. Outwardly her visit was not unlike those she had made to Falmouth when accordion-playing sailors had looked so attractive through the viewfinder of Kemsley man Dermot Fitzgerald's camera. A veteran of the Battle of Jutland and a rare survivor of the Kaiser's High Seas Fleet, she was now a training ship, but she retained her four 240mm guns supplemented by ten more of 150mm calibre. Her magazines were full.

That same week elements the 7th Battalion of the Royal Berkshire Regiment were at Wannock Camp near Eastbourne, where militiamen were enjoying hot days of drill and typical army bullshit. 'A' Company won the Drill Cup and the victors posed for a group photo. The author's father stands near the back. But it wasn't all fun and games. Private Alister Barnes received a telegrammed broadside from his father, Gordon, a marine engineer with the Blue Star Line and a veteran of the Dardanelles campaign of 1915. The prevailing crisis in Europe and Alister's uncommunicative absence combined to worry his mother back home in Stoke Newington. His father, a no-nonsense bloke with little time for trivialities, had had enough of her complaining so he tracked down his errant son and laid down the law. Alister wrote to assure his mother there was absolutely nothing to worry about. Meanwhile, a million-strong army of sixty German divisions supported by over 2,500 tanks were getting into position.

New emergency powers came into effect on 28 August as Britain prepared for war. In Berlin, Sir Nevile Henderson spent time with Hitler attempting to convince him of his country's determination to support Poland no matter what. In Poland there was a deep sense of pessimism that war could be averted. The government began evacuating people from towns close to the German border as air-raid drills took place in Warsaw. British merchant shipping was ordered to steer clear of the Baltic and the Mediterranean by the Admiralty.

Sir Nevile Henderson met with von Ribbentrop on the 29th, where he was presented with a verbal list of sixteen points the Germans demanded be agreed by Poland to avert war. The meeting did not go well. Ribbentrop refused to provide a written list and Henderson went away without getting all the points down on paper. Fortunately, clarity was restored by Goering, who gave a document containing the sixteen points to his friend Birger Dahlerus for delivery to the struggling Henderson.

Meanwhile, both the Dutch and the Belgians made a last-minute push for peace, offering to mediate, but war was now just two days away. All along the Polish border the Germans were busy manufacturing incidents designed to place the blame on Poland for the dire situation. German troops moved into Slovakia to 'protect' the country as the mobilization of Polish forces progressed.

On the evening of 31 August German radio broadcasted the sixteen points on the spurious grounds of seeking a path to settle the dispute. A report of it appeared in *The Times* the following morning, but by then it was strictly old news. At 0447hrs on 1 September the grand old *Schleswig-Holstein* commenced the bombardment of Polish fortifications at Westerplatte. The first shots of the Second World War had been fired.

Mobilization of Britain's armed forces was well in hand and it took an old soldier like Major-General Sir Frederick Maurice, president of the British Legion, to lay it on the line when he used a radio broadcast to warn Germany what lay ahead:

In 1914 you expected to have a quick victory over France. It was we British who helped to prevent that. Speaking as a soldier of experience, I say that it is a vain dream that if you force war upon us it will be a short war. It will be a war which will mean utter exhaustion to you. We are now much stronger than we were in 1914.

That remained to be seen.

War had come, but even as German forces launched their assault the Poles continued to offer direct negotiations on the question of German territorial demands. They were rebuffed. Hopelessly outclassed on land and in the air the Poles would put up a brave fight, but the apogee of Stalin's pact with the Nazis was just a fortnight away. Soviet forces were already preparing for their own invasion.

In the House of Commons, a disappointed Neville Chamberlain rose to respond to the news from Poland;

Eighteen months ago in this House I prayed that the responsibility might not fall upon me to ask this country to accept the awful arbitrament of war. I fear that I may not be able to avoid that responsibility. But at any rate I cannot wish for conditions in which such a burden should fall upon me clearer than they are today as to where my duty lies. No man can say that the Government could have done more to try to keep open the way for a honourable and equitable settlement of the dispute between Germany and Poland. Nor have we neglected any means of making it crystal clear to the German Government that if they insisted on using force again in the manner in which they have used it in the past we were resolved to oppose them by force. We shall stand at the bar of history knowing the responsibility for this terrible catastrophe lies on the shoulders of one man – the German Chancellor, who has not hesitated to plunge the world into misery in order to serve his own senseless ambitions.

... It now only remains for us to set our teeth and to enter upon this struggle, which we ourselves earnestly endeavoured to avoid, with determination to see it through to the end. We shall enter it with a clear conscience with the support of the Dominions and the British Empire and the moral approval of the greater part of the world. We have no quarrel with the German people except that they allow themselves to be governed by a Nazi Government. So long as that Government exists and pursues the methods it has persistently followed during the last two years there will be no peace in Europe.

A full programme of Football League matches took place in England on 2 September after the government signalled the game would face none of the opprobrium heaped upon it for carrying on in August 1914. Nevertheless, there was less of an appetite for soccer than usual as the crowds stayed away in light of the worsening news. Arsenal beat Sunderland 5-2 and Charlton Athletic were too strong for Manchester United, enjoying a 2-0 victory. In the Third Division Bournemouth & Boscombe Athletic put ten goals past Northampton Town. But it all came to nothing for the season was cancelled in view of what was to follow and the results were expunged from the record.

Air-raid precautions were set in train and the blackout was imposed on Britain's cities. It would be a long time before the lights would go on again. The blackout claimed an early victim when the journalist Geoffrey Swaffer was killed when the car he was travelling in collided with a London tram.

In the flurry of activity that followed the German invasion, serious doubts emerged that the Chamberlain government and the French would actually honour their guarantee to Poland. The British issued a warning to Hitler to cease his offensive to avoid war between the two countries, but there was no clear deadline and there was a growing sense that, despite all the fine words, both Britain and France were looking for a way out. The atmosphere in the House of Commons on 2 September was electric as the Prime Minister spoke of an Italian suggestion for a five-power conference to discuss the situation, but the British would not take part while German forces continued their assault. London and Paris were dithering over the time limit to be set for the Germans to stop the invasion and people on both sides of the House were distinctly unimpressed.

In Clement Attlee's absence it was the Labour deputy leader, Arthur Greenwood, who rose in response and he was met with cries of 'What about Britain?' and 'Speak for the working classes', but it was Leo Amery's demand of 'Speak for England, Arthur!' that has gone down in history. Greenwood did not disappoint.

There is a growing feeling, I believe, in all quarters of the House that this incessant strain must end sooner or later, and, in a sense, the sooner the better. But if we are to march, I hope we shall march in complete unity and march with France.

… I speak what is in my heart at this moment. I am gravely disturbed. An act of aggression took place 38 hours ago. The moment that act of aggression took place one of the most important treaties of modern times automatically came into operation.

There may be reasons why instant action was not taken… and I wonder how long we are prepared to vacillate at a time when Britain, and all that Britain stands for, and human civilization are in peril. We must march with the French… I do not believe that the French would dare, or would dream, at this juncture, of going back on the sacred oaths that they have taken.

… Every minute's delay now means the loss of life, imperilling our national interests—

At this point Robert Boothby interrupted, calling out 'Honour!' but Greenwood kept his poise:

I was about to say imperilling the very foundations of our national honour… and I hope that tomorrow morning… we shall know the mind of the British Government, that there shall be no more devices for dragging out what has been dragged out too long. The moment we look like weakening, on that moment dictatorship knows we are beaten. We are not beaten. We shall not be beaten.

At 1100hrs on the morning of Sunday, 3 September 1939, Britain declared war on Germany. Honour had been preserved but Poland would not be saved.

In his broadcast to the nation at 1115hrs Neville Chamberlain could not hide his disappointment.

You can imagine what a bitter blow it is to me that all my long struggle to win peace has failed. Yet I cannot believe that there is anything more or anything different that I could have done and that would have been more successful. Up to the very last it would have been quite possible to have arranged a peaceful and honourable settlement between Germany and Poland, but Hitler would not have it.

In a busy year of alliances and agreements the Pact of Steel between Germany and Italy was signed on 22 May, cementing relations between the fascist powers as their belligerence towards Britain and France continued to mount. One of the champions of the pact was the bellicose Count Dino Grandi, who had joined the Blackshirts in the early days of the fascist movement and had become a leading member of Mussolini's government. Grandi became Italian ambassador to the UK in 1932 and enjoyed a position of influence within the diplomatic circle. He had an eye for the ladies, sharing one mistress, Lady Alexandra Curzon, with her brother-in-law, Oswald Mosley. As much as he favoured the alliance with Germany, Grandi did not want Italy to go to war with Britain and France and his influence waned. He led moves to overthrow Mussolini after the Allied invasion of Sicily in 1943 and lived a life of exile after the collapse of fascism in Italy. He died in 1988. He is pictured during a pleasant afternoon at Claridge's. *Edward Taylor [KN]*

Speaking of Adolf Hitler, Chamberlain faced up to the awful reality: 'His action shows convincingly that there is no chance of expecting that this man will ever give up his practice of using force to gain his will. He can only be stopped by force.'

The time for talking was over.

We and France are today, in fulfilment of our obligations, going to the aid of Poland, who is so bravely resisting this wicked and unprovoked attack on her people. We have a clear conscience. We have done all that any country could do to establish peace. The situation in which no word given by Germany's ruler could be trusted and no people or country could feel themselves safe has become intolerable. And now that we have resolved to finish it, I know that you will all play your part with calmness and courage.

Winston Churchill warned:

We must not underrate the gravity of the task which lies before us, or the severity of the ordeal to which we shall not be found unequal… If these great trials were to come upon our island, there is a generation of Britons here now ready to prove itself not unworthy of the days of yore and not unworthy of the great men, the fathers of our land, who laid the foundations of our laws and shaped the greatness of our country.

Neville Chamberlain's long effort to avert war had ended in failure. As the air-raid sirens sounded in London on the first day of the war he must have had some inkling his health was broken, but he would need all his strength to face the challenges to come in the months ahead.

Adolf Hitler had turned his attention to Poland and the free city of Danzig, along with the corridor of land linking it to the Third Reich. The Nazis had held power in the city for some time where Germans were in the clear majority. The Polish government were no less comfortable with the situation that left a German thorn in their side, but poor relations with all their neighbours had not made them many friends. London had come calling in the wake of Munich, and the possibility of an alliance that might dissuade Hitler from doing anything precipitous was inviting. The growing crisis was the latest to arise from the untidy decisions formalised at Versailles in 1919. Marshal Foch had predicted the treaty was little more than a twenty-year armistice and all this was about to come true as the summer unfolded. *[KN]*

Jittery elements of the Romanian establishment looked to Britain and France to guarantee the country's security in the face of pressure from Hungary and Nazi Germany. That Hitler coveted Romanian oil production was well understood but the country's mutual assistance pact with Poland was also a thorny matter in respect of relations with Berlin. Viorel Tilea, Romania's new envoy in London, created ripples when he claimed Germany had demanded exclusive access to Romanian exports while German forces were massing to invade, but his apparent moment of madness proved entirely unfounded. Tilea's motive for his actions remains uncertain but an attempt to upset Hungarian territorial ambitions is most likely. While Romania eventually succeeded in earning an admittedly futile guarantee from London and Paris, the real effect of Tilea's actions was to drum up support for an accord with Poland within the Chamberlain Cabinet. *William Field [KN]*

William Horton of *The Times* acted as official photographer on the tour of Canada made by King George VI and Queen Elizabeth. Their visit is recognised as being crucial in efforts to shore up support for Britain in the trials to come. Canada was vital to Britain in terms of manpower, raw materials and industrial output, but the country's growing stature as a nation in its own right contributed to doubts over following Britain into another conflict. The experience of the Great War caused some to question the quality of British military leadership, giving Canadian politicians good reasons to secure the power of a veto over how their countrymen and women would be employed if Canada joined in a future conflict. The king and queen were greeted warmly wherever they went. Seventy thousand people filled grandstands along Portage Avenue in Edmonton, Alberta, to cheer the royal motorcade on 2 June 1939. *William Horton [TT]*

Canada's vast natural resources were essential to the manufacture of munitions. Forty per cent of the nickel used in artillery shells produced by the Allies in the Second World War came from the International Nickel Company mine at Frood in Ontario. The king and queen were given a tour of the facility by general manager Donald MacAskill on 5 June. *William Horton [TT]*

The king's visit to the United States was of no less importance, where Britain's intention to stand firm against German militarism was impressed on sceptical US politicians and media commentators. The tour was a great success for the king and queen, but the behind the scenes conversations between the British and Americans mattered even more, however much this displeased isolationists. The royal party paid their respects at the tomb of George Washington at Mount Vernon on 9 June. President Franklin D. Roosevelt and the First Lady accompanied them. *William Horton [TT]*

The US Ambassador, Joseph Kennedy, supported appeasement and increasingly favoured American isolationism. Although he and his family had proved a hit with the British press and high society, doubts about his reliability would grow in London and Washington. The Nazis themselves appeared to misinterpret his position. A report in *The Times* quoting from *Der Angriff* described him as being 'Among the men who have driven England, step by step, into the front place against Germany.' He is pictured with his son Jack earlier in 1939. *Robert Chandler [KN]*

The deteriorating relations between Germany and Poland over Danzig and the British government's interest in making an assistance pact with the Poles found opponents on the left and right. Peace with honour was on the mind of Sir Oswald Mosley when he spoke at a rally held at Earls Court on 16 July, where people heard him speak for an hour without notes. *The Times* reported he told his audience that every member of the British Union of Fascists would fight for Britain if she were attacked, but on the other hand they wanted parties clamouring for war to know 'A million Britons will not die in your Jews' quarrel.' He presented a four-point plan for peace on the basis of 'live and let live' where the Germans would give up interest in Eastern Europe in exchange for Western European disarmament and the return of former German colonies. Britain should concentrate on the affairs of our 'shamefully neglected' empire. The event that had all the trappings of a Nazi rally, including flag and standard bearers accompanied by a uniformed band, was claimed to be the largest indoor political rally in British history with upwards on 30,000 people in attendance, but the true number was said to be lower. *Jack Kirby [KN]*

A busy summer of military exercises and training camps was under way. This would prove to be quite convenient for the three services when the government ordered mobilisation. These members of the Auxiliary Territorial Service are pictured about to board a train at Victoria station. *William Field [KN]*

Militiamen were continuing to take their first steps in uniform. The staff at Kemsley Newspapers were justly proud of their young colleagues going off to serve King and Country and the *Daily Sketch* made features of one of its own; Tom Sole of the Commercial Department. Robert Chandler took a series of images of him preparing to depart for his army training and during the first weeks with the Royal Berkshire Regiment at Reading. *Robert Chandler [KN]*

Tom Sole took to soldiering and had been promoted to corporal by the time the 4th Battalion of the Royal Berks were overwhelmed defending the Albert Canal during the *Blitzkrieg* of 1940. A good number of men were taken prisoner but 21-year old Corporal Thomas Edward Sole of Shoreditch was not among them. He was killed on 29 May 1940 and is buried at Zuidschote Churchyard in Belgium. *Robert Chandler [KN]*

Unlike Tom Sole the men seen here have yet to be issued with the new 1937 Pattern battledress that would replace the uniform that retained all the elements seen during the Great War. Quite a number of old sweats were sorry to see it go. Something that was happening was motorisation and the virtual end of horseflesh in British military service. The vehicles shown are typical products of Britain's motor industry; an Austin 7 field car, two Morris-Commercial CDF 30cwt lorries, a pair of newer 15cwt Morris CS8 trucks and a Norton 16H motorcycle. The conversion had been done at great expense but was seen to create a truly modern army. The picture shows reservists and vehicles of 74th (Yeomanry) Divisional Signals Company taking part in an anti-invasion exercise covering the south of England from Hampshire to Kent. The unit included a large number of London bus drivers and conductors. *Stanley Devon [KN]*

The author's father and his newfound friends were proud winners of the Drill Cup and enjoying life in the great outdoors at Wannock Camp near Eastbourne. Private Alister Barnes was a 20-year-old Militiaman serving with 'A' Company 7th (Stoke Newington) Battalion of the Royal Berkshire Regiment. He is in the third row from the back and eighth from the left. Alister's war was fought against disease. He contracted malaria in India and then tuberculosis. He came through it and retired at the end of an at times wayward life in newspapers in May 1984. He died in 1992. *Author's collection*

Militiamen were also serving in the Royal Navy. These men are on the march at Devonport. *Dermot Fitzgerald [KN]*

War clouds were forming. A Hurricane of No 111 Squadron sits in the late evening light at RAF Northolt during a conveniently prearranged air defence exercise. *Edward Taylor [KN]*

The fighters would need bombers to intercept. Wellingtons of No 214 Squadron provide the opposition. Temporary markings denoting 'Westland' have been painted over the RAF roundel. *Stanley Devon [KN]*

Below: It was all too much excitement for this navigator. *Stanley Devon [KN]*

That the drawn-out negotiations over an alliance between Britain, France and the Soviet Union came to nothing must have been as unsurprising as it was disappointing. Recent events saw London and Paris seek a way of hemming in the Germans and Moscow was keen, but there were too many impediments, not least the flat refusal of the Poles to allow Russian troops into their territory should hostilities between the projected triple alliance break out with Germany. Warsaw was convinced that once Soviet forces marched into the country, they would never leave. The battles of twenty years earlier were etched on their hearts and minds. Another key factor was the British failure to send a big-hitter to lead the negotiations, relying instead on the best efforts of ambassador Sir William Seeds who did not impress Stalin and his court. *Alfred Abrahams [KN]*

The Nazis were also talking to Moscow and a dramatic change in foreign policy leadership in May 1939 would pave the way for the Molotov-Ribbentrop Pact. Maxim Litvinov, the influential People's Commissar for Foreign Affairs since 1930, was both Jewish and in favour of good relations with Britain and France. He came in for sustained attacks from the German media who derided his Jewish background, seeing him as a hindrance to improved German-Soviet relations. Stalin saw an opportunity to remove Litvinov to give him freedom of action to negotiate with Berlin while talking to the British and French. Litvinov's sudden fall from grace on 3 May amid all the usual elements of paranoia within Stalin's court opened the way for Joachim von Ribbentrop to step in. Litvinov (left) is seen in London with Soviet ambassador Ivan Maisky in happier times. *Stanley Kessell [TT]*

Military discussions were also very important to Moscow. The Anglo-French military delegation headed for Russia on a ponderous sea journey at the beginning of August, but much to Soviet resentment the British group also lacked a top name with real power to make decisions. Admiral Sir Reginald Plunkett-Ernle-Erle-Drax (right) led the British Military Mission. He was an experienced staff officer and a veteran of the battles of Heligoland, Dogger Bank and Jutland. *The Times* said of him 'He has a mind at once sound and keen.' With him was Air Marshal Sir Charles Burnett (second right), 'a man of strong decisive mind, with a gift of saying in a few words exactly what he thinks.' Major-General Thomas Heywood (left), whom we saw earlier with General Gamelin, represented the army. He was a much-travelled linguist who spoke French and Russian. During the Great War he served in France, Macedonia, Serbia, Bulgaria, Egypt and Gallipoli. He was part of the British military delegation at Versailles. But all this experience and diplomatic skill would ultimately count for nothing. Ivan Maisky joined the British officers at St Pancras as they set out on their journey to Moscow. *Alfred Abrahams [KN]*

Winston Churchill had been a strident voice against appeasement and his nightmare was about to become reality. It seemed like a good moment to see just how strong the Maginot Line really was. What he saw gave him considerable cause for concern. However impregnable the system was meant to be, there were clear gaps in front of the Ardennes and the French border with Belgium was open. One German installation was so close to the French that they traded jibes using billboards. A *The Times* journalist accompanied Churchill on his tour but Jack Barker did not go. The ubiquitous Monsieur Fryszman got a picture of Churchill with his host General Alphonse Georges as they left Paris for Strasbourg. *M. Fryszman [KN]*

Meanwhile the British cinema industry was playing its part. *An Englishman's Home* was based on a Guy du Maurier play dating from before the Great War and told the story of an ordinary English home attacked by foreign invaders who were patently German but the script never identified a specific power. The film was made at Denham Studios and in this scene Edmund Gwenn and the Australian actress Mary Maguire are in trouble with men wearing what can best be described as an approximation of German uniform. The film was released in 1940, the same year Maguire's husband, Robert Gordon-Canning, was interned. A staunch anti-Semite, he was best man at the marriage of Sir Oswald Mosley and Diana Mitford at the home of Joseph Goebbels in 1936. *William Field [KN]*

Preparations for the blackout were carried out with a minimum of precision at some locations in London. This is the scene outside Verulam Buildings on Gray's Inn Road. *Alfred Harris [KN]*

'Britain is a nation prepared.' Everyone was ready to do their bit. *Robert Chandler [KN]*

An ecstatic overseas trade minister Robert Hudson believed he was the saviour of the planet at the end of July when he dreamt up his plan to entice the Germans with a £100m bribe if only they would be less belligerent towards their neighbours. While the windfall and a return of colonies forfeited at Versailles had some appeal, German diplomacy was already in pursuit of a much bigger prize to underpin Hitler's strategy. In any case, Neville Chamberlain would never countenance a deviation from his own script by a scene-stealing Hudson, whose plan would be quickly disavowed. *William Field [KN]*

The non-aggression pact between Germany and Russia signed on 23 August was a triumph for Joachim von Ribbentrop. On the surface it was all about trade and benign agreements, but secret protocols that would quietly embarrass the Russians for decades had carved up Central Europe between Hitler and Stalin, clearing the way for the German attack on Poland a week later. Stalin would launch his invasion on 17 September. Ribbentrop continued to believe the British would never go to war and dismissed the warning from Lord Halifax that Britain would stand by Poland passed to him by von Dirksen. *Stanley Kessell [TT]*

Two days later the British and Poles signed their mutual assistance agreement after months of discussions begun in the aftermath of the Germans marching into Prague. German pressure on the Poles to surrender Danzig and the Corridor was intense and although wonderful on paper, the new pact with Britain did not offer Warsaw much in the way of immediate military support if the Germans pounced. But, if honoured, it would mean that Germany faced war with Britain and, by extension, France. That Hitler knew all this and didn't care illustrates conclusively that he had only ever been set on war. Foreign Minister Józef Beck led negotiations with Britain. Poland was a country with few friends, being recognised as belligerent and anti-Semitic. The Poles had played games with many of their neighbours and had only recently joined in the dismemberment of Czechoslovakia. A deal with them did not meet with universal approval in Britain. Many politicians at home and abroad cordially disliked Beck but he was prepared to stand up to the Germans no matter what. Using the sort of language that appealed to the anti-appeasers in London, he said, 'Peace is a precious and desirable thing. Our generation, bloodied in wars, certainly deserves peace. But peace, like most things in this world, has its price… We in Poland do not know the concept of peace at any price. There is only one thing in the lives of men, nations and countries that is without price. That thing is honour.'
Geoffrey Keating [KN]

Parliament was recalled in the wake of what the press were now calling the Polish Crisis. Crowds began to congregate around the Palace of Westminster waiting to hear the latest developments or just hoping to see leading actors in the drama. *Stanley Devon [KN]*

Two of them were Britain's War minister, Leslie Hore-Belisha (centre) and Minister for Co-ordination of Defence, Lord Chatfield (left) who were pictured in Downing Street on 24 August by Bill Warhurst. Chatfield had predicted British failure to make an alliance with Russia and that country's subsequent engagement with Nazi Germany would be a 'Mistake of vital and far-reaching importance.' He wasn't wrong. *Bill Warhurst [TT]*

Anti-aircraft defences were being installed on 25 August. Gunners of 90th (Middlesex) Anti-Aircraft Regiment RA (TA) needed a lot of muscle to drag a 3in gun into place at Alexandra Palace. *Stanley Kessell [KN]*

'A Briton on a British gun. What finer type could be found? And need one try, for that matter?' Stanley Devon visited a number of air defence sites on 26 August to take images for an exclusive series by permission of the War Office that were published by the *Daily Sketch* accompanied by stirring captions two days later. Censorship was already taking a hand and no reference was made to units or locations. *Stanley Devon [KN]*

Territorials had been returning from camp but their time back in the civilian world would be brief. These Londoners have stopped on the road at Wisley on their way back from Dorset, much to the interest of a local gent and his dog. The man on the right is aiming a Boys Anti-Tank Rifle, a .55in calibre weapon approved for service in 1937. It was effective against thinly armoured vehicles. The rifle weighed 35lb (16kg) and its recoil was brutal, making it quite unpleasant to operate. *Robert Chandler [KN]*

Mobilisation was under way in France. Reservists were being called up in Paris. *M. Fryszman [KN]*

British and French diplomatic efforts continued to try to persuade Adolf Hitler to hold off from his threat to wage war on Poland. A series of carefully prepared deceptions purporting to show attacks on Germans by Polish police and border forces had given the Führer the pretext he needed, and the charade of Hitler appearing open to negotiation continued while German forces massed on the Polish frontier. Sir Nevile Henderson arrived at the Foreign Office in the late afternoon of Friday 26 August carrying the message from Adolf Hitler to Neville Chamberlain pretending to seek improved relations with Britain and preserve peace. *Robert Chandler [KN]*

Large crowds continued to gather along Whitehall and in Downing Street itself as the crisis reached its point of no return. These scenes are unthinkable in our modern world where security gates and armed police protect the Prime Minister's residence save for carefully managed occasions. *William Field [KN]*

A prankster took the opportunity to register his disapproval at all the voyeurism. The man threw a suitcase full of tennis balls into the crowd in Downing Street, causing a degree of panic. *Stanley Devon [KN]*

Adolf Hitler had only ever intended war, but Neville Chamberlain had little option but to try and bring the Germans to the negotiating table. Sir Nevile Henderson departs from Croydon to make a last attempt to dissuade Hitler from war. *Alfred Abrahams [KN]*

The strain on him was immense. *Failure of a Mission*, Henderson's account of the crisis published in 1940, offers a sanitised account of the Chamberlain government's dealings with Nazi Germany that is considered to be a whitewash. It was written while he continued a four-year battle with cancer that ended with his death, aged 60, on 30 December 1942. *Alfred Abrahams [KN]*

An air-raid shelter is dug in the communal area of an un-named block of council flats in London on 31 August. *Alfred Abrahams [KN]*

Grace under pressure! No matter what was happening, the Prime Minister would find time for a quiet walk in St James's Park with Mrs Chamberlain. They would head out across Horse Guards into the park followed by one or two minders. It provided a good opportunity to photograph a man with the world on his shoulders, but the scene illustrates the sense of calm that pervaded Chamberlain throughout the crisis. His efforts to ward off disaster were unceasing, but Hitler's generals had distributed their final orders and the charade of the Germans offering talks in a broadcast from Berlin on 31 August would create more false hope. *Robert Chandler [KN]*

'KEEP CALM – WAR IS NOT INEVITABLE' – Official. The *Daily Sketch* continued to pin faith in the efforts of the Prime Minister even as the evacuation of children from the capital was well in hand. 'These children will leave London today. Mother tells them to behave and not forget to fill up their printed cards saying they're safe. She knows, as you do, that on the word of Mr Chamberlain this does not mean war must come.' Mrs E. Rowsell of 75 Coldbath Mansions, Clerkenwell instructs her children Sylvia, 7, Lawrence, 5 and Sheila, 4, as they attend an evacuation rehearsal at Hugh Myddelton Primary School. *Geoffrey Keating [KN]*

The Deutschland class battleship *Schleswig-Holstein* was launched in 1906 but by the time she entered service she was made obsolete by the arrival of HMS *Dreadnought*. She was, nevertheless, kept on in the *Kaiserliche Marine* and was involved in several operations before attending the Battle of Jutland in 1916. She was flagship of the *Reichsmarine* in 1926 and became a training ship in Hitler's *Kriegsmarine*, although she retained a good part of her armament. This less than ideal image shows her on a visit to Falmouth in March 1938 ahead of her day of destiny firing the opening shots of the Second World War. *Schleswig-Holstein* was sent on a spurious goodwill visit to Danzig at the end of August but the real intention was for her to begin the bombardment of Polish positions, heralding the assault by German forces. She opened fire at 0447hrs on 1 September. *Dermot Fitzgerald [KN]*

News of the German attack made the early editions of the London evening papers, seen for sale at Clapham Common underground station. Bill Warhurst cannot resist a hint of a smile as he buys the *Evening Standard*. Eric Greenwood [TT]

King George VI called in on his Prime Minister to be briefed on the state of affairs and to offer encouragement on the day when Chamberlain's work unravelled. *Bill Warhurst [TT]*

'Speak for England, Arthur!' Leo Amery's demand of Arthur Greenwood set up the challenge to what many in the House saw as Chamberlain's prevarication when national honour was at stake. The opposition Labour benches were staunch anti-appeasers and the party had found little to approve in the government's dealings with the Poles, whose authoritarian leadership and widespread anti-Semitism were anathema to their ideals. But a line in the sand had been drawn and now it was time for Britain to live up to her agreement. Greenwood is seen on the right talking with Labour leader Clement Attlee. *Herbert Muggeridge [KN]*

'I am speaking to you from the Cabinet Room of 10 Downing Street. This morning the British Ambassador in Berlin handed the German Government a final Note stating that, unless we heard from them by 11 o'clock that they were prepared at once to withdraw their troops from Poland, a state of war would exist between us. I have to tell you now that no such undertaking has been received, and that consequently this country is at war with Germany… It is the evil things that we shall be fighting against – brute force, bad faith, injustice, oppression and persecution – and against them I am certain that the right will prevail.' – Neville Chamberlain. *Bill Warhurst [TT]*

Neville Chamberlain is pictured after his fateful broadcast to the nation. Behind him is his Parliamentary Private Secretary, Lord Dunglass, who as Alec Douglas-Home would serve as Prime Minister from 1963–64. Chamberlain now had the invidious task of leading the government through the first months of a war that would see a sequence of disasters in 1940. Divisions in the Conservative Party meant his replacement, Churchill, had the need to retain him in his first war cabinet. But by then Chamberlain was terminally ill and he would not live to see his conviction that the right would prevail come to pass. *Bill Warhurst [TT]*

The king's speech: HM King George VI speaking to Britain and the Empire in a formal photograph taken by William Horton. The photograph is nothing like the actual scene of the broadcast, where the king stood up in front of the microphone as he was prompted by his speech therapist Lionel Logue. Such a scene was never likely to be captured for public scrutiny. The king reached out to his audience, lamenting that war had come again, but he spoke firmly about the need for Britain to stand up to the threat of force, although he never mentioned Germany by name. 'The task will be hard,' he warned. 'There may be dark days ahead, and war can no longer be confined to the battlefield, but we can only do the right as we see the right, and reverently commit our cause to God.' *William Horton [TT]*

'War can no longer be confined to the battlefield…' The king's warning would prove to be prescient. An air-raid warning sent Londoners into the shelters and they would learn to get used to them as time progressed. *William Horton [TT]*

The king's proclamation ordering conscription of all men aged between 18 and 41 is read from the steps of the Royal Exchange in London. This scene was repeated in cities across the United Kingdom. *Edward Taylor [KN]*

Winston is back! Chamberlain appointed the coming man First Lord of the Admiralty in his first wartime cabinet. The three-word telegram announcing his arrival to the Fleet was sent just minutes after instructions to commence hostilities against Germany. The man himself strode across Horse Guards followed at a discreet distance by his bodyguard, Walter Thompson. The sinking of the liner *Athenia* by a U-boat a few hours into hostilities was the start of a battle that would cause him much anxiety amid so many other trials to come. *Bill Warhurst [TT]*

Below: The gathering storm had broken. War had come. To end this narrative here are some lines from Shakespeare's *King John* that summed up the mood of much of the country as the first day of a war so many Britons dreaded came to close. *[KN]*

O, let us pay the time but needful woe,
Since it hath been beforehand with our griefs.
This England never did, nor never shall,
Lie at the proud foot of a conqueror,
But when it first did help to wound itself.
Now these her princes are come home again,
Come the three corners of the world in arms,
And we shall shock them. Nought shall make us rue,
If England to itself do rest but true.

6

OUR HANDS ARE CLEAN

·······································

NEVILLE CHAMBERLAIN served in Winston Churchill's first wartime government as Lord President of the Council but stood down in October 1940 when his health failed. Even as his prodigious powers ebbed away, Chamberlain's most faithful supporters argued that the pursuit of peace through appeasement was worth every effort in its own right but in doing so the policy had given Britain time to prepare for war; thus creating the impression that appeasement and rearmament were in some way interconnected. It was an assertion that wilfully ignored their champion's long-established aversion to rearmament and his frequent obstruction of it.

'The prize was so infinitely precious that no humane statesman could, with due regard to his country's honour and interests, leave anything undone that might help in winning it,' wrote Lord Kemsley on 6 October 1940.

If the pursuit failed, if the prize eluded our grasp, we should, at any rate, be no worse off than before. We are indeed, far better off, for not only are the country's defences vastly stronger, but there is the intangible, immeasurable asset of moral prestige... If the worst comes to the worst, blood-guiltiness will not be with us. The whole world will know that our hands are clean.

And the whole world does know. The record is plain and unalterable that before Britain took up the sword her Government had used all honourable means to preserve the peace. Those efforts were pursued to the very last minute of hope. In that policy, which will forever be associated with his name, Mr Chamberlain was a faithful steward of British interests and honour.

Rightly or wrongly, the policy of appeasement was conducted to save Britain and Europe from the horror of another world war. Neville Chamberlain had been ruthless in pursuit of peace and his willingness to confront Hitler face to face should not be discounted in any assessment of his performance however misguided the policy he embraced is perceived to be. He died of cancer on 9 November 1940.

When paying tribute to him in the House of Commons three days later, Winston Churchill said:

'Whatever else history may or may not say about these terrible, tremendous years, we can be sure that Neville Chamberlain acted with perfect sincerity according to his lights and strove to the utmost of his capacity and authority, which were powerful, to save the world from the awful, devastating struggle in which we are now engaged. This alone will stand him in good stead as far as what is called the verdict of history is concerned.

PRESS GALLERY

THE STARS of this book are the photographers. The men shown here were responsible for the majority of the images we've seen. The collection holds portraits of a number of others, but the set is incomplete and in sharing this selection it cannot be emphasised enough that all the photographers whose work appears here are greatly admired today. Their legacy fills the News UK photographic archive and it has been an honour to be able to share their work through this book.

Alfred Abrahams was born in 1881 and joined the *Daily Graphic* in 1907. His long career came to an end when he suffered a stroke in 1950. He died in 1954. *[KN]*

An image made from the sole surviving negative of **Patrick Brown.** He took the superb images of British troops in the Rhineland featured in chapter one along with many other excellent photographs during his time with Allied and Kemsley. *[KN]*

Jack Barker was the son of the manager of *The Times* Paris office and began taking pictures for the paper in 1931 when he was just 17 years old. He served in the Army Film and Photographic Unit during the war and was a noted photographer of royalty after 1945. He died, aged 59, on 16 March 1973. *[TT]*

According to Stanley Devon, the popular **Robert Chandler**, who was born in 1899, had joined the Royal Naval Air Service as a 16 year old and he clearly thought highly of him. Bob moved on to the *News of the World* as head of the photography department in 1946 and although he officially retired in 1964, he was still there doing Saturday shifts until 1977. *Robert Field [KN]*

Ernest Victor Barton was noted for his work following Gandhi on his travels in India but his untimely death on 22 May 1932 occurred when he was covering another icon of the era in the shape of Amelia Earhart, when she made her solo transatlantic flight from Newfoundland to Ireland. Barton was returning by plane to London with his films but the aircraft crashed in heavy fog, killing him and the pilot, Major I.N.C. Clarke, DSC & Bar. *P. James [KN]*

Gerald Cook, seen here in 1936, had joined the *Daily Sketch* two years earlier. He covered some of the Spanish Civil War and grew a moustache that makes him look older in a slightly later portrait. He came back to Kemsley after war service and became news picture editor. He moved on in 1950. *J.W. Eggitt [KN]*

Reginald Coote – always Reggie to his colleagues – was a photographer who often helped out on the *Daily Sketch* picture desk assisting Tom Noble and later F.R. Donovan. Reggie encouraged Stanley Devon to move to the *Daily Sketch* from the Associated Press. He was an official photographer with the Royal Navy during the war, covering major events such as the Allied landings in French North Africa in 1943. *Gerald Cook [KN]*

William Field was better known as Billy and considered an expert horseracing photographer. He continued to work until he was 70 years old. *Jack Kirby [KN]*

The award-winning **Stanley Devon**, MBE, is pictured just as he was poached from the *Daily Sketch* by the Air Ministry to become an official photographer in October 1939. His work with the RAF during the Second World War was some of the finest of an exceptional career. His entertaining autobiography *Glorious* takes its title from the name given to Stan by wags he impressed with his skills and humour while in the RAF. *[KN]*

Dermot Fitzgerald moved from London to Plymouth, where he found regular work photographing the comings and goings of the Royal Navy during the 1930s. He provided a regular stream of negatives and prints to the *Daily Sketch* and joined the permanent staff just after the Second World War, but only stayed a year. He is pictured here in 1935. *Alfred Harris [KN]*

Born in 1890, **F.R. Donovan** had been based in Paris from 1927, where he covered a number of events seen in this book. He returned to London in 1936 and eventually became night picture editor of the *Daily Sketch*. *Robert Chandler [KN]*

Eric Greenwood joined *The Times* in 1921, progressing via the picture library and darkroom to become a photographer in 1927. He was adept with Autochrome stock, taking notable colour images of the Royal Family, including King George V making his Christmas radio broadcast in 1934. He covered major events during the war, including the Battle of Britain, the Blitz and the D-Day landings. He also took a variety of much admired images on VE Day. He enjoyed a busy and varied career after the war and retired in 1966. *[TT]*

The earliest work of **Robert Field** found in the News UK archive dates from the end of the Great War. He was still busy at the start of hostilities in September 1939. He was a typically versatile photographer who covered a wide range of subjects. *[KN]*

Alfred Harris pictured in the Photographers Room in January 1937. Like many snappers of the period, he began his career working in the darkroom before moving up to be a photographer in 1934. He retired in 1971. *[KN]*

William Horton joined *The Times* in 1926 and secured a strong reputation as a landscape specialist. He was much favoured for his discretion by the royal family and was official photographer to HM King George VI on his pivotal tour of Canada and the United States in 1939. He got into uniform at the start of the war and became an official photographer to Winston Churchill. His notable post-war work included coverage of Roger Bannister breaking the four-minute mile in 1954. He died, aged 67, in May 1961. *[TT]*

Robert Chandler took this generic image of a press photographer for the *Sunday Graphic* in July 1939. The process of elimination suggests the model was **Charles Maxwell**, for whom no portrait images survive in the News UK collection. He was killed while on Home Guard duty on 24 September 1940 during the air raid that did much damage to Kemsley House and the company's glass plate collection in particular. *Robert Chandler [KN]*

Born in 1914, **Geoffrey Keating**, MC, was a much-travelled photographer and soldier who was an early member of the Army Film and Photographic Unit during the Second World War. He was instrumental in creating publicity for the rising star 'Monty' – Lieutenant General Bernard Montgomery. He took some of the best-known images of him from the war. Geoffrey was wounded in action on several occasions and awarded the Military Cross in 1942. He worked for BP after the war and died in 1981 aged just 66. *[KN]*

Herbert Muggeridge pictured in 1938. He enjoyed a busy career but the heavy demands of working through the Second World War with so many other photographers away contributed to his untimely death in 1948. *[KN]*

Cathal O'Gorman followed the traditional route moving from the darkroom to behind the camera. He developed a reputation as a first-class aviation photographer capable of getting superb air-to-air pictures. He survived a flying bomb hitting his home in 1944 that killed his wife and other family members. Although he struggled with the aftermath for the rest of his life, *The Times* stood by him and he continued to produce excellent work until his retirement in October 1968. This image was taken in 1934. *[TT]*

Stanley Hedley Kessell came from a Cornish family. He joined *The Times* in 1924 and enjoyed a solid career until the start of the Second World War, when he became one of the official photographers who went to France with the BEF. He was evacuated from Boulogne but went straight back with the reinforcements Churchill sent to bolster the French. He was evacuated a second time but was killed on 14 December 1940 while photographing an army demolition exercise. The author was able to have Stanley added to the database of war dead maintained by the Commonwealth War Graves Commission after he noticed he had been omitted. *William Horton [TT]*

Fred Roper spent most of the 1930s with Allied Newspapers covering a wide range of subjects including the beginning of the Italo-Abyssinian War. He moved on to the *Daily Herald* in time to produce splendid work on the Home Front during the Second World War. *Robert Chandler [KN]*

Edward Taylor – Eddie – cut a dashing figure when he was about to leave the *Daily Sketch* to be an official war photographer in 1939. The work by him in this book must surely mark him out as one of the great 'unknowns' of press photography. *Alfred Abrahams* [KN]

Right: **Herbert William Warhurst**, forever known as Bill, was one of the true giants of Fleet Street. He became only the second photographer to be employed by *The Times* and stayed with the company until his untimely death in 1953.
His extensive career included coverage of military exercises, the royal family, the salvage of bullion

from the SS *Egypt*, the Abyssinian War (as seen here in *Indiana Jones* mode), the excavation of Tutankhamun's tomb and an encounter with Adolf Hitler. He was *The Times* photographer covering the North-West Europe campaign of 1944–45, where he produced some of the best-known images of the war. Much travelled with a deserved reputation for superb work, Bill is recorded as being an immensely modest man and the fact his death was given some prominence in *The Times* shows just how highly he was thought of by his peers. *[TT]*

Official correspondents leave for France, October 1939. Stanley Kessell, left, is distinguishable by his Great War medal ribbons. A veteran of the Argyll & Sutherland Highlanders, he was about to experience a busy time of it. He had just over a year to live. Eddie Taylor, centre left, seems keen to get going. *[TT]*

BIBLIOGRAPHY

Bass, Gary Jonathan, *Stay the Hand of Vengeance: The Politics of War Crimes Tribunals*, Princeton University Press, Princeton, New Jersey 2002.

Beckett, Ian F.W. and Gooch, John, eds, *Politicians and Defence: Studies in the Formulation of British Defence Policy*, Manchester University Press, Manchester 1986.

Blaxland, Gregory, *Destination Dunkirk*, Pen & Sword, Barnsley 2018.

Bouverie, Tim, *Appeasing Hitler: Chamberlain, Churchill and the Road to War*, The Bodley Head, London 2019.

Boyd, Ruth, *Stanley Devon: News Photographer*, Derek Harrison 1995.

Breyer, Siegfried and Skwiot, Mirosław, *German Capital Ships of the Second World War*, Seaforth Publishing, Barnsley 2012.

Bridgeman, Brian, *The Flyers: The Untold Story of British and Commonwealth airmen in the Spanish Civil War and Other Air Wars 1919 to 1940*, self-published, Swindon 1989.

Burn, Michael, *Turned Towards the Sun: An Autobiography*, Michael Russell, Norwich 2003.

Burt, R.A., *British Battleships 1919–1945*, Seaforth Publishing, Barnsley 2012.

'Cato', *Guilty Men*, Faber & Faber, London 2010.

Choules, Claude, *The Last of the Last*, Mainstream Publishing, Edinburgh 2011.

Cluett, Douglas, *The Fast and the Furious*, Sutton Libraries and Arts Services, Sutton 1985.

Cornwell, Peter D., *The Battle of France Then and Now*, After the Battle, Hobbs Cross 2007.

Cotter, Jarrod, *Bristol Blenheim Owners' Workshop Manual*, Haynes Publishing, Yeovil 2015.

Creedy, H.J., for the Army Council, *Manual of Military Vehicles (IC Engined)*, His Majesty's Stationery Office, London 1930.

Crew, Danny O., *Ku Klux Klan Sheet Music: An Illustrated Catalogue of Published Music, 1867–2002*, McFarland & Company, Jefferson, North Carolina 2003.

Davidson, Eugene, *The Unmaking of Adolf Hitler*, University of Missouri Press, Columbia, Missouri 2004.

Devon, Stanley, *Glorious*, George G. Harrap & Co, London 1957.

Faber, David, *Munich: The 1938 Appeasement Crisis*, Simon & Schuster, London 2008.

Edwards, Robert J., *Tip of the Spear*, Stackpole Books, Mechanicsburg, Pennsylvania 2015.

Fletcher, David, *British Light Tanks 1927–45 Marks I–VI*, Osprey Publishing, Oxford 2014.

French, David and Holden Reid, Brian, eds, *The British General Staff: Reform and Innovation, 1890–1939*, Frank Cass Publishers, London 2002.

Gilbert, Martin, *Winston S. Churchill, Companion Volume V, Part 3: The Coming of War 1936–1939*, Heinemann, London 1982.

Gruner, Wolf and Osterloh, Jörg, *The Greater German Reich and the Jews*, Berghahn, New York 2015.

Hadley, W.W., *Munich: Before and After*, Cassell and Company, London 1944.

Hart, Peter, *The Last Battle*, Profile Books, London 2018.

Henderson, Nevile, *Failure of a Mission*, G.P. Putnam's Sons, New York 1940.

Hobart, Malcolm C., *Badges & Uniforms of the Royal Air Force*, Pen & Sword, Barnsley 2012.

Horne, Alistair, *To Lose a Battle*, Penguin, London 2007.

Kaufmann, J.E., Kaufmann, H.W., Jankovič-Potočnik, Aleksander and Lang, Patrice, *The Maginot Line: History and Guide*, Pen & Sword, Barnsley 2011.

Keynes, John Maynard, *The Economic Consequences of the Peace*, Macmillan & Co, London 1919.

Kirkpatrick, Ivone, *The Inner Circle*, Macmillan & Co, London 1959.

Koop, Gerhard and Schmolke, Klaus-Peter, *German Light Cruisers of World War II*, Seaforth Publishing, Barnsley 2014.

Lister, David, *Forgotten Tanks and Guns of the 1920s, 1930s and 1940s*, Pen & Sword, Barnsley 2018.

McDonald, Iverach, *The History of The Times Volume V, Struggles in War and Peace, 1939–1966*, Times Books, London 1984.

Moran, Peter J., *Wreck Recovery in Britain: Then and Now*, After the Battle, Hobbs Cross 2018.

Mühlberger, Detlef, ed., *The Social Basis of European Fascist Movements*, Routledge, Oxford 2015.

Paice, Edward, *Tip & Run: The Untold Tragedy of the Great War in Africa*, Weidenfeld & Nicolson, London 2008.

Petruskevich, Edward, *The MS Wilhelm Gustloff – Construction to Maiden Voyage, August 4th 1936–April 20th 1938*, Norfolk, Virginia 2016.

Pitt, Barrie and Liddell Hart, Basil, eds, *Purnell's History of the Second World War*, British Printing Corporation, London 1966 onwards.

Powis, Mick, *The Defeat of the Zeppelins*, Pen & Sword, Barnsley 2018.

Rankin, Nicholas, *Telegram from Guernica*, Faber & Faber, London 2003.

Robertson, E.M., *Hitler's Pre-War Policy and Military Plans 1938–1939*, Longmans, London 1963.

Robinson, Derek, *A Splendid Little War*, Quercus, London 2016.

Shirer, William L., *The Rise and Fall of the Third Reich*, Pan Books, London 1964.

Smith, Peter C., *Combat Biplanes of World War II*, Pen & Sword, Barnsley 2015.

Southworth, Herbert R., *Guernica! Guernica! A Study of Journalism, Diplomacy, Propaganda and History*, University of California Press, Oakland, California 1992.

Thomas, Hugh, *The Spanish Civil War*, Pelican Books, Harmondsworth 1986.

Townsend, Peter, *Duel of Eagles*, Weidenfeld & Nicolson, London 1970.

van der Vat, Dan, *The Grand Scuttle: The Sinking of the German Fleet at Scapa Flow in 1919*, Grafton, London 1988.

Vanderveen, Bart, *Historic Military Vehicles*, After the Battle, London 1989.

Vauvillier, François, *The Encyclopaedia of French Tanks and Armoured Vehicles 1914–1940*, Histoire & Collections, Paris 2014.

Wachsmann, Nikolaus, *KL: A History of the Nazi Concentration Camps*, Farrar, Straus and Giroux, New York 2015.

Williamson, Gordon, *German Pocket Battleships 1939–45*, Osprey Publishing, Oxford 2003.

Wynn, Kenneth G., *Men of the Battle of Britain*, Frontline Books, Barnsley 2015.

Zaloga, Steven J., *Early US Armor: Tanks 1916–40*, Osprey Publishing, Oxford 2017.

"Here we go, again." *Robert Chandler [KN]*